UNIVERSITY OF CALIFORNIA PUBLICATIONS IN INTERNATIONAL RELATIONS

VOLUME V
1957

EDITORS

R. H. FITZGIBBON
E. C. BELLQUIST

SOVIET DIPLOMACY AND THE SPANISH CIVIL WAR

BY

DAVID T. CATTELL

UNIVERSITY OF CALIFORNIA PRESS
BERKELEY AND LOS ANGELES
1957

Reprinted with the permission of The Regents of the University of California

JOHNSON REPRINT CORPORATION
111 Fifth Avenue, New York, N.Y. 10003

JOHNSON REPRINT COMPANY LTD.
Berkeley Square House, London, W.1

University of California Publications in International Relations

EDITORS: R. H. FITZGIBBON, E. C. BELLQUIST

Volume 5

Submitted by editors September 7, 1956

Issued November 7, 1957

University of California Press

Berkeley and Los Angeles

California

◇

Cambridge University Press

London, England

First reprinting, 1966, Johnson Reprint Corporation
Printed in the United States of America

TO

PHILIP E. MOSELY

PREFACE

IN HIS REPORT to the 17th Party Congress in January, 1934, Stalin declared: "We never had any orientation towards Germany, nor have we any orientation towards Poland and France. Our orientation in the past and our orientation at the present time is towards the USSR, and towards the USSR alone. And if the interests of the USSR demand rapprochement with one country or another which is not interested in disturbing peace, we take this step without hesitation. . . ."

At the beginning of 1934 Stalin was still playing the "lone wolf" in international relations, but at the same time keeping open the possibility of an alliance with one of his enemies. The Soviet Union, as yet deep in the throes of a political, social, and industrial revolution, was beginning to fear her isolation. To the east and to the west there were developing military, aggressive regimes with strong anti-Communist orientations backed by industrial systems superior to her own. By the end of 1934 when Hitler had ended all democratic, socialist, and Communist opposition in Germany, Stalin dropped the bipolar policy of the USSR against the "bourgeois capitalist" world and was calling for collective defense with the democratic states against fascism and militarism.

This volume is the second part in a study of the Soviet Union's most consistent attempt to apply the doctrine of "collective security" as a means to her own defense. The first volume [*Communism and the Spanish Civil War* (Berkeley and Los Angeles: University of California Press)] analyzed the Soviet Union's direct relations with Spain on the governmental, party, military, and secret police levels. This volume analyzes the Soviet attempt to use the Spanish crisis to strengthen her relations with England and France and to defend herself against German aggression. The two parts are closely related as double facets of a single policy. This does not mean, however, that the policy was consistent in its ends and means. The authoritarian habits of force and terror and the refusal of the Communists to abandon, even for the moment, their goal of subversion and world domination worked to undermine the Soviet goal of a popular front and collective security with England and France against the "Fascist" aggressors.

Having decided as a major step in her new line to support the Spanish Republic and use it as a means to involve and ingratiate herself with England and France, the Soviet Union in police-state fashion mobilized all the instruments at her control. All channels of Soviet and Communist communication were soon filled with reports on the Spanish Republic and Soviet diplomacy in its behalf. Daily throughout the war a part of the four-page *Pravda* and *Izvestiia* was devoted to communiqués from Spain, as well as to frequent feature articles and editorials. Not until after the Munich crisis in September, 1938, did the momentum of propaganda and comment on the Spanish crisis diminish, but even then it was often recalled as a prime example of the democratic states coöperating with the "Fascists" to encircle the Soviet Union (see page 175 n. 29).

After the Nazi-Soviet pact in August, 1939, Spain and nonintervention, being a part of a policy now rejected, were rarely mentioned, and when they were, the role of Germany and Italy was passed over and the responsibility for defeating the Spanish "people" was placed on England and France [M. E. Airapetian, *Vneshnei politiki SSSR 1917–1940gg* (*The Foreign Policy of the USSR 1917–1940*) (Moscow: Voenizdat., 1941), p. 78, and *Politicheskii slovar'* (*Political Dictionary*) (Moscow: Gos. Izdat. Politicheskoi Literatury, 1940), pp. 225 f.]. Even in the period of the grand alliance during the Second World War down to 1948 the issue was largely overlooked. For example, in the three-volume *Istoriia diplomatii* [*Diplomatic History*] edited by V. P. Potemkin (Moscow: Gos. Izdat. Politicheskoi Literatury, 1945), only about ten pages were devoted to the Spanish conflict and these followed closely the Soviet interpretation of about 1937. Not until the cold war and the publication in 1948 of the Nazi-Soviet documents of 1939–1941 did Soviet writers renew their interest in the diplomacy of the Spanish Civil War. They seized upon this issue as an argument of Western duplicity in favor of Hitler and as a justificatior of their own *rapprochement* with Nazism. Because the United States had subsequently become the Soviets' leading antagonist, she was now included as a major accomplice of "Fascist" intervention in Spain [A. M. Nekrich, *Politika angliiskogo imperializma v Evrope oktiabr' 1938–sentiabr' 1939 (The Policy of English Imperialism in Europe, October 1938–September 1939)* (Moscow: Gos. Izdat. Politicheskoi Literatury, 1953), p. 223]. They also used the issue as a means to discredit the socialists, who were again being denounced as an enemy, stressing the weak and ineffective support of the moderate left on behalf of the Spanish Republicans [R. Varfolomeeva, *Reaktsionnaia vneshniaia politika frantsuzskigh pravygh sotsialistov (1936–1939gg.) (The Reactionary Foreign Policy of the French Right Socialists [1936–1939])* (Moscow: Gos. Izdat. Politicheskoi Literatury, 1949), and N. N. Nikolaev, *Vneshniaia politika pravygh leiboristov Anglii v period podgotovki i nachala vtoroi mirovoi voiny 1935–1940gg. (The Foreign Policy of the Right Labourites in England in the Period of Preparation and the Beginning of World War II, 1935–1940)* (Moscow: Gos. Izdat. Politicheskoi Literatury, 1953)]. And for the first time Soviet writers were permitted to mention that the Soviet government had sent military aid to the Loyalists, although no specific amounts were named (see page 175 n. 44).

On the Western side, the Spanish Civil War likewise occupied a great deal of attention at the time. Hundreds of accounts were written and many hours spent in Parliament and the Chamber of Deputies debating intervention and nonintervention. But when it was over and new crises had come to overshadow Europe, the issue was forgotten and the eclipse has persisted to the present time. Postwar writers who have dealt with the interwar period and the events leading to the Second World War have been only briefly concerned with the Spanish issue and in some instances not at all.

At the time of the Civil War varying interpretations were expressed on the manner in which the French and British governments were handling the crisis: (1) Prime Minister Chamberlain's continued support of the Non-Intervention Agreement and his policy of wooing Mussolini represents *realpolitik* and the only way to stave off war, pending democratic rearmament [Viscount Templewood, *Nine Troubled Years* (London: Collins, 1954), p. 258, and Duncan Keith-Shaw, *Prime Minister Neville Chamberlain* (London: Wells Gardner, Durton and Co., Ltd., 1939), pp. 83 f.]. (2) "What everyone must condemn in the light of history, is our [British] failure to reach any decision at all about the Spanish war and our own proper action in regard to it" [Douglas Jerrold, *Britain and Europe, 1900–1940* (London: Collins, 1941), p. 137]. (3) It is correct for the democracies to stay out because intervention "would run counter to our firm resolve not to become entangled in any aggressive Fascist or Communist bloc, resting upon warring 'ideologies' which we reject as almost equally false and objectionable." Let them fight it out alone [Robert William Seton-Watson, *Britain and the Dictators* (New York: The Macmillan Co., 1938), p. 386]. (4) England and France are too deeply divided on the Spanish question ever to tolerate active support for one of the warring factions. In France even civil war is a threat (see pages 9–12). (5) Franco and his Fascist allies must be encouraged in their fight to destroy the Communist menace in Spain [General A. I. Denikin, *World Events and the Russian Problem* (Paris: Impr. Rapide C.-T., 1939)] (6) Chamberlain is obtuse and a fool, and his policy of appeasement in Spain and elsewhere is bringing the democracies to the brink of disaster (see pages 126–127).

The consequences of the Munich crisis and the war itself apparently vindicated the last of these judgments and the laborious negotiations over the Spanish crisis seemed best forgotten. Few Western analysts have bothered subsequently to challenge this verdict. But such an all-inclusive conclusion lumping together the British policies toward the Munich, Austrian, and Spanish crises is too hasty, because even Chamberlain's most bitter opponent on foreign policy, Winston Churchill, basically agreed with him on Spain (see page 92). Although this study does not attempt to analyze the British-French policies in detail, it does suggest that writers have been too swift with their verdicts and reopens the questions of whether Chamberlain really committed a gross error in respect to Spain, an error which his opponents could and would have avoided, and whether his policy in fact proved a failure.

I should like to express my gratitude to the Royal Institute of International Affairs and the International Institute of Social History in Amsterdam for their help during the research phase. In editing the manuscript I am indebted to the useful criticism of Mrs. Jane Degras and Professor Julian Towster. Mrs. Jane Degras was particularly helpful in pointing out opposing views and editorial deficiencies. I am also grateful for the patient and helpful coöperation of Miss Susan Haverstick as editor and to my wife.

CONTENTS

[ix]

CHAPTER I

THE GREAT POWERS AND THE OUTBREAK OF WAR IN SPAIN: JULY, 1936

THE SOVIET UNION AND SPAIN BEFORE 1936

IN THE DECADES before the Civil War, Spain played a minor role in European politics. After its long years of relative isolation from great-power politics, however, the crisis of 1936 unexpectedly made Spain the arena of a bitter struggle for hegemony in Europe, brought a smoldering friction between the Fascist and non-Fascist states to a blaze, and almost set all Europe aflame.

The Communist International had, in contrast, for several years followed developments in Spain because of its economic and political instability.[1] In spite of this interest, however, the Communist party made very little headway in Spain and numbered fewer than 1,000 members by 1931, as against the million and more adherents of the Anarchist movement. The proclamation of the Second Republic in 1931, followed by political maneuverings between the right and left for supremacy, opened the way for the Communists, like all other parties, to increase their activities and strength, although by February of 1936 they still claimed only 35,000 members. Because of the victory of the Popular Front in February, 1936, after two and a half years of governments of "black reaction," international Communist interest in affairs in Spain became even more marked. This heightened interest overflowed from the publications of the Communist International to the pages of Soviet periodicals and newspapers. The Communist party as a member of the winning Popular Front, although distinctly a junior partner in it, hoped to increase its prestige and influence. But more important to the leaders in the Kremlin was the fact that the successes of the Popular Fronts in Spain and France were the two bright spots which stood out against the ever more menacing shadows cast by Nazism and the mounting danger of German aggression.

Before 1931 the government of Primo de Rivera had refused to recognize the Soviet regime. The inauguration of the Republic in Spain, however, brought with it a new foreign policy and negotiations for recognition were begun. Just before the swing to the right in the elections of 1933, the Azaña government exchanged notes of recognition *de jure*

---

[1] For notes to chap. i, see pp. 135–138.

and *de facto*. The notes provided for the exchange of ambassadors; Julio Alvarez del Vayo, formerly ambassador to Mexico, was to become ambassador to Moscow and A. Lunacharsky Soviet ambassador to Madrid. The victory of the rightist parties in November and December, 1933, however, forestalled the carrying out of the exchange of ambassadors, although the successive governments of the right did not withdraw Spanish recognition of the Soviet regime. The exchange of ambassadors finally took place only after the outbreak of the Civil War.

The months immediately preceding the onset of Civil War in July, 1936, had been marked by the deterioration of civil order. Along with the other far larger parties of the left, the Communists had increased their following and by July claimed 117,000. In addition the Communists had made some progress in closing the gap between the Communists and Socialists by the campaign to establish a united front. The most promising step in this direction was the creation of a united Communist and Socialist youth movement, the *Juventudes Socialistas Unificadas* (JSU). Rumors spread by the right proclaimed the presence of numerous agents from the Comintern and the spinning of a Red plot backed by Soviet arms to take over the government and establish a Soviet republic. Although it is not unlikely that the number of Comintern agents in Spain did increase in this period, the rebels and their allies were unable to present any concrete or reliable evidence that the Soviet government was taking a direct and vital role in the activities in Spain. The sympathies of the Soviet press were for the Popular Front and it expressed concern about a possible return to the "domination of the landowners and Church," but the Soviet government itself remained neutral. The Soviet government only became directly interested as a result of the persistent complicity of Germany and Italy with the rebel generals.

THE ROLE OF GERMANY AND ITALY

The outbreak of hostilities on the Iberian Peninsula in July, 1936, was welcomed by Italy and Germany as a means of increasing their power and influence in a strategic area of Western Europe.[2] Mussolini had just finished his conquest of Abyssinia and was anxious for another opportunity to prove the valor of his soldiers and to affirm the role of Italy as the dominant power in the Mediterranean.

Since 1931 Mussolini had shown a special interest in the affairs of Spain, going as far as to agree secretly in 1934 to help the Monarchists restore the Monarchy.[3] Mussolini coveted Spain as part of his dream to make the Mediterranean an Italian lake, as it had been in the days of ancient Rome. A strong ally in Spain with direct control over bases in the Spanish Balearic Islands would have given Italy an important position in the western Mediterranean and would have made this area untenable for British and French forces.

Only a few months before, in March, 1936, Germany successfully challenged France by remilitarizing the Rhineland in repudiation of the Versailles Treaty. The Nazis were also rapidly infiltrating Austria, now that Italian efforts to prevent such a move had been ended for the most part through Mussolini's involvement in Ethiopia and his increasing reliance on Hitler's support.[4] Encouraged by its successes, Germany was looking for further opportunities to isolate France. An ally in Spain would increase Germany's threat to France and would surround France almost completely by hostile states. An increase in German influence in Spain furthermore would enhance Hitler's prestige and be a step toward reëstablishing German interest and possible hegemony over North Africa.[5]

Both Germany and Italy looked to Spain as an important source of certain raw materials needed for armaments, such as mercury, lead, zinc, and copper and iron ore.[6] Both dictatorships claimed the domination and victory of the Popular Front in Spain would mean the spread of communism into Western Europe. It is difficult to evaluate the degree to which the German and Italian leaders were affected by their own propaganda in this direction. From the German and Italian documents it would appear, however, that communism in Spain constituted a real phobia in the minds of the German and Italian leaders.[7]

It was General Franco who first tried to turn the Spanish conflict into an international issue. In a press communiqué issued on July 21, two days after the beginning of the military insurrection, he declared:

Our movement has come at the right time because the conditions aboard certain warships have shown how intense is the Communist propaganda in the naval forces and how necessary it was to act swiftly and energetically as we have done. Civilization in Western Europe would otherwise have suffered a most serious setback. . . .

Among the ships that attacked Ceuta was a Russian oil tanker on which two guns were mounted. This shows once again how we have been betrayed by former Spanish Governments and how they have bowed to the mandates of Moscow. The interests of Spain therefore are not alone at stake as our trumpet call sounds across the Straits of Gibraltar.[8]

Franco, immediately finding himself in difficulties, requested help from Germany and Italy. Since the Spanish navy and air force had remained mostly loyal to the government, he was at a loss to transport his troops, consisting of 5,000 members of the Spanish Foreign Legion and 17,000 Moors, from Africa across the Straits of Gibraltar to help the other rebel forces meeting heavy opposition from the troops remaining loyal to the government and from the masses of armed workers. Germany and Italy responded to the call and, by July 27, German and Italian transport planes, fighters, and bombers were transporting and protecting the movement of rebel troops from Morocco to Cádiz. Thus in the crucial first ten days of the rebellion Hitler and Mussolini, supported by the Antonio de Oliveira regime of Portugal, took the first step and aided the rebels to profit by the confusion and the inability of the government to consolidate its forces. Once committed, Germany and Italy not only continued to lend support throughout the war, they greatly increased the scope of their aid to include sending entire fighting divisions. For example, by January of 1937, Italy had 211 pilots, 238 specialists, 777 ground officers, 995 noncommissioned officers, and 14,752 troops in Spain fighting for Franco.[9] By April, 1937, the total number of troops had increased to 70,000. The German forces in Spain, however, remained only a fraction of the size of the Italian contingent.[10]

During the first months of the war both Germany and Italy together with Portugal tried to wear the coat of respectability and sought to hide from their own people and the world their intervention, an action contrary to the generally accepted rules of international law.[11] They particularly wanted to conceal their role for fear of arousing the western democracies, because their interference in Spanish affairs was a direct threat to the security of France and Great Britain. Consequently, both Italy and Germany persistently denied sending aid to the generals despite contrary evidence. For example, when three Italian planes were forced down in French Morocco on their way to join General Franco on July 30, the Italian government categorically denied intervention. Even in November and December, 1936, while large numbers of their troops were being sent to Spain, Germany and Italy refused to admit support of Franco. From the beginning, however, they realized that it would be impossible to prevent knowledge of their help from spreading abroad regardless of denials and attempts to cover up. As a result, following General Franco's lead they chose the already successful tactic of arousing fear of communism in Spain, charging in tirades of propaganda and objections that the Soviet Union was sending aid to the Republican forces and attempting to install a Red government in Spain.

The Reaction of the Soviet Union

Against charges of Red aggression, the Russians did their best to retaliate. They denied all intervention by themselves[12] and countercharged Italy and Germany with complicity in plotting the insurrection. K. Radek in an article in *Izvestiia* on August 4, 1936, gave the pattern of Soviet countercharges:

... Exploiting the fear of revolution by the ruling classes of the world, the German and Italian Fascists are preparing to intervene against the Spanish revolution in order to place into their hands the important trump-cards for the preparation of a world war and a new territorial redistribution of the world. The Fascists express themselves loudly against Soviet intervention, although they know that the USSR is far from Spain, and although they were unable to name a single Soviet active man who could be found in Spain....

Their aims are clear.... Herr Hitler argues as follows: ... if with the help of German bombers General Franco succeeds in defeating the Spanish masses and establishes a Fascist government, the latter in order to obtain further help would be obliged to act jointly with Fascist Germany against France.... [Therefore] the German Fascists protest not only against Moscow interference ... they also make the same charges against the French government simply because the legal Spanish government, which came to power on the basis of democratic elections, is allegedly trying to import some airplanes from France. But a German company of Junkers is sending dozens of planes to the Spanish rebels....

Thus the general propaganda pattern of bitter recrimination which lasted during the entire civil strife in Spain was established at the beginning by the Soviet Union and Italy and Germany. The battle of "documents," "proofs," and propaganda continued to the end of the war and even afterward. The Nazi and Fascist accusations of Soviet intervention were groundless during the early stages of the struggle.[13] The Soviet countercharges also were for the most part prefabricated although they had some basis in fact. The actual extent of German and Italian aid was not known at first except for a few instances such as the forced landing of Italian military planes in French Morocco. The Communist press initially accused not only Hitler and Mussolini of helping the rebels, but also the Conservative government of Great Britain of indirect support:

If further proof of the National government's attitude was needed, it was found in the refusal of the British authorities at Gibraltar to permit the Spanish Fleet to refuel. It was further freely asserted in papers like the *Telegraph*, which is usually well informed as to the diplomatic moves of the government, that Baldwin and Eden had brought pressure on the Left government of France, in order to restrain it from helping the Spanish government.[14]

Although not directly concerned with the Spanish crisis, the Soviet Union was very much alarmed by the international political and strategic implications should Spain come under Fascist and Nazi influence and accepted without question the major role of Germany and Italy in the revolt. Politically, a pro-Fascist Spain would increase the prestige and strength of the aggressive anti-Communist bloc. But this was not so disturbing as the strategic effect it would have on France's power position. France and Russia had only recently concluded an alliance against possible German aggression. Many elements in France still opposed the treaty and succeeded in delaying its ratification for ten months,[15] and the French government refused to supplement the treaty, as they had promised, with military conversations. Nonetheless the Soviet Union still considered it the important and essential cornerstone of her security program. As a result, articles in the following vein began to appear frequently in the Soviet press soon after the outbreak of hostilities:

If during a world war Germany could use Spanish ports as bases of operation it would mean that the war activities of the Entente countries would be made particularly difficult. (*Izvestiia*, Aug. 3, 1936).

...It is absolutely essential to submit to serious study the possible consequences of the Spanish events "for the future, for the independence and for the security of France." (*Pravda*, Aug. 14, 1936).

This stress on Spain's strategic importance to Great Britain and especially France continued to dominate Soviet editorials on the Spanish conflict throughout the war.[16]

Contrary to the propaganda of the rebels, many conservative groups, Nazis, and Fascists, the Soviet Union did not decide to intervene immediately in Spain and maintained official neutrality during the first months.[17] The reasons for this were probably several. Strategically Spain had no immediate value for the protection of the Soviet frontiers; Soviet interest in Spain lay in protecting her ally France against encirclement. Since the threat was directed against France, the USSR felt France should make the first move to help the Loyalist government. Furthermore, the Soviet Union, in the process of trying to industrialize rapidly and to rebuild her defense against the rising threat of Nazi aggression through a series of five-year plans, could little afford an adventure on the other side of Europe. Even though to support the Loyalist government meant to uphold a government of the Popular Front, Stalin had long put the advancement of Socialism in Russia ahead of revolution and the cause of the working classes elsewhere. Stalin would intervene in Spain only if it was to Russia's direct betterment to do so.

While maintaining an official attitude of neutrality, the Soviet Union nevertheless unofficially gave moral and monetary aid.[18] The Soviet press was full of praise for the Loyalist government and for the Spanish people "courageously resisting the rebel onslaught." Immediately the trade unions in the USSR organized collections for Spain. During the first days of August, 1936, *Pravda* and *Izvestiia* both published pages of speeches and pledges by factory workers, collective farmers, and academicians urging solidarity with Spain. N. Shvernik, head of the Soviet trade unions, led the drive and in a speech before the All-Union Central Council of Soviet Trade Unions on August 3, 1936, analyzed the Spanish crisis in detail and urged the collection of money for Spain: "The All-Union Central and the Moscow Regional Councils of Trade Unions calls upon the workers and people of the Soviet Union to give material aid to the Spanish fighters who, with guns in their hands, are defending the democratic republic."[19] Three days later Secretary Shvernik reported that 12,145,000 rubles (about $2,400,000) had already been collected and that he had sent 36,435,000 French francs to the Spanish Prime Minister Giral.[20]

Thus a review of the publications in the Soviet Union indicates that the Soviet government did not treat the events in Spain as just another attempted *coup d'état* so common in that country and the Latin American republics. Aware of the importance of Spain in the European balance of power, the Soviet newspapers daily devoted a sizable section of their four-page editions to reports from and editorials on Spain. It was not merely because the revolt of the generals was an attack on the legitimate government supported by the Popular Front. The reports, speeches, and editorials stressed, rather, the defense of a democratic republic against fascism. That the Popular Front was leftist and contained as part of its coalition the Communist party was only rarely mentioned and generally played down. A further indication of the importance of the conflict to the Soviet Union can be seen in the fact that very soon after the outbreak the leading foreign correspondents of the Soviet Union, Ilya Ehrenburg and Michael Koltsov, were sent to Spain.

The Division of Opinion in France

Significantly, the Nazi and Fascist charges of military aid to the Loyalist government were directed against France as well as the Soviet Union. The outbreak of hostilities in Spain was very discomfiting to France and to the newly created Popular Front government of Leon

Blum in particular. No country was more aware of Spain's significance to European politics than France. France was the only great European power to have a common border with Spain and it was therefore her special concern who controlled that country. A friendly power on the Pyrenean border would simplify France's defense problems. Who held authority over the Spanish Mediterranean coast and the Balearic Islands was also important to France for the protection of her communications with her African colonies. Some in France remembered Spain's influence on European affairs during the Franco-Prussian War of 1870. One of the causes of the war had been Bismarck's desire to put a "Hohenzollern candidate" on the Spanish throne.

Each year with the growing strength of Hitler, France was witnessing the gradual collapse of her security system which, in turn, made the Spanish problem all the more acute. Poland, formerly the key to the French alliance system in Eastern Europe, had signed a nonaggression pact with Hitler as early as 1934. Many of the other states in Eastern Europe were also being persuaded to coöperate with Hitler by the success of the Polish-German alliance, a deep-seated fear of Communist Russia, and the dynamics of Hitler's politics and economics. Only Czechoslovakia, who had the most to lose by German resurgence, remained closely allied to France. France had sought to overcome these losses in part by an agreement with Russia, but the *rapprochement* never bore fruit because France was unable to abandon her suspicions of Russia's motives and goals.

Under the leadership of Pierre Laval, France had further sought to isolate Germany by winning over Italy to the *status quo* powers. However, the bad reception of the Hoare-Laval pact by French and British public opinion, and the British insistence on the imposition of light sanctions on Italy for her invasion of Abyssinia, alienated Italy from coöperation with either France or England. France faced the dilemma of choosing an alliance with Italy against Germany, thus accepting the Italian conquest of Ethiopia, or an alliance with Great Britain—Great Britain assuming the leadership.[21] Mussolini was, after all, a doubtful ally and France for the last thirty years had based her policy on a close alliance with Great Britain. France had really no choice but to accept Britain's lead. Thus France lost the initiative and when Germany in violation of the Versailles Treaty remilitarized the Rhineland in March, 1936, France took no action beyond verbal protest, even though the move was a direct threat to her security. It has been argued that France at the time was under a caretaker government pending the elections in

May and was not in a position to take the initiative. Nevertheless, even the new, popularly elected government of Blum, when it came to power in June, took no decisive action. Britain felt unwilling and unable to stop German rearmament and France bowed before her leadership.[22]

France's attitude toward the rise of Nazism in Germany had from the first been highly ambivalent. As most of the rest of the world, France did not fully understand Nazism, either its strength and hold on the German people or the extremes to which it was capable of going and, consequently, underestimated its force and danger until much too late. Many groups in France praised Hitler for his dynamism and concluded that decadent, divided France also needed just such an energetic leader to revive her previous glory and greatness. Some saw Hitler also as a bulwark against communism and possible Soviet aggression. The fear of communism was still strong among the conservative elements in the West.

In addition, many Frenchmen, in spite of their strong nationalism, wanted the end of the Franco-German hostility that had helped bring on two recent wars. They hoped that Hitler would further this aim in spite of his words to the contrary in *Mein Kampf*. They allowed themselves to be deceived by Hitler's statements that he wished for only peace and friendship because they so ardently wanted to believe him; the French were weary of war. For them it no longer meant glory for France or a settlement of international disputes. The memory of the First World War was still too acute for them to look upon the possibility of a new war with anything but horror. As a result the pacifist movement was very strong in France. The Socialist party, the largest party in the Chamber of Deputies, exhibited particularly strong strains of pacifism as did its leader and the new premier, Leon Blum. The Socialists were repelled by the contemplation of rearmament because of its costs and because its end result would inevitably be war, and the suffering would fall to the working class.

French internal politics and problems were also ill-suited to a new armaments race and a strong, energetic foreign policy. The government of the Popular Front, which came into being on June 5, 1936, just a few weeks before the beginning of the Spanish revolt, was not a stable government, although the elections of May had shown a strong turn to the left (five out of nine million votes). Neither the Socialists nor the Popular Front government, however, held a majority in the Chamber of Deputies, but depended for their continuance on the votes of parties outside the government. Furthermore, the Popular Front had been formed as an election alliance and its program was essentially negative—an attack on previous governments. When it came to deciding on a ruling policy, the differences between the parties were great. Leon Blum was further hindered by the omission of the Communists from the government. Being a part of the ruling bloc and yet not participating in the government gave them an enviable position. They could in general take credit for the successes of the Popular Front, but had to assume none of the responsibility for its mistakes.

The internal economic problems that had burdened previous ministries were still unsolved when Blum took office. Financial instability, high costs, low incomes, and the flight of gold and capital abroad constituted the most serious problems. To solve them Blum wanted to be free of international complications and demands on the energy and resources of the government. The memory of recent riots by Fascist and semi-Fascist organizations was also very fresh in the minds of the French leaders. Leon Blum wanted stability both at home and abroad in order to prevent the recurrence of rioting and the possible increase of fascism in France.

Thus the outbreak of hostilities in Spain found France in a delicate and difficult situation. The natural sympathies of Leon Blum and the Popular Front were with the Spanish government, which was also a government of a Popular Front. But large segments of the French population did not share these feelings. The parties of the right "bloc" looked to the generals to save Spain from communism. They felt that a victory of the Popular Front in Spain would further increase and encourage the revolutionary tendencies of the left in France. Thus the Spanish Civil War threatened to open a serious schism between the right and left in France.[23] As was so often true in France, political enmities were further complicated by a religious conflict. A large part of the senior Catholic hierarchy in France openly began to support the rebels in their fight against the "anti-Christs" of the Spanish government who would not even allow Mass to be said in their zone.

The Spanish government at the very beginning of the insurrection decided to take advantage of its friendship with the Popular Front government in France. José Giral, the Spanish prime minister, telegraphed on the night of July 20 or 21 to the French government asking for arms and ammunition.[24] In negotiating Spain had two strong advantages, a large gold reserve of about $600,000,000, a part of which she immediately sent to Paris to pay for any arms purchased, and a secret clause in her 1935 treaty of commerce with France providing for the purchase of twenty million pounds' worth of arms and ammunition. The Spanish government, in order to follow up its request, sent Ferdinando de los Ríos to Paris on July 24 to negotiate the purchase of arms.

The French press was fully informed of all the moves of the Spanish government through rebel sympathizers in the Spanish embassy in Paris. Alarmed by the intention of Blum's government to send arms to the Loyalists, the newspapers of the right raised a furor against intervention on behalf of the legal Spanish government.

Shortly after his arrival in Paris, Ferdinando de los Ríos reported on Leon Blum's attitude toward aiding the Spanish government. He quoted Blum as saying, "My soul is torn. . . . I shall maintain my position at all costs and in spite of all risks we must help Spain that is friendly to us. How? We shall see."[25] The significant concept in this statement was not that he desired to aid Spain, but that his soul was torn. Blum was subjected to pressures from all sides. His own cabinet was divided on the advisability of selling arms to Spain. The president of the French Republic is reported to have said to Blum, "What is being planned, this delivery of armaments to Spain, may mean war or revolution in France." While Blum's inclination was to support the Spanish government, he was a pacifist who wanted to do nothing that might upset the peace of France or Europe. In addition, he longed to be free of international entanglements in order to deal with the internal problems of France.[26]

Four days after the outbreak of hostilities, July 23, Blum flew to London to participate in the meeting of France, Belgium, and England concerning Germany's violation of the Locarno pact in the Rhineland on March 7. Undoubtedly, at this conference the British made known their views on the Spanish conflict. From subsequent official statements and actions, as well as from newspaper reports at the time, it is clear that the attitude of the British Foreign Office was strict neutrality. Furthermore, the British government, being Conservative, was in many ways sympathetic to the rebel cause. Winston Churchill, although not a member of the government at this time, summarized the Conservative attitude: "French partisanship for the Spanish Communists, or British partisanship for the Spanish rebels, might injure profoundly the bonds which unite the British Empire and the French Republic."[27] It was just such a danger that Leon Blum most feared. Having only the nebulous alliance with Russia as a basis for a continental security system, France dared not lose British friendship now that Germany was rearming.

The French cabinet on July 25 decided "not to intervene in any manner whatever in the internal conflict in Spain." This, nonetheless, did not solve the important question whether or not to sell arms to the Loyalists. A compromise solution was finally devised: the French government refused to furnish war material, but did not prohibit private firms from selling to Spain.[28] The compromise was destined, however, to be unsuccessful because Italy and Germany actively and persistently intervened on the rebel generals' behalf and because French policies toward Spain were to be determined in the long run in London, not in Paris.

The British Attitude toward the Civil War

Great Britain was less disturbed than France by the outbreak of the Civil War in Spain. In the first place, she was a greater distance from Spain. Because of Gibraltar, she hoped the government of Spain would be, if not entirely friendly, at least not hostile, and from her point of view neither of the two forces fighting appeared likely to challenge her position in the Mediterranean. Although she was certainly aware of the immediate possibility of an Italian- and German-dominated Spain, she refused to be panicked into rash action and felt confident she could settle differences by appeasement and negotiation, just as she had successfully made an agreement with Germany in 1935 in respect to naval strength, assuring for herself continued superiority. Up to this point Great Britain was not alarmed over the possibility of German aggression and expansion.

Furthermore, the British government throughout the war never felt that the Axis influence in Spain would be anything more than temporary at best. Speaking at the Foreign Press Association dinner on January 12, 1937, Anthony Eden declared:

> ... I know that there are some who believe that as the outcome of this civil war Spain inevitably must have a government either fascist or Communist. That is not our belief. On the contrary, we believe that neither of these forms of government being indigenous to Spain, neither is likely to endure. Spain will in time evolve her own Spanish form of government.[29]

From a United States diplomatic report it would appear that the attitude of the government leaders in Great Britain went even further:

> ... The British Government's attitude towards the Spanish situation has been from the beginning that a decisive victory by either of the contending sides would endanger European equilibrium—rather peace without victory was preferable, with the situation ending in stalemate after withdrawal of foreign volunteers, leaving a settlement to be negotiated between the contending elements in Spain on a basis of provincial autonomy.[30]

Great Britain in some ways had become an isolationist power similar to the United States. She had allowed her military strength to lapse and even failed to keep her navy at its top efficiency and potential. She refused to tie herself to the continent and instead tried to restore the pre-first World War balance-of-power concept without maintaining the military force to back it. She hoped to recreate the balance merely by diplomatic maneuvers. From the press and from the few polls taken at the time it would appear that the overwhelming mass of the British people wanted to remain completely neutral in the Spanish conflict. Even those Labour leaders who favored selling arms to the Spanish government would have been horrified by the idea of Great Britain ever becoming actively involved.

If the Conservative leaders in Great Britain had been forced to choose one side or the other, their sympathies would probably have been with the rebels. They were inclined to believe the hypothesis that the Comintern was attempting to retrieve its falling fortunes in Spain. Furthermore, they feared that the triumph of the Spanish left might upset the Salazar regime in Portugal. For centuries Britain and Portugal had maintained close relations and the spread of revolution to Portugal from Spain would have disturbed this friendship.

Though Great Britain was still suffering from economic depression in 1936, there was no serious division between the right and left as in France. Consequently the government, in formulating its policy of neutrality in the Civil War, had little difficulty from internal conflicts and pressures. The Labour party favored help to the Spanish government, but was not yet aware of the importance of the conflict and only very moderately pressed the government to act on behalf of the Loyalists. Also, the British government was firmly in the hands of the Conservative party and could easily ignore the demands of the Labour leaders. Though many individual Conservatives and industrialists favored support to the generals, if only for the protection of large British interests in Spain,[31] they did little to encourage the government to take an active part. Reportedly, however, they lent support to Franco privately and urged the government to put pressure on France not to help the Loyalists.

Consequently, British policy from the beginning was to stay absolutely clear of any involvement and to advise France to do the same. They also cautioned France and the world against hysteria over rumors of Communist and Fascist intervention.[32]

CHAPTER II

THE NON-INTERVENTION AGREEMENT: AUGUST, 1936

The French Appeal for European Neutrality

THE FIRST INTERNATIONAL INCIDENT related to the Spanish conflict came on July 30, 1936, when three Italian planes made a forced landing in French Morocco on their way to aid General Franco. From the outset rumors had been spreading that Italy and Germany were aiding the rebels. This event gave the rumors substance and the French government realized they were not just the fabrication of Communist propaganda or loose talk on the part of correspondents.[1] Positive evidence that Italy was aiding Franco put the Spanish crisis in an entirely different light. It appeared to be the beginning of a frantic and costly European armaments race and, perhaps, the first battle of a new European war. Blum feared that if France gave arms to the Loyalists and Germany and Italy did the same for the rebels, it might be very difficult to confine the war to Spain. Rumors were already rife that Mussolini had his air force in readiness to intervene openly in Spain if France continued to aid the Madrid government.[2] Above all, Blum was anxious to avoid an armaments race with Germany and Italy. The cost would have made his program of increased social services impossible and might have disrupted completely the already unstable French finances. The situation was more acute as Germany was considered most likely to be the winner. Nor did Blum want to become involved in a contest with Germany and Italy without the complete support of Great Britain, which he was not at all sure would be forthcoming. Like most Frenchmen at the time, he valued peace very highly. War was to be avoided if France were to survive, and the keys to French security and peace were a close alliance with England and the Maginot line.

Blum with the support of the British government sought, as the only conceivable solution to the Spanish crisis, to neutralize the conflict internationally by obtaining the agreement of all interested powers not to intervene in Spain.[3] During the first week of August notes were sent to Italy, Great Britain, Germany, Soviet Russia, the Netherlands, Czechoslovakia, and Poland requesting their adherence to a policy of nonintervention. France, to make clear the seriousness of her intention

---

[1] For notes to chap. ii, see pp. 138–139.

to isolate the conflict, on August 8 announced that, effective the next day, she would stop all military exports to Spain. The transit of war material bought in other countries, however, was not prohibited until September 8. While this embargo on military aid showed French sincerity, it left France with little bargaining power in respect to Italian and German aid to the rebels. Hitler and Mussolini were now free to delay their adherence to nonintervention indefinitely. From the German and Italian documents, it is clear that procrastination was to be their main tactic in sabotaging the Non-Intervention Agreement.

The reaction of the leaders of the Soviet Union to the nonintervention proposal is unknown. From the information available it is difficult to conclude whether they received the proposal with disquiet or relief. There are factors that could explain either reaction. The Non-Intervention Agreement deprived states of the legal right to give aid to the legitimate government of Spain, and Russia's acceptance of the proposal would deny her the right to aid the proletariat and the Popular Front. This, in the eyes of the revolutionaries all over the world, would put her on the side of the reactionaries and the capitalist powers. Furthermore, Hitler and Mussolini were not likely to consider the pact binding. In fact, before the agreement was proposed, they were already circumventing international law by giving military supplies to the rebel generals. The addition of a mere pact of nonintervention thus was not likely to deter them, as the Communists well knew. On the other hand, something had to be done to try to stop Germany and Italy from turning Spain into a colony. Since Russia herself was not interested at this time in intervening in Spain and making it a satellite,⁴ she was perhaps willing to let France try by peaceful negotiations to remove the threat by offering as a *quid pro quo* the noninterference of the democratic states and the Soviet Union. In her position as a self-professed supporter of revolution and the Popular Front, the Soviet Union would have had difficulty proposing nonintervention herself. For the proposal to come from the democracies was also advantageous because, in event of failure, the stigma would fall on the democracies and not the Soviet Union, who could claim simply to have gone along with the majority of states.

Thus acceptance offered certain difficulties to the Soviet leaders. On the one hand they had two very valid reasons to refuse: a loss of prestige among the revolutionaries for refusing to aid the Spanish Popular Front; and well-founded scepticism about its effect on the activities of Germany and Italy in Spain. On the other hand there were even more compelling reasons for accepting the proposal. Refusal to comply would be considered by the West as an admission that Russia was intervening or intended to intervene in Spain, and so make the Nazi propaganda about saving Spain from Communism much more plausible.[5] This in turn would increase the fear of Communism in the West, which the Soviet Union had been trying to dispel for the last year in pursuit of her policy of an alliance with France and England. To refuse France's request would have serious effects on the Franco-Russian treaty of alliance recently ratified by the French Chamber of Deputies, and it was because of France that Russia was most concerned about German and Italian influence in Spain. In spite of the weakness of this move, France was still attempting to deal with the problem collectively and, as a strong supporter of collective security at this time, Russia felt obliged to coöperate. Finally, the Soviet Union may have felt that a system of nonintervention backed by rigorous inspection and control could be effective in spite of Germany's and Italy's wishes to the contrary.

The Soviet government answered on August 6, 1936, agreeing in principle to the French proposal:

> The government of the USSR subscribes to the principle of noninterference in the affairs of Spain and is ready to take part in the proposed agreement. The government of the USSR desires also that, in addition to the states mentioned in the French appeal, Portugal should also join in the agreement, and secondly, that the assistance rendered by certain states to the rebels against the legal government of Spain should be immediately discontinued.[6]

Although the Soviet government accepted nonintervention in principle, she attempted to hedge and save face with the left throughout the world. The Communist parties abroad did not reverse their policy of advocating intervention on behalf of the Spanish people. They merely refrained from directly attacking the Non-Intervention Agreement while demanding the end of neutrality by the masses and urging all democratic forces to rally to the support of the Spanish government. Harry Pollitt, a leader of the British Communist party, wrote in the *International Press Correspondence* on August 8, 1936:

> It is no exaggeration to declare that, just as the coming to power of fascism in Germany in 1933 opened up a new and gravely dangerous international situation that has disturbed the peace of the whole world, so in Spain a struggle is now being fought out, the outcome of which will decide the future of democracy, social progress, collective security, and peace all over the world.
>
> For this reason there can be no question of any attitude of neutrality on the part

of any person claiming to have the slightest respect for democracy, the will of the people, and constitutional government.

The key to success for the democratic forces in Spain lies in the hands of the people of France and Britain above all others, and if we had used half the energy and power to support the legally elected Spanish government that the Fascists and reactionaries in Italy, Germany, France, and Britain have done to support the Spanish Fascists, decisive victory would already have been won.[7]

From this seemingly ambivalent attitude of the Soviet Union it is possible to conclude that her acceptance of the agreement was owing primarily to the pressure and needs of her ally, France. The evidence shows further that, almost from the beginning, the Communist leaders were highly doubtful of the outcome. The continued attacks by foreign Communists on the neutral policy of the democratic masses and the Soviet decision as early as the end of August to circumvent the pact by clandestine aid to the Loyalists is a strong indication that the Soviet Union never considered it possible to counteract Hitler and Mussolini by a mere agreement not backed by police controls.

As each day passed, the Soviet government became more and more skeptical about the consequence of the nonintervention policy. Even the Soviet press began to voice doubts. An editorial in the *Journal de Moscou*, French language newspaper published by the Foreign Affairs Commissariat in Moscow, on August 11, 1936, questioned whether Germany would give up her plans in Spain:

If only the French proposition had a more substantial result than some platonic statement of neutrality, it would have meant for Fascist Germany that she would have to abandon her project of establishing a military base on the other side of the Pyrenees, a project which she has been elaborating for a long time.

The unilateral blockade of France and Great Britain against military aid to the Spanish government, while Germany and Italy still refused to accept nonintervention and continued to supply the rebels, intensified the protests of Moscow's subsidiaries, the Communists abroad, against neutrality, and they demanded the blockade be lifted and the leadership be assumed by the Communists in the struggle to help the Spanish people:

The present blockade of Republican Spain must be raised at once. . . . It is high time to grant the Spanish Republic that assistance which those who are falling there in the cause of freedom have every right to demand, those who are protecting France from the horrors of war by their heroic fight; and in the first place, the intervention of Hitler and Mussolini must be stopped. The Communists will take the lead in this fight for the support of the Spanish people, to which they have a right.[8]

While outside Russia the Communists were openly attacking the policy
of neutrality, the Soviet government maintained a diplomatically correct attitude in line with its acceptance of the French proposal. The
press stopped reporting mass meetings in favor of the Spanish Republic
and the Soviet newspapers still made no direct attack on the policy of
neutrality, nor did they advocate that communism lead in the fight for
democracy in Spain. They showed their misgivings only indirectly. The
Soviet press emphasized that Italy and Germany were purposely delaying their answer to France's note[9] and continued to publish the evidence
of uninterrupted "Fascist" intervention.[10]

The growing doubts of the Soviet leaders concerning the advisability
of nonintervention were probably the most influential cause for their
demurring final ratification of the Non-Intervention Agreement. Negotiations between M. Payart, the French ambassador in Moscow, and
Litvinov were allowed to drag on for many days. A French embassy
official in Moscow also indicated to an American colleague other reasons
for the delay. He reported that:

. . . it was extremely difficult to get the Soviet authorities to agree to the exchange
of notes. Even Litvinov often found it necessary to refer certain points to his
government. The hesitation was probably caused by the feeling that the Kremlin
might be criticized by the more militant revolutionary forces of the world and the
fact that the Soviet Government might eventually be pushed into a position which
would permit it to be said that it had assumed obligations on behalf of certain
organizations resident on its territory over which it has hitherto professed to have
no control.[11]

The USSR was, however, firmly committed to accept the agreement by
her earlier adherence in principle and by her alliance with France.
Consequently, on August 23, notes were finally exchanged between the
Soviet Union and France. The Soviet Union, however, made certain
that her adherence was subject to a similar acceptance by Germany,
Italy, and Portugal:

The Government of the USSR, so far as they are concerned, will put this declaration in force as soon as, in addition to the French and British Governments which
have already exchanged notes under date of 15th August on this subject, the Italian,
German and Portuguese Governments have also acceded to it.[12]

The Soviet press announcing the exchange of notes warned that mere
adherence to the proposal was not going to be enough. The *Journal de
Moscou* declared (August 25, 1936):

But, even when these countries shall have subscribed to the French proposal, it
will be necessary to exert every effort in order that the adopted declaration may not
be a dead letter; in order that, for the same reason, it may become obligatory for
all the countries which shall have signed it.

Soviet suspicions were not lessened by Germany's adherence on August 24; and the Soviet leaders persistently refused to associate themselves too closely with the democracies in support of nonintervention. They also tried to minimize as much as possible their abandonment of the legal government of Spain. An editorial in *Izvestiia* on August 26 attempted to rationalize the Soviet government's reasons for support of the agreement and showed clearly its increasingly hostile attitude toward the policy:

. . . It must be stated frankly that a declaration of neutrality in connection with events such as those taking place in Spain is not our idea, but a special type of innovation in international theory and practice. Up to the present time there has been no precedent whereby a government of any country elected in accordance with its laws and recognized by all powers, is put on a level both juridically and in practice with rebels.

We have every reason to suppose that if an uprising of left and progressive elements should burst forth anywhere against a reactionary Fascist dictatorship, the majority of those who are now hypocritically ranting for neutrality and nonintervention would take up an opposite point of view. They would not only demand a renunciation of aid to the rebels, but would do all in their power to aid the reactionary government. For this reason it is necessary not to close one's eyes to the fact that in the present concrete example of Spain, the theory of neutrality is in fact a general retreat before Fascist governments and their supporters in various countries. . . .

The declaration of neutrality worked out by the French government is apparently directed toward the cessation of this [Fascist] aid to the rebels and to the guaranteeing of the actual nonparticipation of other countries in Spanish affairs. For this reason, the motives which led the Soviet government to accept this declaration are understood. . . .

Although France, as proof of good faith, had on August 8 prohibited French citizens from sending arms to Spain, and Great Britain had followed suit on August 15, the Soviet Union took no specific measures until August 28 after decrees halting armament shipment had been issued by Italy, Germany, and Portugal.[13] The "illogical" attitude of England and France was additional fuel to the Kremlin's dissatisfaction which the Soviet press was beginning frankly to admit. On August 24 *Pravda* declared:

As a result [of the British and French embargoes] there has developed a situation in which the rebels unimpededly receive war material from Italy and Germany while the legal Spanish government, if it tried to buy equipment from France and England, is virtually deprived of the opportunity. This situation will not improve even if Germany and Italy adhere to the Non-Intervention Agreement since there is no guarantee whatsoever that the Fascist countries will not violate it.

THE FORMATION OF THE NON-INTERVENTION COMMITTEE

Continued reports and rumors from Spain of war materials still being sent in large quantities to both sides were a clear indication that the mere exchange of notes was not going to be sufficient to stop intervention. In order to strengthen the commitments, the French government proposed a committee to implement and amplify the Non-Intervention Agreement. The French suggested it meet in London because they hoped that the British government would thereby take a strong interest and an active lead in seeing that the agreement was honored. The role of the Soviet government in the formation of the committee is unknown. It may be the Soviet Union in fact warned France she would not abide by the commitment unless it were strengthened by some system of control preventing supplies from going to the rebels. Or it may be that the growing restlessness of the Soviet Union about Spain made a break appear imminent. However, it would seem the French were motivated primarily by the continued and expanded aid from Hitler and Mussolini to the generals, and the fear of a German-Italian-controlled Spain.

The Soviet Union immediately backed the idea of a committee as the only chance of implementing the agreement, although she held little hope for its success. Nevertheless the Soviet leaders, while supporting the committee, were unwilling to wait to give it time to function; about this period the Soviet Politbureau decided to intervene in Spain on behalf of the Republic. It is unknown whether this dual policy arose from a division within the Soviet leadership or a double-edged policy common to Russian diplomatic maneuvers. The latter would seem the more likely interpretation. Even if a program of police control did grow out of the committee's deliberation, the Soviet leaders knew Germany and Italy would do everything possible to delay its application and would in the meantime send as much material as possible to the rebels. These munitions and supplies would throw the balance of military strength to the side of the rebel generals while the legal government of Spain would be unable to augment its military strength. Consequently, it is probable that the Soviet government backed both tactics as part of one consistent policy; intervention to counteract Italian and German aid until a system of effective control could be inaugurated, and support of the London committee as the ultimate method of eliminating Spain as a source of European rivalry.

The first meeting of the Non-Intervention Committee on September 9 merely established it as formal organization. At the second meeting, held on September 14, a chairman's subcommittee was appointed to do the real work since the full committee of twenty-six nations was considered too unwieldy. The chairman's subcommittee was composed of Belgium, Britain, Czechoslovakia, France, Italy, Germany, Sweden, and Russia. It was further resolved, on the suggestion of the USSR, that complaints concerning violations of the nonintervention pact should be considered by the subcommittee and then reported to the full committee. The permanent chairman for the committee was Lord Plymouth, Parliamentary undersecretary at the Foreign Office, and the committee's secretary was Francis Hemming, a British civil servant.

The operation of the committee was hindered from the very beginning by two factors. First, not until the end of September did the combined influence of France and Great Britain, exercised not only through diplomatic channels but also through conversations at Geneva, succeed in inducing the Portuguese government to waive objections to its participation in the Non-Intervention Committee. Without Portugal, its work would have been ineffective; the strongly prorebel government in Lisbon was not only supplying material, but permitting transshipment of German and Italian supplies across its country. Second, the meetings were immediately charged with hostility as shown by the dialogue between Samuel B. Kagan (Cahan), representative of the USSR, and Dino Grandi, representative of Italy, at the second meeting on September 14:

M. Cahan: I was saying that we know that the Spanish Government has drawn the attention of the British and the French Governments to the case of the delivery in Italian boats of twenty-four Italian military airplanes at Vigo. We have also heard a report that in Spanish Morocco there are ten Italian heavy bombers being assembled. I propose that in fullfillment of those important tasks which are entrusted to this Committee, these reports and similar reports, and any information of a similar nature in the possession of the Governments represented here should be the subject of an immediate investigation by this Committee.

S. Dino Grandi: I would like to make a very short observation upon what has just been said by the honorable representative of Soviet Russia. I quite agree with what is just proposed, that the Committee should be charged with the full investigation of any information which reaches it, concerning any kind of foreign activities in Spain. I am sure that when the Committee will be in full possession of this information, it will be easy to ascertain that many European countries are, or at least have been, carrying out all sorts of activities and forms of intervention in Spain, which cannot be considered in accordance with the Agreement of Non-Intervention, and first amongst all these countries, the Union of Soviet Russia.[14]

Thus the pattern of recrimination in the committee, primarily between the representatives of the USSR and Italy, was established from the outset.

CHAPTER III

THE LEFT AND NONINTERVENTION

LEON BLUM DEFENDS HIS POLICY

NEITHER THE Non-Intervention Agreement nor the committee, although acceded to and joined by all interested powers, did anything to remove the Spanish conflict from European politics as Blum had hoped. The delaying tactics of Italy and Germany, the many reservations of Portugal, and the continued circumstantial reports from Spain of aid to the rebels disturbed and exasperated the Communist and democratic left; clearly Mussolini and Hitler were not being deterred by the non-intervention pact.

On the other side, Italy and Germany still accused Russia and France of aiding the Madrid government. This claim found strong support among the French rightists. Propaganda about Communist attempts to establish a satellite in Spain almost reached the level of hysteria during the Nazi rally at Nuremberg in the first weeks of September. Mussolini began to rattle the saber. He boasted that Italy could mobilize eight million troops, intimating that if France chose to support the Madrid government he would not stand idly by.

More and more the various factions in European politics began to take sides. It was obvious that even the Pope, though declaring his neutrality in the conflict, favored the rebels because he was distressed by the anti-Church activities in the Loyalist zones.[1]

France was the political arena where these views clashed and divided the country. Leon Blum, in spite of his efforts, found the issue overshadowing and undermining his domestic program. Most alarming, Blum by appeasing the noninterventionist views of the Radical Socialists and the British government was losing the support of his own Socialist party and one of his Popular Front allies, the Communist party. On August 5, Leon Jouhaux, the secretary-general of the *Confederation Generale du Travail* (CGT), outlined in a speech at Lille the opinion of the opposition within the Socialist party to Blum:

In the face of the Spanish situation there can be no neutrality for the conscientious worker. The old dogma of non-intervention has cost us dearly and now threatens to cost us even more. The defeat of the Spanish workers may well prove our defeat, not only from the social point of view, but even the defeat of our own country.[2]

---

[1] For notes to chap. iii, see pp. 140–143.

On August 13, the French Communist party addressed an open letter to the Socialists:

It is intolerable that we should watch the rebels being supplied by Italy and Germany while the legal government of Spain sees a political blockade raised against it—a kind of sanctions regime which, in spite of international decisions, was not put into operation against Italy, although she was guilty of invading Abyssinia.

We are of the opinion that in the present situation it would be useful for our two parties to make a common step in favor of united international action to support the Spanish people in their glorious fight for liberty and peace.[3]

The CGT, although not officially connected with the French Socialist party (SFIO), nevertheless was composed mostly of Socialists and headed the Socialist opposition to the policy of nonintervention. On August 21 the Administrative Committee of the CGT issued a statement reaffirming "complete solidarity with the Spanish proletariat and people" and insisting on the right of French workers "to come to the aid of their Spanish comrades by every means in their power." This growing opposition finally forced Blum to take his case in person before his party during the first week of September. Against shouts of "Des avions pour l'Espagne!" Blum gave his view of the Non-Intervention Agreement:

...I assume the entire responsibility for the Government's actions. Our policy will lead to the salvation of Spain and the maintenance of peace....

The result was, it is true, that we found our hands tied for a long time, while others were enabled to supply the insurgents. That injustice of continued supplies to one side embittered you, as it did us, but weigh up the advantages of the Convention. Had we not suggested an international convention and secured adhesions to it where should we have been?

Remember the declaration of one of the insurgent chiefs who was prepared to throw Europe into an inferno rather than accept defeat. Our suggestion saved Europe from a general conflagration.

There is no proof of any Government adhering to the Convention having violated its signature. Yet a strong trade union delegation yesterday urged me to declare in favour of a policy of assistance to Spain. We decline to dishonour our signature to the convention.

It is impossible to act otherwise without causing an European crisis of which it is difficult to foresee the consequences....

* * *

I will never admit that war is inevitable and will labour until the last minute to avoid it. I will never despair of maintaining peace.[4]

In this same speech Blum attacked the Soviet Union for its two-faced approach:

Do not let us forget that the international convention of non-intervention in Spain bears the signature of Soviet Russia. Yet one political group [the Communists] which adhered to this contract by the Popular Front parties appears to be criticising our actions. Does it wish to repudiate the contract?

But Blum's persuasive words were not enough to turn popular feeling in his favor. Although his party was forced to support him, the daily reports of German and Italian planes flying to rebel Spain nullified his words. The very next day 200,000 metal workers in the Paris region went on strike for an hour in protest.

Because the CGT and Communists could not persuade Blum's government to abandon its policy of neutrality, they found themselves in a serious dilemma. Refusal to support the Blum government would mean its collapse and very likely the end of the Popular Front's control of the government. Consequently, on September 8, in the face of more strikes, the Administrative Committee of the CGT passed a face-saving resolution. On the one hand it affirmed its solidarity with the Blum government, while on the other it declared:

... the committee recognizes that the possibility of arriving at total non-intervention is compromised by the attitude of countries who have taken sides with factions of Spaniards against the regular Spanish Government and by the diplomatic reserves and effective action of Germany and Portugal which are jeopardizing the principle of neutrality.

Under these conditions, and continuing its action in favor of the Spanish Republic, the committee esteems it as its duty to request the French Government to reconsider, in accord with the English and other democratic governments, its policy of neutrality. . . .[5]

The Communists also bowed to the pressure. They stated they would not vote against the government but declared their views remained unchanged. Maurice Thorez expressed the Communist views in a fiery editorial in *L'Humanite* on September 9: "For the honor of the working class, for the honor of the Popular Front, for the honor of France, the blockade that is killing our Spanish brethren and that is killing peace must be lifted."

Even though compromise was forced momentarily on the French working classes by the Blum government, the French Communists were not deterred and refused to give up. At the end of October they again appealed to the Socialists to abandon nonintervention and repeated their demand periodically thereafter,[6] but the Socialists, however reluctantly, continued to support Blum. For example, in February, 1937, in the face of continued large-scale intervention by Germany and Italy, the National Council of the Socialist party approved the government's policy of nonintervention by a vote of 4,661 to 732. Even in July, 1937, when the Non-Intervention Agreement had unquestionably failed to prevent the transport of arms and troops to Spain, Blum declared to the Socialist Congress: "I accept full responsibility for what we have done in this matter, though I agree that many of our hopes have been deceived. Thanks to the line of non-intervention, peace has been preserved."[7]

The French Socialists were thus willing to sacrifice Spain and appease the right and German and Italy in order to continue in power and maintain peace both in France and in Europe.[8] Not until June of 1938 did the Socialists abandon their support of nonintervention.[9]

THE BRITISH LABOUR PARTY AND NONINTERVENTION

During August and September, 1936, the British Labour party was faced with much the same problem as the French left in respect to Spain.[10] The circumstances and reactions among British labor circles, however, were very different from those in France, although the final policy was in fact similar. In the first place the Labourites were not troubled with the problem of actual participation in government, as were Blum and the Socialists, and could sit in the much more comfortable position of the Opposition and merely criticize the government's policy of nonintervention. Another very significant difference in the position of the two groups was the attitude of the rank and file of the labor movements. While in France they staged daily demonstrations in favor of the Spanish workers and frequent strikes against Blum's policy, the British workers manifested only the slightest interest. W. Lawther of the Mineworkers' Federation and B. A. Bagnari of the Clerks and Administrative Workers described this apathy at the Trade Union Congress held in Plymouth during September, 1936:

> *Mr. W. Lawther:* ... It is now nearly eight weeks since the rebellion started in Spain, and before going further into the question I should like to draw the attention of the Congress to the fact that while the Spanish workers are sacrificing their lives in defense of democracy it cannot be said that the Trade Union and Labour Movement of this country has done all it could have done in support of the Spanish workers. ... It is true that already some £13,000 has been collected, but it is also true that there has not been one big meeting or one big demonstration organised by the General Council or by the National Council of Labour in support of Spain and to explain the facts of the situation. ...
>
> * * *
>
> *Mr. B. A. Bagnari:* ... The General Secretary told us we have raised £13,000. Let us analyse what that means. ... It means almost exactly seven-eighths of a penny per member of the Trade Union Congress. Is your democracy worth seven-eighths of a penny? ...[11]

The result of this indifference was that neither the rank and file nor the labor leaders desired to take a strong stand on the Civil War, even though their general sympathies were for the Spanish workers. In France Blum had barely been able to persuade his party to support him and then only reluctantly; in Great Britian the decision to support the nonintervention pact was approved by the great majority of the leaders, the individual members of the party, and especially the trade unions.[12] Many British Labourites by tradition were pacifists as were a large minority in the Socialist party of France. Furthermore, there prevailed throughout England a desire for peace and a peaceful solution; the British people were willing to fight only if their country was directly threatened but not if the cause was collective security.

Consequently, from the first days the various organs of the labor movement in Great Britain passed resolutions supporting their Spanish comrades and condemning Nazi and Fascist intervention,[13] but they side-stepped the important issue of whether or not to support the policy of nonintervention. Not much enthusiasm could be found for the agreement, especially in view of its continued sabotage by Germany and Italy, yet the British labor movement was unable to bring itself to the position of denouncing it. At the Labour Party Conference at the end of August, 1936, the debate on the issue was indecisive. Finally on September 9 the National Council of Labour at a special meeting at Plymouth adhered to the policy of nonintervention and at the same place next day the decision was endorsed by the Trade Union Congress.[14]

The debate in the Trade Union Congress clearly shows the attitude and reasoning of the British labor movement. Sir Walter Citrine, General Secretary, presented the defense in support of the resolution. One of the arguments used was that failure to support nonintervention would bring about the collapse of the Blum government and destroy the solidarity between the French and British Socialists who had maintained close contact with each other throughout the crisis. But Sir Walter very clearly expressed the real reason for the decision:

... You have all read in the papers how a deputation consisting of Mr. Greenwood, Mr. Middleton and myself met Mr. Eden on August 18. We argued the case that you would put. We argued that in Spain they had a democratically, properly constituted Government. We argued that that Government was entitled to the supplies of munitions it needed. We argued that that agreement, while on paper preventing the Fascist Powers from supplying munitions, was in fact being held up in such a way as to give those Governments all the opportunities they needed for supplying arms. We also said that all the evidence proved that you could not trust the word of Mussolini or of Hitler, irrespective of what they signed or what they promised. ...

The Government never left the slightest doubt in our minds that they regarded it as absolutely imperative, if the peace of Europe was to be preserved, to back up to the fullest of their power, the proposals of the French Government. They said it was essential to avoid war, and whatever the rights or wrongs of the situation might be, whatever the technical rights of the Spanish Government, they had to be considered against a much larger and much greater and graver question. They foresaw that in the event of the Powers supplying munitions to Spain you would have the Powers in Europe forming into two rival blocs. . . . They felt that would inevitably mean that sooner or later there would be conflict in Spain between the Powers, which would rapidly spread to other countries and perhaps to the whole of Europe itself. They also claimed that the agreement would succeed. . . .

If there is no other means except naval action or military action to restrain a Hitler and a Mussolini, dare I tie the British Labour Movement, dare I tie British public opinion to take that sort of action? Frankly, friends, I could not say "Yes" to that. . . . I thought to myself even in the British Labour Movement we shall require some heart-searching before we can give a definite clear reply as to what we should do on that question. . . .

I would remind you of the fact that there are no Governments in the world today who are in a better position from the point of view of military, naval and air equipment than Italy and Germany. They have spent hundreds of millions of pounds in equipping their forces, and if anybody could supply munitions it would be those two Powers. The democratic Governments, on the other hand, have their own domestic needs to consider. Some of them are very apprehensive indeed that before very long they may have to use all the resources at their disposal to defend their own frontiers. . . .

May I remind you of the "Kamerun" incident. When the Spanish Government in the pursuit of its rights stopped the "Kamerun," the German merchant ship, and searched her, you remember what happened. The German Admiral, Admiral Carls, commanding the warships in Spanish waters said, "I have instructed my fighting ships to reply with force to every unjustified act of force of your ships." That is the type of thing that leads to war. . . .[15]

Even the small group who opposed nonintervention in the Trade Union Congress was not consistent and expressed the same intense desire to avoid war. For example, the Furnishing Trade Association led the movement to oppose nonintervention and at the same time sponsored a resolution "that on no account whatever shall the Trade Union Movement assist the Government in its desire for conscription, either in the armed forces or in the industrial field, in the event of war."[16] This was the approach also of the British Communists who demanded that the government use the threat of force, but refused to support the rearmament program needed to back these threats.

In spite of the basic inconsistency of the Communists, their attacks on neutrality and their demands for collective security vexed the peace of mind of the left in England. The mass demonstrations and the collections of large sums from Soviet workers, forced or voluntary, disquieted the conscience of the left. Sir Walter tried to dismiss the Communists by saying, "we wondered . . . how it was that the Communist Party of France could demand that the French Government should send munitions to Spain, and that the same Communist Party never raised its voice to ask that one of the greatest Powers in the world, from which it draws its inspiration and its help, should do anything of the kind—a most significant omission."[17]

Thus the labor movement in Great Britain, as in France, in the beginning supported the government's nonintervention policy and rejected active help for the Loyalist cause. By October the British Labourites began to doubt the wisdom of their decision.[18] Throughout October the Labourites expatiated the problem within labor circles and with the government. By the end of the month, although they still did not support direct intervention on behalf of the Loyalists to counteract Italian and German aid to the generals, they advocated international resumption of free trade of arms with the legitimate government of Spain. The new resolution of the British Trade Union Congress and Labour party leaders in joint session adopted on October 28 declared:

In view of the fact that the Non-Intervention Agreement has proved ineffective in its operation, this joint conference calls upon the British Government, acting in collaboration with the French Government, immediately to take the initiative in promoting an international agreement which will completely restore to democratic Spain full commercial rights, including the purchase of munitions, and thus enable the Spanish people to bring their heroic struggle for liberty and democracy to a victorious conclusion.[19]

As noted before, the British Labour party as the Opposition could easily reject the policy of nonintervention, in contrast to the French Socialists who as a member of the Popular Front government had to assume governmental responsibility. The Labour party was merely performing its duty in challenging and criticizing governmental policy. It committed the labor movement to no positive action in favor of the Loyalists, thus giving the Communists occasion to complain: "Four months ago the Labour Party's national conference passed a resolution calling for all possible steps to be taken to get the 'neutrality' farce ended. Since then, as a national organization, it has done precisely nothing."[20]

The British Socialists during the ensuing ten months condemned Fascist and Nazi intervention and alternated between advocating the complete abandonment of nonintervention and urging strong measures of control to effectuate the Non-Intervention Agreement. They never, however, dropped their neutral view in favor of a policy of direct support of the Loyalists.[21] They upheld at most only the traditional right of states to trade with the legitimate government of Spain.[22] In arguing against the Non-Intervention Agreement, the Socialists found it very difficult to get around the government's contention that although the pact may not have stopped intervention, it had prevented the war from spreading. Peace had, after all, been maintained in the rest of Europe. This rationale struck a responsive chord in the British people whose primary interest in foreign affairs was to keep the peace.[23] It was not really until Anthony Eden resigned from the Foreign Ministry that the Labour Party consistently opposed the government's foreign policy.

THE CIVIL WAR AND THE SECOND AND THIRD INTERNATIONALS

The Socialist International and the International Federation of Trade Unions followed the lead of their two most important sections in France and Great Britain. At first they supported the Non-Intervention Agreement,[24] but through a joint meeting of the leaders on October 26, 1936, they declared that the pact had failed and complete commercial rights should be restored to the legitimate government in Spain. While the Comintern complimented the Socialist International for finally making a positive resolution, it exhorted, "But to-day such declarations no longer suffice; it is necessary to act, for the last hour has struck. But nothing is said precisely regarding the intended action."[25] The next step the Comintern leaders wanted the Socialist groups to take was positive and common action with the Communists, as they had urged from the beginning:[26]

... to organize in every country a joint campaign of the C.I., the L.S.I. and the I.F.T.U. in order to evoke a great popular mass movement in favor of the legitimate Spanish government. This joint action should compel the democratic governments to lift the blockade now operating against Spanish democracy; all international working-class organizations should join hands to prevent the production and transport of war materials to the Fascist rebels; clothes, food, and medical stores should be sent to the champions of Spanish liberty by joint effort, and a joint relief committee should be formed to assist the wives and children of the militiamen fighting against the Fascists or killed in that struggle.[27]

The Socialists, however, resisted and continued to resist throughout the war all Communist invitations for joint action in respect to Spain. Neither the Socialist International nor the Socialist organs of the separate countries, except in Spain, accepted the Comintern offer. Although they were willing on occasion to discuss Spain with the

Communists, they refused common cause with them. The Third International met such refusals with bitter denunciations. For example Georgi Dimitrov, head of the Comintern, protested:

At a time when the fascist rebels in Spain are slaughtering Socialist and Communist workers who are fighting shoulder to shoulder at the front, when they are spreading death and destruction throughout the country, the leadership of the Socialist international persistently refuses to organize aid for the Spanish people jointly with the Communist International.[28]

The Communists did not criticize the inactivity of only the French and British sections of the Socialist International. In July, 1937, after the Comintern had again failed in new negotiations, they censured the Socialists of the smaller nations as well:

First of all, they [the opponents of united action] assert that they have themselves already done everything necessary for Spain, and that for that reason common action with the Communists is superfluous. . . .

* * *

Social-Democrats are members of the governments of Belgium, Czechoslovakia, Denmark, Sweden and Finland. Have they adhered to their own decision and acted this way in relation to their own governments? No, they have not; at any rate the behavior of these governments towards Spain does not as yet show this. Perhaps the Right Social-Democrats will object: "Yes, our countries are not big, their relative weight in the League of Nations is insignificant. So long as England and France do not change their line, we can do nothing."

That is not quite true. Of course, very much in the Spanish question depends upon the attitude of England and France. But collective action on the part of the small states in support of Spain would undoubtedly make a big impression upon the governments of England and France, and would have its influence upon their attitude towards Spain. . . .[29]

Perhaps there is a certain amount of truth in the accusations that the small states hid throughout this period behind the excuse of English and French appeasement. If instead they had banded together in resisting Hitler and urging the French and British governments to resist, they might have acted as a significant force in international relations.

Communist recriminations against the Socialists continued unabated throughout the Civil War.[30] Except in France the sections of the Communist International in Western Europe were relatively small. Therefore, it is doubtful that a united program of the two Internationals would have added significantly to the Loyalist cause. In fact, it might have done just the opposite. The leaguing together of Socialists and Communists would certainly have aroused the suspicions of the moderate and conservative groups in Western Europe and would have made it much more difficult for the Socialists to influence government policy.

The Socialists also had other good reasons for not accepting the Comintern's invitations. The methods of the Communists had long alienated the Socialists and the purges then current in the Soviet Union convinced them even more that the ways of Communism were incompatible with democratic socialism. The Socialists of the West had adopted democratic means to accomplish their ends, and the Communists' allusions to more drastic measures to force changes in the policies of the democratic governments toward Spain were not to their liking. From the very beginning the Socialists, particularly the British Labour party, had not been won over to the Comintern's united front program and had immediately rejected any idea of adopting it on an international level. Furthermore, they were apprehensive that the Communists might use the united front for infiltration into the Socialist ranks. The successful application of this technique by the Communists in Spain confirmed their fears.[31]

Finally, it must be recognized that there existed among all the Socialist parties a tendency toward pacifism and a willingness to appease Hitler and Mussolini in the cause of peace. While some groups on the left wanted to use the general strike and other vigorous measures to force the democratic governments to take a positive stand against German and Italian intervention in Spain, even larger groups were much less concerned about the fate of Spain and more interested in maintaining peace at almost any cost. The strength of the latter was often exemplified in Great Britain by the rather academic opposition of the Labour party to the government's policy of nonintervention. Between the two extremes the Socialist leaders of Western Europe steered a middle road and refused to join the Communists' whole-hearted adoption of the Loyalist cause.

CHAPTER IV

THE SOVIET UNION INTERVENES

THE EVIDENCE INDICATES that the Soviet Union during the last week of August or the first week of September decided to intervene actively in Spain on the side of the Popular Front.[1] What caused the Soviet Union to act alone when the Socialists of France and Great Britain together with their governments resolved against aid to the Loyalist government? Why did she break the Non-Intervention Agreement as soon as she signed it in order to support almost singlehandedly the Spanish government's fight against the rebel generals aided by Portugal, Italy, and Germany? The Fascists and many conservative circles claimed that the Communists were intervening to set up a Soviet satellite. The Communists in contrast asserted that they were merely aiding bourgeois democracy in Spain. Neither of these explanations, as discussed in the first volume of this study, *Communism and the Spanish Civil War*, seems to approach the truth. A thorough investigation of the internal activities of the Communists in Spain does not substantiate the charge that the Soviet leaders intended setting up a Communist government in Spain. Even when the opportunity for power presented itself time and again, the Soviet agents prevented the Communists from taking over the reins of government. That the Soviet Union intervened purely to save bourgeois democracy was equally unlikely and was believed by only a few, even at the time.[2] The Soviet Union before and afterward never showed such altruism toward the democratic movements of the West, and her acts of terror and violence in Spain are sufficient evidence that her goals were not humanitarian. The whole purpose of the Comintern was to prepare for the overthrow of bourgeois society, and the doctrines of the Popular Front as laid down in the 1935 Congress of the Comintern did not abandon this objective.[3] The explanation of the Soviet move, therefore, must lie somewhere between the two extremes.

The immediate stimulus for the Soviet action was, of course, the continued support of the rebels by Italy and Germany; the Soviet Union intervened to counteract this aid.[4] But why Stalin was willing to engage in a semiwar with Hitler and Mussolini in Western Europe is difficult to answer.

From the statements in *Mein Kampf* down through nearly all the

---

[1] For notes to chap. iv, see pp. 143–144.

pronouncements of the National Socialist party, Hitler had made known his explicit hate for the Communists and his desire to overthrow the Soviet regime. He also made no secret of his wish to develop a German empire out of Soviet territory. After Hitler's victory in 1933 and 1934 and the complete subordination of the German nation to his will, including the annihilation of the Communist and Socialist parties, the Soviet leaders could not fail to realize the danger of Nazi aggression toward themselves. The desire to overthrow the Communist regime in Russia was not unusual though rather academic in the West, but behind it in Germany there lurked the driving force of a fanatical movement and leader backed by rapid rearmament.

Hitler's anti-Comintern crusade appeared all the more menacing considering the state of military unpreparedness in the Soviet Union. The Soviet Union was in the midst of a second social, political, and economic revolution, and all her energy and resources were needed to untangle it. The Communist party and government also were in the initial stages of a purge and reign of terror that was already beginning to rock the foundations of political power, including the entire military command. Forced collectivization among the peasants and the uncertainty and ruthlessness of the purge were creating a social discontent which made doubtful the loyalty of large segments of the Soviet population to the regime. Amid such internal conflicts the Soviet leaders were in no position to build a military force to compete with a rapidly arming, economically strong Germany. Already by 1936, and perhaps much earlier, the German military machine was superior to Russia's and the disparity was likely to increase unless the Nazi menace could be stopped.[5]

In this distinctly unequal armaments race with Germany, the Soviet Union had three alternatives: (1) to develop a system of collective security with the Western democracies for the joint suppression of German aggression, (2) to engage Hitler in war early in his career before he was ready for aggression to the East and wear down his forces by attrition, or (3) to try to appease Hitler. Probably Stalin put his hopes in these alternatives in the order given above, the first representing the most positive and sure means of extricating Russia from her predicament and the last representing the highest cost with the least insurance. It may also be argued that in the period from 1936 to 1939, as a good strategist, Stalin never excluded any of these alternatives absolutely, though this is impossible to prove. The first expressions of a Soviet policy of collective security began in 1934–5 with the signing of the Franco-Soviet Pact, the entrance of the Soviet Union into the League of Nations, and the launching of the Popular Front program in France. Until 1939 the statements of Commissar of Foreign Affairs Maxim Litvinov reiterated the paramountcy of the Soviet desire for collective security and never failed to stress the need to stop "Fascist" aggression in Ethiopia, the Rhineland, Spain, China, Austria, Czecho-slovakia, and elsewhere.[6]

The Spanish Civil War was the first engagement of Hitler's arms and troops in combat for the expansion of German hegemony and the Soviet leaders considered it, therefore, the best opportunity to employ the doctrine of collective security. The theory of collective security is based on the idea that a threat to the peace and security of any nation any-where is a threat to the security of every other peaceful nation; in other words peace is indivisible. It would thus follow that even though Spain was remote from Russia, the loss of its independence would be a threat to the Soviet Union. However, to make this system work against Ger-many with her rapidly expanding military force would require the support not only of the Soviet Union but also of France and England. Stalin, consequently, felt the coöperation of France and England was essential for the containment of Germany. It is not unlikely that he considered the Iberian Peninsula a particularly fortunate area in which to inaugurate a working system of collective security. Although Spain under German and Italian control was only a minor threat to Russia, it was a direct threat to France and even Great Britain. Thus Stalin probably felt especially confident that he could influence France to take an active interest in her own security by his intervention in Spain. During the 1920's France had been the leading proponent of collective security. Stalin also knew the sympathies of the Blum government were with the Madrid government, and the vast majority of the Socialists and workers were not in favor of Blum's policy of nonintervention. By his action Stalin may have hoped to throw the balance against Blum and force him to abandon his belief in neutrality, if only to insure that the Loyalist government would not be dominated by the Communists through exclusive Soviet aid. No doubt by this time Blum himself had serious doubts about the feasibility of his policy. Stalin may also by his action have hoped to influence the British Socialists in the same way. Stalin probably planned that his initial intervention would prevent the immediate victory of Franco and his German and Italian allies and save Madrid, thereby giving the slower-acting democracies an opportunity to see the seriousness of the threat. But that Blum, backed by the

British government, would stubbornly stick to his support of nonintervention, in spite of increasing evidence of its violation, could not have been foreseen.

Another possibility is that Stalin may not have expected help from France and England and, therefore, the second alternative of engaging Hitler in a war of attrition, no matter how small, to delay his aggression to the east was the main motive.[7] It is well known that Stalin had a very low opinion of the capabilities and revolutionary instincts of the laboring masses of Western Europe. From the beginning he may have counted on going it alone and saw the Spanish affair merely as a delaying tactic for Nazi aggression against himself. Even before the Spanish Civil War the Communists had predicted Hitler's next move would be against Czechoslovakia. For example, *Pravda* reported on July 19, 1936, on the basis of a Tass communiqué from Paris that Germany, in an agreement with Poland, had formulated a plan of aggression against Czechoslovakia.[8] By keeping Germany involved in Western Europe, Moscow may have hoped to restrain Germany from advancing to the east and threatening the very borders of the Soviet Union. Intervention would also show Hitler that Russia could not be bluffed by a show of force and was not willing to appease him as were England and France. Stalin, as a dictator himself, must also have recognized the importance of success and an aura of invincibility to Mussolini and Hitler for keeping a hold on their followers. Litvinov in a speech in June, 1938, alluded to this factor: "Because of their internal weaknesses and insufficient resources, the present aggressors require rapid military successes."[9] If Stalin could undermine them by defeats in Spain, the task of destroying them would be much easier. Therefore, it is not unreasonable to assume that the Soviet leaders saw a good opportunity in the Spanish crisis to initiate a battle of attrition or at least delay. Spain was a long way from Russia and, by using Spanish workers, the Soviet Union did not have to commit herself to an open war with Germany. Soviet troops thus remained out of the fighting while the Spanish Loyalists served as mercenaries. When the Spanish partisans were not sufficient, the Communists recruited young liberals in the democracies and unwanted foreign Communists to fight for the Loyalist cause in the International Brigades. Thus all the Soviet Union needed to supply was a minimum of equipment and technical assistance, just enough to keep Loyalist resistance from collapsing.[10] As a secondary interest, the Soviet Union also was able to observe and test the technical aspects of modern war, particularly the new techniques being developed by the Germans.[11]

Although Stalin may have wanted to wear down Germany's military strength, it is impossible on the evidence to go so far as some commentators and conclude that Stalin was trying to involve Germany in the West and thereby entirely turn away Hitler's ambitions from the Soviet Union.[12] If the Russians had wanted to direct Hitler westward, they would more likely have given him a free hand in Spain. This in turn would have opened up North Africa for German colonization and would have made an attack on France much easier. Furthermore, it is difficult to see how in any general war that might develop Stalin could have easily withdrawn, since, by giving aid and instruction to the Loyalist troops, he was already in part committed. If he wanted to escape the risk of being a part of the big war, his neutrality from the beginning was essential.

Some commentators have gone even further to claim that Stalin's primary interest was to form a pact with Hitler dividing the world into spheres of influence, bribing Hitler with a free hand in the West. For example, Walter Krivitsky, the former Soviet Chief of Military Intelligence in Western Europe, wrote: "To Stalin the fusion of these two dictatorships is the climax of all he has striven toward for years." And in respect to Spain: "His idea was—and this was common knowledge among us who served him—to include Spain in the sphere of the Kremlin's influence. Such domination would secure his ties with Paris and London, and thus strengthen, on the other hand, his bargaining position with Berlin. Once he was master of the Spanish Government—of vital strategic importance to France and Great Britain—he would find what he was seeking. He would be a force to be reckoned with, an ally to be coveted."[13] The rationale of this thesis is that Stalin, weak militarily, intensely adverse to and distrustful of the capitalist powers, had only the one alternative of negotiating a pact with Hitler. Stalin's problem was to show Hitler that Russia had something to offer and was a power of enough consequence to negotiate with Hitler as an equal. However, it is very unlikely that Stalin this early seriously considered an alliance with Hitler. The evidence to support this view is very meager, all indirect, and based mostly upon a process of reading double meanings into Communist statements. Against this thesis are the explicit statements and actions of the Soviet leaders, seeking collective security with the democracies and heaping venom on the Nazis and Fascists, as will be seen in their role on the Non-Intervention Committee. Even the tactic of the Popular Front was basically directed toward attracting the bourgeois governments into closer relations with the Soviet Union. The difficulty and reason for the failure of the Popular Front program came from the fact that it could not be reconciled with the long-range Communist aim of undermining and destroying the bourgeois states. It does not logically follow from this inconsistency, however, that Stalin refused to drop his basic hostility toward the Socialists and democrats for the purpose of making a pact with Hitler. His continued support of the overthrow of the bourgeois state can be more simply and obviously explained by his desire to retain his leadership over the revolutionary and leftist elements of the world and his faith in the eventual Communist world revolution or conquest led by Soviet Russia.

In contemplating the three-cornered struggle developing among Nazism-fascism, communism, and democracy, and the need to side with one or the other for fear of a Nazi-democratic pact against himself, it is logical that Stalin should have first looked to the democracies for support and alliance. Stalin had little or nothing to fear from the bourgeois democracies, which after 1921 had never attempted to renew their intervention in Soviet Russia even though the Soviet government had been weak and almost totally unarmed during the 1920's and early 1930's. On the other hand, Hitler was arming and calling for a crusade against communism. Certainly Stalin had less chance to achieve and no grounds to trust an alliance with Hitler. As Litvinov pointed out, "history teaches us that aggression and expansion are insatiable."[14] Nevertheless, it is not inconceivable that Stalin, in preparing for all contingencies, left open a possible alliance with Hitler as an alternative, though a distinctly less attractive one, in case an entente with England and France did not materialize and Hitler did not become bogged down in Spain.

Thus the Soviet Union aided Loyalist Spain not from a sense of altruism, but from a need for security. She used Spain as the focal point, the pawn, to bring about a coalition between Russia and the democratic and leftist governments to collectively thwart German aggression, and to delay and deplete Hitler's armament on the battlefield before he became too powerful. These two purposes, mutually beneficial to Russia, could be pursued simultaneously.

CHAPTER V

SOVIET DIPLOMATIC MANEUVERS: SEPTEMBER AND OCTOBER, 1936

THE LEAGUE ASSEMBLY: SEPTEMBER, 1936

THE SPANISH QUESTION was not on the agenda of the Assembly of the League of Nations when it met in September, 1936, because England and France were not in favor of having the League consider the matter. The prestige of the League at this time was at a low ebb owing to the successful Italian conquest of Abyssinia, followed swiftly by the German occupation of the Rhineland. The French and British did not want to embarrass the League further.[1] Also, two of the most interested powers, Germany and Italy, were no longer members of the League and any solution of the Spanish strife would require their complete coöperation. Since the Non-Intervention Committee comprised all the interested powers and was set up specifically to deal with the problem, the democratic powers saw no reason to involve the League. The Spanish Republican delegates at Geneva, however, insisted that the matter be brought up. The Civil War was rapidly approaching a critical stage and the Republican government desperately needed outside help. In addition, the Loyalists were not represented on the Non-Intervention Committee and, consequently, their only chance of putting their plea directly before an international assembly was in the League.

Although the Spanish question was not formally debated in the Assembly, Spain was given a hearing in which she appealed for League intervention on the basis that the Civil War was a danger to peace, and the aid given to the rebels by certain states "whose political regime coincided with that to which the rebels are wedded ... implied the negation of the most elementary and essential principles and rules of international cooperation."[2] The Secretariat of the League, however, refused to publish the Spanish allegations of intervention by Germany and Italy, so the Spanish delegation printed the documents at its own expense and distributed them independently.

The Soviet Union used the opportunity of the Spanish plea to urge the strengthening of collective security and to express her growing dislike of the Non-Intervention Agreement. In respect to the Non-Intervention Agreement, Litvinov had the following to say:

---

[1] For notes to chap. v, see pp. 145–149.

The Soviet Government associated itself with the declaration on non-intervention in Spanish affairs only because a friendly country feared that an international conflict might otherwise ensue. It did so in spite of its opinion that the principle of neutrality does not apply in a case where mutineers are fighting against the lawful government and contradicts the principle of international law, in which view it fully agrees with the statement made to us by the Spanish Minister of Foreign Affairs. It understands that the unjust decision referred to was thrust upon it by those countries which, though they consider themselves the mainstay of order, have created a new situation, fraught with incalculable consequences, as a result of which it is permitted openly to assist mutineers against their lawful government.[3]

At the same time, outside diplomatic circles the Communists were increasingly more outspoken in their condemnation of the democracies for their continued support of the policy of nonintervention. "But France is following blindly—to put it mildly, in view of the present political conditions—behind London. And London is acting cleverly with a view to satisfying Hitlerite ideals. So at Geneva, Mr. Eden did not conceal the objective of this policy."[4] Within the Soviet Union the Communists showed their impatience by launching on September 12, after several weeks of quiescence, a new drive among Soviet workers to collect relief funds for Spanish children and mothers.

THE WORK OF THE NON-INTERVENTION COMMITTEE

The Non-Intervention Committee moved very slowly. Delays were constant. The refusal of Portugal until September 28 to participate made it difficult for the committee to complete its organization. Only after Portugal joined the committee was it possible to determine the procedure by which complaints as to violation of the agreement should be dealt with, and these procedural questions required frequent reference back to the twenty-six governments represented. The burden was relieved somewhat by the chairman's subcommittee, but even with this inner council the work went slowly—such delays, however, were not unusual in an international organization. Finally, the procedure ultimately agreed upon was itself cumbersome. When a complaint on the violation of the nonintervention pact was placed before the committee, it was necessary first to relay it to the accused government for refutation. Several days or weeks later when the answer was received from the accused, the exchanges were distributed among the members. The members in turn required time to examine the refutation before a meeting could be held to consider any action. Consequently, by the middle of October, over two and a half months from the beginning of the war and from the time Italy and Germany first started sending munitions, no complaints had been considered by the committee. Some of the delays in the work of the committee may have been fostered, but most of them were explainable and unavoidable.

But the war in Spain was not moving slowly. The military campaign was quickly approaching a climax. The rebels with German and particularly Italian aid were rapidly consolidating their forces. On September 28 Toledo fell and several Nationalist armies began to converge on Madrid. The fall of Madrid would have dealt a serious blow to the Republican cause and very likely would have made it almost impossible for the Loyalists to rally their forces into an effective defense. The war might have been over in a matter of a few weeks.

Under these circumstances the Soviet Union could not stop or slow down shipment of arms to the Loyalists. She apparently felt it was impossible to wait for the London committee to prove its worth. The longer intervention was delayed, the more difficult and the more costly would it be to save the Popular Front in Spain. By the middle of September the Soviet Union was already finding herself at a serious disadvantage vis à vis Germany and Italy. The prompt aid of Germany and Italy had allowed the rebels to take advantage of the confusion of the Spanish government during the first weeks and provided the means for General Franco to send his troops across the straits from Morocco to Spain and prevent the Loyalist government from stamping out the rebellion immediately. Also to the advantage of Germany and Italy was the delivery of the bulk of their initial aid during the early days prior to the Non-Intervention Agreement. This alone made it almost impossible for the Republican supporters to prove conclusively until much later in the war that Germany and Italy gave aid after August 28, the effective date of the agreement. Russia, on the other hand, did not arrive at the decision to intervene until early September. Consequently all the Soviet aid was in direct contravention of the agreement and she, therefore, was forced to utilize extra precautions in an effort to hide her actions.

Having thrown in her lot with the Loyalists, the Soviet Union became increasingly restless about the slow progress of the London committee. She was more than ever anxious that the committee or preferably England and France immediately act to end German and Italian intervention.[5] A note of warning to London and Paris was implied in the editorial by A. Sedovski in the *Journal de Moscou* on September 28, 1936:

The initiative in this agreement belongs to France and England. Because of the position assumed by these countries, they have brought about the adherence of other countries to this policy as being the least undesirable in the circumstances. But if France and England consider that this policy is the best, they must do everything in their power to make this policy of nonintervention in the affairs of Spain an effective means for avoiding the danger to peace resulting from Fascist intervention in Spanish affairs.

Through Great Britain as intermediary the allegations of the Spanish government against Germany and Italy were brought before the committee at its sixth meeting on October 9. The Italian and German representatives categorically denied the accusations. The committee, following its procedure, however, would not discuss the complaints until they had been submitted in writing to the governments concerned and a written answer was received for consideration by the committee. The Soviet Union argued that the statement by the Italian representative in denying the charges should be accepted as the answer of the Italian government and the committee should proceed from there to take action. The committee, however, overruled this procedure and asserted that an answer in writing was needed.[6] The Soviet proposal was rejected because by proceeding in the agreed fashion there could be no complaints of prejudice or illegality. The French and British governments also hoped Italy and Germany in their written answers would take a more conciliatory attitude. The most important reason, however, was that the committee did not know how to determine the values or how to act in the situation. Was it to accept the word of Germany and Italy or the Republican government? Should it carry on an independent investigation of the matter? And if the accusations were proved correct, what then? Here lay the crux of the nonintervention scheme. The democratic states had instigated and entered into the Non-Intervention Agreement solely on the basis that they individually would do everything to prevent arms from their countries from going to Spain with the hope that the USSR, Germany, and Italy would do likewise. The agreement committed their countries no further. It was not a collective security agreement in which they pledged themselves to see that none of the adhering countries sent arms. The French representative, Charles Corbin, stated this clearly:

Permit me to recall first of all that the requisite principle of the Non-Intervention Agreement is its strict execution by all members of the committee assembled here. It is only if this principle is rigorously upheld and if the spirit of it is universally respected that the agreement has its purpose.[7]

The nonintervention scheme as it stood depended for its success upon the good faith of all the participating powers. France and Britain had hoped that the Non-Intervention Agreement followed by the formation of the Non-Intervention Committee would show Hitler and Mussolini the deep concern they had for any interference into their sphere of the Iberian Peninsula so the dictators would at least minimize their participation. The failure of this warning to deter Germany and Italy had not been contemplated by its originators. The agreed procedure in the Non-Intervention Committee which was inspired by England and France made this clear—a fact not lost to Hitler and Mussolini. In its investigation of alleged breaches, the committee was never intended to be a court to judicate widespread violations by the governments; rather, it was set up to relay and publicize complaints of infractions to the interested governments so they would better enforce the agreement and their own laws. In fact, the final step in the procedure contemplated by the committee was that "(i) on receipt of the observation of the government against which the complaint has been preferred the Committee should take such steps as may appear proper in each case to establish the facts." Thus the committee was to act as little more than an instrument to rally moral force against German and Italian and later Soviet intervention. It was not to consider the case of violation by an entire country backed shamelessly by the government, or what action should be taken in such an event.

Thus when Mussolini and Hitler refused to acknowledge Spain as a French-British sphere and limit their intervention, a new approach was required. But with the isolationist attitudes prevailing among the European democracies, particularly Great Britain, and with the *de facto* collapse of collective security through the League of Nations, it was by no means certain the participating powers would be willing to take the next logical step in the nonintervention scheme, that of policing other powers. At least such a policy was not to be rushed into without prior intensive consultations and careful consideration of the consequences. England and France wanted to be absolutely certain moral force and warnings would not be sufficient. Too precipitous action, it was also feared, might lead to the withdrawal of Germany and Italy from the committee, as they had walked out of the League.

Consequently, when the Soviet Union suggested that, in order to speed up matters, the committee should accept the statement of the Italian representative denying all charges of the Spanish government and proceed from there, the other powers balked.[8] It went beyond what had been contemplated for the committee by most of its members.

THE SOVIET "ULTIMATUM"

At approximately the same time the British government relayed to the committee the allegations against Italy, the Soviet Union presented her own bill of complaints concerning intervention on behalf of the rebels but refrained from attacking Germany and Italy directly. The Soviets chose the least consequential member in the league of rebel supporters, Portugal,[9] as the object of their attack, hoping to knock out the smallest first.[10] The USSR also suspected that Portugal served as the main channel of rebel supplies particularly from Nazi Germany. The note condemning Portugal did not stop with accusations but, attempting to mold the pact into a system of collective security, made several suggestions to the committee. The Soviet Union had never doubted that it was primarily states who were violating the agreement and not individuals. And she was certain more would be required to halt Hitler and Mussolini than pious declarations and accusations that could easily be denied. In line with her charges against Portugal, therefore, she recommended to the committee that "(a) an impartial commission be sent to the Spanish-Portuguese border to investigate on the spot the true state of affairs there, and that (b) this commission should leave there some of its members to control the fulfillment of the Non-Intervention Agreement on that border in the future."[11] Again the committee bypassed the problem by deferring any discussion of these suggestions until it had first received from Portugal a written answer to the complaints.[12]

Not content with the slow pace of the committee or willing to await the outcome of its deliberations on the charges, the Soviet government decided to force the issue by throwing a bombshell into the proceedings. In a letter presented to the committee along with the Russian accusations against Portugal, Soviet representative S. Kagan declared:

> The Soviet Government can in no case agree to turn the Non-Intervention Agreement into a screen shielding the military aid given to the rebels by some of the participants in the Agreement against the legitimate Spanish Government.
>
> The Soviet Government is therefore compelled to declare that if violations of the Agreement for Non-Intervention are not immediately stopped the Soviet Government will consider itself free from the obligations arising out of the Agreement.[13]

This Soviet "ultimatum" was the signal for all the sections, including the Russian section, of the Comintern to attack the failure of the Non-Intervention Agreement.[14] Stalin reënforced this determined stand by the Soviet Union when he wrote to the Spanish Communists: "The toiling classes of the USSR are merely carrying out their duty when they give all possible aid to the revolutionary masses of Spain. They realize that the liberation of Spain from the yoke of Fascist reactionaries is not the private affair of Spaniards but the general concern of all advanced and progressive mankind."[15]

The Soviet Union had several reasons for trying to force the issue at this time.[16] She was well aware of the hypocrisy of Hitler and Mussolini and the reluctance of England and France to face forcefully the true state of affairs in Spain. By her veiled threat she may have hoped to force France and England to take decisive action before it was too late. The events in Spain, furthermore, could not wait indefinitely for the Non-Intervention Committee to awaken to the needs of an adequate system of control. The Soviet government may also have hoped to win over the British Labour party and the French leftists whose support for the Non-Intervention Agreement seemed to be waning. The most important consideration, however, was probably that the Soviet Union needed to justify before the committee and the world her own intervention in Spain. While she was doing everything to keep her actions secret, in a country in the throes of a civil war like Spain, this was virtually impossible. Already all Europe was aware of Soviet intervention. Consequently, the Soviet Union wanted to make it quite clear that she had intervened only because of German and Italian intervention on the side of the generals. The Soviet representative stated the Russian attitude on this point:

... I repeat that, if there is an Agreement, *we want that Agreement to be fulfilled.* If the Committee or the countries represented on the Committee can secure that the Agreement is fulfilled to stop violation, well and good, if it cannot, let the Committee say so and everyone will draw the proper conclusions. As far as we are concerned, we say that unless the breaches are stopped we shall consider ourselves freed from the Agreement.[17]

The possibility that Stalin wanted to destroy the nonintervention scheme cannot be overlooked. He was becoming increasingly embarrassed by Russia's commitment to the Non-Intervention Agreement and more and more convinced of its futility. Thus the motivation was there. Furthermore, empirical grounds for such a conclusion can be found in the persistent demands of the French and British Communists for the end of nonintervention and in the fact that the Soviet Union overwhelmed the committee with two impossible demands and an "ultimatum" before it could begin actually to function.

Regardless of the reasons for which the Soviet Union considered this move necessary at this particular time, it turned out badly for her. First of all, by immediately publishing the letter to the committee in the newspapers, for the purpose of giving it greater impact, the Soviet Union violated the rules of procedure of the committee concerning secrecy of the proceedings.[18] But much more serious was the timing; the Soviet Union took this step at the same meeting she presented her accusations against Portugal and her suggestions that control measures be adopted, and at the same time the Loyalist charges against Italy were presented to the committee. Nevertheless, England and France dismissed the Soviet "ultimatum" not so much because of the manner in which it was presented, but because of their own unreadiness to commit themselves to a system of control or other measures necessary to enforce nonintervention. Thus all three attempts of the Soviet Union to strengthen or destroy the committee on its first day of real operation failed.

THE AFTERMATH OF THE SOVIET "ULTIMATUM"

Italy and Germany successfully used the Soviet "ultimatum" for their own purposes. Count Grandi, Italy's representative, immediately turned it against the Soviet Union:

> The Soviet Government, with a peculiar and suspicious haste, would like to force us to tear up the established rules, and goes so far as to threaten us all with its immediate withdrawal if the Committee does not work miracles of speed. Why this haste? Why this sudden zeal? ...
>
> * * *
>
> The Soviet Government wishes to sabotage our Committee and make it impossible for it to work.
>
> The Communist Government of Russia has not found recent events in Spain satisfactory to its wishes.[19]

The British government was very much alarmed by the Soviet moves and portended that instead of strengthening the agreement, they would bring about its early collapse. The London *Times* on October 9, 1936, made the following comment:

> ... The Russian declaration, technically delivered to the Committee but published textually in Moscow, inevitably assumed the character of a manifesto appealing to Communist sentiment everywhere, challenging the Fascist Governments, and rousing precisely those antagonisms which it is the whole purpose of the Committee to moderate.

The British government was convinced that the Non-Intervention Agreement and Committee were the only means of modifying Mussolini's and Hitler's aims in Spain without precipitating war. Furthermore, Germany, the Conservative leaders repeatedly insisted, was too strong and would easily win the armaments race unleashed by the failure of the agreement. Consequently they feared above all the collapse of nonintervention and were very much concerned by the reports of increasing Communist aid to the Loyalists, which they felt would only strengthen Hitler's desire to intervene by giving him additional cause—to stop the spread of communism. They were determined that the Soviet attempt to "break up the nonintervention scheme" should not be successful.[20]

In addition, most British Conservatives for their own part were alarmed by the possibility of a Communist government in Spain and wanted it even less than a German- and Italian-dominated regime. Thus they had all the more reason to want to maintain the Non-Intervention Agreement, without which Russia could openly and legally aid the Loyalists. Although their apprehension, as discussed previously, was probably groundless, it was one more source of friction between the USSR and Great Britain.

The difference in the British and Soviet outlook on the Spanish problem did not in fact end here. Except for a common desire to see Hitler and Mussolini out of the area, there were few issues or policies on which the two governments could or were likely to agree. The Kremlin was seeking the immediate and vigorous enforcement of the Non-Intervention Agreement, the active support of the Loyalist government, or some collective ultimatum to Germany and Italy to get out. Although the British government was cautiously considering a policing scheme of its own, it was apparently absolutely opposed to any scheme or ultimatum which was likely to alienate Hitler and Mussolini. If the nonintervention scheme had to be abandoned, the evidence indicates the British were contemplating a policy of supporting not the Loyalists but rather the rebels. Some evidence in this direction had already come to the attention of the German government. The German chargé d'affaires in Spain reported that *sub rosa* the British were aiding the rebels:

As for England, we have made the interesting observation that she is supplying the Whites with ammunition via Gibraltar and that the British cruiser commander here has recently been supplying us with information on Russian arms deliveries to the Red Government, which he certainly would not do without instructions.[21]

Such an alternative course was calculated not to challenge Hitler but to compete with him for influence. By concurrently supporting the rebels the British would allow General Franco to escape all obligations to Hitler and Mussolini and thus keep himself free from all outside influence, exactly what the British wanted. The main difficulty with this course was that it assumed Franco actually preferred to be free from ties with Mussolini and Hitler and did not want to use such an alliance as a means to build an empire.

The Soviet Union, despite the unfavorable reception of her declaration, did not retreat from her stand. *Pravda* on October 11 declared: "The position of the Soviet Union is unchangeable and unshaken. The Soviet government demands the immediate cessation of the continuous violations of the Non-Intervention Agreement and concrete measures by the committee in this direction." The international Communist press went a step further calling for the end of the agreement.[22]

However, the Soviet "ultimatum" was not completely without its advantages to the Soviet Union. The action did not receive such hostile treatment in the Liberal and Labour presses in Great Britain or by the left in France.[23] In fact, many in France rejoiced at the Soviet's boldness but feared perhaps it was too late to benefit Spain. Even more important the committee a few weeks later began to consider the problem of establishing a system of observers in Spain under the committee's auspices. To what extent Soviet pressure was responsible for this and to what extent it came about as a result of the general awareness that the committee was not functioning satisfactorily, is difficult to ascertain. On the one hand Francis Hemming, secretary of the Non-Intervention Committee, in a conversation with the author said that the Soviet threat actually helped push through the control plan and thus was more of an advantage than a detriment. Many of those groups which had looked with equanimity on German and Italian alignment in Spain were alarmed at the intervention of the Soviet Union, fearing a Communist-dominated government. In this respect the Communists were effective in arousing further the desire by England and France to halt all intervention in Spain. Regardless of the outward attitude of France and England in rejecting and ignoring the Soviet ultimatums, they were secretly apprehensive lest the Soviet Union leave the committee and break up the Non-Intervention Agreement. Consequently, the Soviet note did in effect spur them to speed up consideration of control measures.

On the other hand, the continuous stream of reports from Spain made England and France well aware of continued intervention by Germany and Italy and the new intervention by the Soviet Union. Consequently, at the time of the Soviet "ultimatum" they had already realized the necessity of some scheme of observation as additional pressure to deter large-scale German and Italian intervention and influence. In contrast to Russia, they wanted to proceed slowly, being very careful to keep the continued adherence of Germany and Italy at least in theory. If Germany and Italy left the committee, any peaceful solution would have been more or less frustrated, as the problem of the Abyssinian war in the League had already demonstrated.

CRIMINATIONS AND RECRIMINATIONS

Before the Non-Intervention Committee could consider new measures of prevention, it was necessary to dispose of the allegations made by the Spanish government against Italy and Germany; by the USSR against Portugal; and by Germany, Italy, and Portugal against the USSR. This battle of recriminations occupied the committee during most of October and November. France and England stood more or less between the two sides trying to find the facts and clear the stage for new action by the committee. To avoid unnecessarily alienating Mussolini and Hitler in the publicizing of the facts, France and England acted as if the infractions were only minor and able to be remedied quickly once they were made known to the government of the offenders. For its own part, the British government carefully investigated the actions of the British ship *Bramhill*, alleged to have carried arms to the Spanish government, and assured the committee that, within the capacity of its power, it would prevent further violations by British subjects.

In the battle of charges the Soviet Union emerged the worst. Her accusations against Italy, Germany, and Portugal fell flat and she was unable to defend herself against the counter-indictments.[24] In part this was owing to the lack of support given by England and France who did not want to arouse Hitler and Mussolini unfavorably and felt little concern about Soviet reaction. The primary reason, however, was that the Soviet government which possessed a world-wide organization in the Comintern plus a comprehensive secret police network, failed to use them to uncover concrete evidence against Germany and Italy. The Soviet relied for her charges rather on the proof supplied by the Spanish government, whose information was none too complete or accurate, and on newspaper accounts.[25] Most of the charges were easily repudiated for lack of substantiating evidence, or for lack of proof that the material was sent after the Non-Intervention Agreement came into operation on August 28. As a result, Portugal, Italy, and Germany came out of the attack almost unscathed. That the Soviet Union herself did not contribute one piece of evidence that would put these powers in a bad light is surprising. The British government supplied the most reliable evidence against Italy—the landing of planes and ammunition at Palma, Majorca, on September 7, 1936.[26] It is difficult to understand the failure of the Soviet Union. Either the Communist intelligence network of that time has been greatly overrated or Russia did not wish to use it for fear the release of information might lead to its exposure. Regardlesss of the reason, the Soviet Union was at a great disadvantage trying to convince the democracies and world opinion that Spain was coming under the hegemony of Hitler and Mussolini.

The USSR fared even more poorly in defending herself against Italian and German charges.[27] She was having a very difficult time concealing her military shipments to Spain. Most of the material was shipped from Odessa by sea and had to pass through the Turkish straits where it was easily detected. Its passage from there could be watched and plotted by the Italian navy and air force to its destination in Loyalist Spain. After arriving in a Spanish port, its unloading could be checked by the very large rebel fifth column in existence throughout Loyalist Spain and by the extensive intelligence service of both Italy and Germany. As a result Italy and Germany were able to present some damaging evidence against the Soviet Union. In addition there was evidence presented by the British government.[28] The Soviet Union was frequently at a loss to refute the accusations during the cross-examination in the committee. For example, there was the case of the Soviet steamer *Kuban* which the Italian government charged was carrying munitions to the Loyalists as well as foodstuff to the women and children from the Russian people. From a Soviet newspaper report the Italian government collected the information that 2,500 tons of foodstuffs were loaded on the ship and the cargo "was so enormous as to occupy not only all available space, but even the captain's cabin, the seamen's bathroom and the refrigerator used by the crew." The loading capacity of the *Kuban* was known to be at least 5,000 tons and when it was loaded in Odessa for this particular voyage, the draft of the ship was reported to be at the Plimsoll line. The Italian representatives also pointed out that the type of foodstuff carried by the *Kuban* weighed approximately the same as its volume; therefore, it should not have been necessary to use the crew's quarters for loading space.[29] Thus on two counts, space and draft, over 2,000 tons were not accounted for. The Soviet Union absolutely denied this reasoning, but was unable to prove to the satisfaction of all the powers that the Italian charges were false.

The Soviet defense at this time both in and out of the committee was reduced to flat, unsubstantiated denials. For example, *Pravda* on October 24 denounced all German and Italian charges by saying "the intervention of Germany, Italy and Portugal has been proved ... and the attempt of the German Government to assume the role of the accuser of the U.S.S.R. and to blame the latter for sending ammunition under the disguise of food, is simply miserable." At the same time the Soviets attempted to distract the world's attention from her violations by the tactic of the counteroffensive, that is, the slandering of certain members of the committee:

> Lord Plymouth acts clumsily. This *haut* landlord, known in England most of all as the appraiser of good racing horses, and a gourmet, member of the aristocratic "beefsteak" club, apparently does not give himself a clear account of the seriousness of the mission entrusted to him by the British government in the cause of peace.... Instead of studying the facts which would bear evidence on the intervention, Lord Plymouth hastened to declare that the explanation given by the German government fully satisfied him.[30]

The other charges of Russian intervention discussed in the committee besides the *Kuban* case proved equally embarrassing to the Soviet Union and the committee was faced with the problem that in spite of denials the Soviet Union was violating the agreement. The Soviet Union's earlier threat to repudiate the agreement only further encouraged this conviction. Germany, Italy, and Portugal, on the other hand, were able publicly to clear themselves sufficiently to leave at least some doubt as to how extensively they were still aiding the nationalists.

Renewed Threats by the Soviet Union

Even after the hostile reception of her "ultimatum" at the meeting of the Non-Intervention Committee on October 9, the USSR did not cease to press on the committee her argument that unless all powers adhered to the agreement, none was obliged to abide by it. Having declared herself no more bound by the agreement than Germany and Italy, the Soviet Union did not make a move to leave the committee, although she intimated the possibility in her declaration. There is some evidence that at one time she actually contemplated such a step.[31] It is believed that Litvinov was able to persuade the antidemocratic and rasher elements among the Soviet leaders to remain at least temporarily. France very likely also brought a great deal of pressure to bear on her ally. An exit at this time would have constituted open admission that she was aiding the Loyalists. Finally, it would have put an immediate end to any Soviet hope of a close alliance with the democratic nations and might have opened the way to a four-power arrangement of England,

France, Germany, and Italy which the Soviets feared above anything else. Thus the USSR soon relinquished the idea of withdrawing from the committee, especially since her ultimatum had elicited little sympathy from the governments of England or France.

Instead, the Soviet Union stressed pursuit of another course referred to in her note regarding alleged violations by Portugal—the establishment of a system of control over Portuguese imports and exports. On October 12 the representative of the USSR sent a note to the chairman of the committee, Lord Plymouth, urging the prompt summoning of the committee to consider the Soviet demand for the "immediate establishment of control over Portuguese ports," and "this control should be entrusted to the British and French Navies—or both."[32] The Russians were still unwilling to wait the several weeks until the committee could first deal with the specific charges of intervention against various members. Either the Soviet Union felt time to be too pressing for the Loyalists or she anticipated her own defenses against the charges of intervention to be weak and ineffectual, and her best escape was to turn the committee to other matters before the debate on the violations. By urging enforcement measures she may also have hoped to convince the committee of Russia's sincere desire to isolate the Spanish insurrection.

The new Soviet demand to the committee met with no better response than the earlier one. As discussed previously, the democratic powers were not to be rushed into a hasty position which might force Italy and Germany out of the committee. As a result Lord Plymouth answered the Soviet note as follows:

As you know, all the specific complaints, which have been brought against the Portuguese Government, of violations of the Agreement for Non-Intervention in Spain were submitted to and discussed by the Committee at the meeting on October 9 and the Portuguese Government has been requested, in accordance with the rules of procedure laid down by the Committee on September 21st, to supply, at as early a date as possible, "such explanations as are necessary *to establish the facts.*" Since the reply of the Portuguese Government has not yet been received and since, moreover, your note of October 12th contains no additional evidence whatsoever to show that the Agreement is in fact being violated, I do not think it would be proper for me to summon a further meeting of the Committee at this stage to discuss this matter.[33]

Rebuffed, the Soviet Union tried for a second time to jolt or break up the committee. In a note to the committee dated October 23, 1936, she demanded return to the legitimate Spanish government of the right to buy arms freely abroad and reiterated her stand that she would not be bound by the agreement to any greater extent than the other participants. In this new note the choice of words was even stronger, implying more directly that the Soviet Union might abandon the agreement and leave the committee unless it acted immediately to stop intervention by Germany and Italy.[34] England and France, however, still could not be persuaded and the Soviet note was bypassed by the plenary session of the committee on October 23, and referred to the chairman's subcommittee for further elucidation by the USSR.

The members of the subcommittee at their next meeting centered their interest upon learning whether the Soviet Union intended to remain on the committee and whether she would abide by the pact. There was no thought of appeasement. Lord Plymouth expressed the opinion of most of the members when he said:

> ... As has been pointed out by others who have spoken this afternoon, the situation has been complicated as a result of the letter addressed to me by the Soviet Ambassador on 23rd October.
>
> ... what I should like to know and what I think everybody here wishes to know is, whether, until these conditions are fulfilled which the Soviet Government has laid down, the Soviet Government will consider itself bound by the Agreement, or are they going to judge for themselves what the position is, and if in their opinion war material is being imported into Spain on behalf of the rebel generals, do they intend on their part to consider themselves absolved from the Agreement and will they take action such as is foreshadowed in this statement as the result of it.[35]

The Soviet representative refused to give direct answers to these questions. Nevertheless, it is significant that these same meetings of the committee and subcommittee for the first time took up the question of neutral observers to be stationed in Spain to report on violations of the agreement—the first step toward a system of control.

Having by her ultimatums elicited from the members not outward sympathy but only resentment, the Soviet Union still did not carry out her implied threats to leave the committee.[36] She had no wish for the onus of being the power to break up the agreement and thus play right into the hands of Germany and Italy. Rather, the Soviet Union decided to change again her tactics.

CHAPTER VI

PROPOSALS ON ENFORCEMENT: NOVEMBER AND DECEMBER, 1936

A Change of Soviet Tactics

By the middle of October, 1936, England and France were becoming increasingly disquieted by the trend of events; it looked very much as though a new world war was threatening in Spain with Germany, Italy, and Russia pouring in arms. As a result on the urgent suggestion of the French and British representatives the Non-Intervention Committee at its meeting on October 23 agreed that the chairman's subcommittee should meet the next day "to discuss the general position of the work of this Committee." From its discussions the subcommittee presented the following proposal to the full committee on October 28:

> The establishment, subject to the concurrence of the two parties in Spain, of an impartial body of persons, stationed on Spanish soil, at the principle points of entry (by sea and by land) for the purpose of reporting, when called upon to do so by the Committee, on any specific case.[1]

This development heartened the Soviet government and, in another statement to the committee on October 28, clarifying her note of October 23, she renewed her plea for control over the Portuguese ports and readily agreed to the British suggestion of control of all Spanish ports and frontiers. She also reiterated her ambiguous threat to ignore the agreement to the same extent as other powers.[2] This note, however, was expressed in much milder terms than the one of October 23 and did not contain the implied threat that the Soviet Union might walk out of the committee. It marked a significant change in the attitude of the Soviet Union toward the committee—from one of hostility to one of coöperation.[3] The democratic powers had by this new plan relieved the Soviet Union of the necessity of deciding either to assume the extremely unpopular task of breaking up the committee, which would have been largely to the advantage of Germany and Italy, or to admit defeat by remaining on the committee contrary to all her own terms.

The reversal of the attitude of the USSR supports the hypothesis that, after her initial decision at the time of her first ultimatum on October 7 not to walk out of the committee, the Soviet leaders never really wanted to break up the agreement but merely wanted to make

---

[1] For notes to chap. vi, see pp. 149–151.

it effective. Further credibility is given this hypothesis by the subsequent full coöperation of the Soviet Union in working out a control system, as reported by the secretary of the Non-Intervention Committee. See pages 60–63. It also coincides with the activities of the Soviet Union within Spain itself.[4]

CONTROL AND MEDIATION

The committee's investigation of alleged violations by the various powers in Spain came to nothing. After the accusations were categorically denied, the committee could do little since it had no way to check or prove the facts. Lord Plymouth expressed the committee's frustration. Discussing the substantial evidence concerning the unloading of arms by the Soviet ship *Kuban* and the denial by the Soviet government, he said:

> ... On the one hand we have charges supported by evidence which I think members of the Committee will feel, as I do, is more detailed and circumstantial than any which we have had before us in previous cases. On the other hand, we have a flat denial of the charges by the Government concerned, who contest the reliability, and indeed the honesty, of the evidence adduced. I cannot feel that in these circumstances the Committee is in a position to take a decision, because it does not possess the material which will be necessary to enable the validity of the two opposing cases to be investigated. This merely goes to show, as I pointed out earlier in our proceedings, how necessary it is that we should pursue with the greatest possible energy our proposal for some system of supervision in Spanish territory which will enable us to have placed at our disposal reliable evidence on instances of this kind.[5]

Because the committee's investigations were useless and because the meetings had degenerated into propaganda polemics by the German, Italian, and Soviet representatives, it was tacitly agreed by the powers near the end of November to refer no more complaints to the committee, but to concentrate on a scheme of observers to report violations.

Toward this new role of the committee the Soviet Union was generally well-disposed. Maisky expressed the attitude of the Soviet Union during the meeting of the committee on November 12:

> After weeks of aimless wanderings our Committee has eventually come to a practical task; it has elaborated a scheme for the more or less effective control of the Non-Intervention Agreement.... This is a very gratifying fact. It brings something of a new atmosphere into the Committee, and gives hope of practical and concrete results of its work.[6]

The Soviet Union's new policy generally took the form of working closely with France and England on the committee.[7] She supported the three main projects initiated by the two countries during December: to push forward the scheme of control already under consideration; to bring the question of volunteers within the scope of the Non-Intervention Agreement;[8] and to attempt a mediation between the contending parties in Spain.

In marked contrast to previous meetings, the sessions of the committee and chairman's subcommittee during November and December concerning the formulation of an observation scheme were characterized by a general harmony of purpose. Germany and Italy did not consider it necessary to obstruct because during November Franco, already occupying parts of Madrid, seemed well on the way to a rapid victory.[9] Furthermore, it was part of their tactics to lull the suspicions of the democratic powers while recognizing Franco's regime as the *de jure* government of Spain and establishing diplomatic relations with him.[10] France and England were disturbed by what they considered to be a premature recognition of the rebel regime; Franco had not yet taken Madrid and consequently it could be interpreted as an aggressive act against the Loyalist government. But more important from the point of view of European politics, it committed Hitler and Mussolini publicly to the side of the rebels.[11] Even during the meetings in December when Franco's victory was no longer so certain, Italy and Germany continued their policy of outward coöperation in the committee. They were relying on Franco to put a stop to any control plan by extended negotiations and by ultimately refusing to allow observers into the Nationalist part of Spain.

The Non-Intervention Committee, as a result, worked with surprising swiftness and was able to send to the Spanish parties a draft plan of supervision on December 4. The Spanish government on December 16 replied accepting in principle, but reserved its final decision until details of the plan were known. The rebel Burgos government, on the other hand, answered with a series of questions designed to demur negotiations. From the documents of the German Foreign Office it is clear that the Nationalist answer was part of a conscious and well-planned pattern of tactical delay.[12] The four governments of Germany, Italy, Portugal, and Nationalist Spain alternately delayed and impeded the operations of the Non-Intervention Committee throughout its lifetime.[13] By thus interchanging the responsibility, Italy, Germany, and Portugal were generally able to escape the onus of obstructing the progress of the committee. When this failed, they tried to implicate the Soviet Union as the encumbrance.

Although the Soviet government, in its new course of coöperating with France and Great Britain, even pledged support of the December Anglo-French proposal to mediate the dispute in Spain, it was obvious from Soviet press comments that it held little hope and considered the attempt a waste of valuable time:

> The Soviet Union does not believe that the Anglo-French proposal indicates a right way out of the extremely menacing situation that has come to exist as a consequence of the Fascist intervention in Spain.
>
> * * *
>
> Nevertheless, because of its unchangeable desire for peace and taking into account the position of England and France and other states, the Soviet government acceded to the said proposal of the French and English governments; it expressed in principle its readiness to participate in the attempt to put an end to the armed conflict in Spain by means of mediation....[14]

The proposal proved to be impractical, as the Soviets predicted.[15] The division in Spain was too wide and bitter, and neither side was willing to yield as long as it had the support of outside powers.

THE SPANISH GOVERNMENT ATTEMPTS TO INTERFERE

A factor which the French and English governments felt to be particularly disturbing to their negotiations was the Spanish government's insistence in December of 1936 on bringing her plight before the League Council under article 11 of the League Covenant, naming Italy and Germany as aggressors.[16] England and France did not want the League to disturb the discussions in the Non-Intervention Committee. There is evidence the Soviet Union in line with her new policy also suggested confidentially to Spain that a plea to the Council would not be effective, but publicly she supported the right of the Spanish government to bring its case before the League.[17] The Spanish government could not be dissuaded. With the two most important members of the Council in opposition, it is doubtful whether Spain really expected action, but it at least offered her an opportunity to attract world-wide attention and possibly sympathy.

France and England, with the coöperation of most of the other members on the Council, were ultimately successful in side-stepping the issue, securing the passage of an innocuous resolution supporting the Non-Intervention Committee, and urging all powers not to intercede in the affairs of other nations. The Soviet Union was the only country which supported the Spanish government and was willing to name Germany and Italy as aggressors. Beyond this, the Soviet Union did not press her point or make any dramatic moves to force the Council toward action. She merely used the debate to restate her position concerning the policy of nonintervention.[18] It is perhaps significant that along with the foreign ministers of France and England, Commissar of Foreign Affairs Litvinov did not attend the Council meeting.

CHAPTER VII

FOREIGN VOLUNTEERS AND A CONTROL SCHEME: FEBRUARY–APRIL, 1937

THE QUESTION OF VOLUNTEERS

ON THE SUGGESTION of the Soviet Union in a letter dated November 11, 1936,[1] the committee considered the matter of prohibiting foreign troops and volunteers from going to Spain to fight in the Civil War as a part of the Non-Intervention Agreement. It was immediately supported by England and France. The new proposal embarrassed Italy and Germany because both countries, Italy to a greater degree, were in the process of moving large numbers of troops into Spain to help Franco.[2] The arrival of Russian aid at the end of October had enabled the Loyalists to stop Franco's offensive and save Madrid. As a result, Hitler and Mussolini found it necessary to supply the rebels with troops as well as war material to insure their victory. However, if Germany and Italy were to obstruct the committee openly by refusing to prohibit the sending of "volunteers" to Spain, it might cement an alliance between Russia, England, and France—a step Hitler had long sought to prevent. England and France were particularly sensitive in this direction because the growing Fascist-Nazi friendship had resulted in the signing of the anti-Comintern Pact on November 25, which the French and British had reason to fear was aimed at them as well. Under these circumstances the new Rome-Berlin Axis counterattacked with accusations against the Soviet Union and France, claiming 35,000 Russians and 25,000 Frenchmen to be in Spain fighting for the Loyalists.[3] Then it agreed in principle to the interdiction of foreign volunteers as part of the Non-Intervention Agreement, but insisted on the prohibition of all indirect intervention at the same time.[4] By coupling the two factors they hoped to delay action indefinitely. The debate on the definition of what constituted indirect intervention was calculated to extend over several sessions of the committee. In any event, restriction on indirect intervention would be difficult for the democratic countries who could not legally control all the actions of their citizens or the press.

Italy and Germany also emphatically reminded the committee that in August and September they had originally suggested the prohibition against allowing volunteers to go to Spain. At that time they had

---

[1] For notes to chap. vii, see pp. 151–155.

not contemplated sending troops and had feared the influx of revolutionaries from all over the world into Loyalist Spain. By December the situation had completely changed—Italy was sending whole divisions.[5] By claiming the original idea, the Axis powers hoped to earn credit for the proposal and also obscure their attempts to obstruct the committee.

As a further example of its tactics of delay, the Italian government withheld its answer to the committee's December 9 questionnaire on volunteers and indirect intervention until December 24, just before the Christmas holidays when the committee would be recessed.[6] In addition the answer declared Italy would still not accept forbiddance of volunteers without the inclusion of the prohibition against indirect intervention.[7] Even after the Christmas recess Italy and Germany appeared to be unprepared to proceed on the question of volunteers and, in an attempt to sidetrack the issue, insisted on the appointment of two special technical subcommittees to further study both questions.

Although the Soviet Union was also an intervening power in Spain, her attitude displayed a marked contrast to Italy's and Germany's on the question of "volunteers." In this race to build up the manpower of both sides in Spain, the Soviet Union could not compete since she refused to send any Russian troops, except instructors, to assist the Spanish Loyalists. The Communists depended solely on recruitment for the International Brigades to increase the Loyalist strength. This was necessarily a slow process and not nearly as effective as sending organized troops to Spain. As a result, the answer of the Soviet government to the committee's questionnaire of December 9, delivered early on December 18 was in complete agreement with the proposal drawn up by the committee.[8] At the meeting of the subcommittee on December 22 the Soviet Union also urged a system of control be immediately established to check fulfillment by the member states.

The British and French governments were equally anxious to push through the agreement on volunteers, but for the purpose of limiting the war without regard for one side or the other. They had become more and more alarmed about events in Spain as a result of continuous reports of German[9] and Italian troops landing in rebel ports, increased public association of Hitler and Mussolini with Franco's cause as exemplified by German and Italian recognition of the Burgos regime, and public statements by prominent Nazis and Fascists to the effect that Franco was helping abolish communism in Spain.[10] In fact, Hitler's foreign minister, Baron von Neurath, left no question about the Nazi position in his conversations with the British and French ambassadors: "I had to declare in all seriousness, and with the request that my statements be reported verbatim to their Governments, that we would in no case tolerate the establishment of a Soviet Communist government in Spain."[11]

In an effort to break the deadlock over volunteers, the British government coöperating with France decided to appeal directly to the interested governments (Germany, Italy, the USSR, and Portugal). Telegrams were sent to the four capitals on December 24.[12] The Soviet Union sent an answer on December 29 promising full support, though she demanded "that all measures of control should be taken as rapidly as possible, and independently of the consent or lack of consent of the insurgent generals."[13]

Germany and Italy, as usual, delayed their answers to the Anglo-French note until January 7; the replies consented only in principle and did not commit their governments to final action unless agreement was also reached on indirect intervention. Seizing on the earlier Soviet demand, they furthermore predicated their acceptance "upon the condition that ... all participating Governments agree to a completely effective control, on the spot, of the prohibitions to be agreed upon," and suggested a system be inaugurated to remove all foreigners already fighting in Spain.[14]

The French and British governments, still anxious and determined to bring about an immediate agreement on this matter, tried a new strategy. In a new note dated January 10, 1937, to the interested powers the British ignored the Italian and German conditions for agreement and declared:

4. In the meanwhile His Majesty's Government are themselves of the opinion that the general desire expressed in the replies received from the other Governments for the exclusion of foreign volunteers and military personnel from Spain would warrant the immediate adoption by each Government within their own territories of the prohibitory measures required for that purpose, even in advance of the establishment of a complete system of control for Spain.

5. As evidence of their sincere desire to reach international agreement at once on this aspect of indirect intervention in Spain, His Majesty's Government is, spontaneously and without further delay, issuing a public notice in which attention is drawn to the fact that it is an offense punishable under the Foreign Enlistment Act for British Subjects to accept or agree to accept any commission or engagement in the forces of either side or for any person to recruit volunteers in the United Kingdom for service in Spain.[15]

The French government on January 13 notified the British government that it was immediately introducing the necessary legislation.

The Soviet Union sent an answer to the new British *démarche* on January 15. She reiterated her approval of a prohibition on volunteers and, as a conciliatory move, no longer insisted on the prerequisite of effective control as mentioned in her earlier memorandum of December 29. By this concession Russia hoped to isolate the Axis powers who were also insisting on effective control. She, however, refused to accept the policy of unilateral measures by the various powers as a solution to the problem:

Finally I consider it necessary to point out that in the opinion of the Soviet Government unilateral measures of prohibition on the part of certain participators on the London Committee at a time when other participators are not only free from obligations but in fact continue to send military contingents to Spain not only would not achieve the desired result but would be tantamount to intervention in the aid of the Insurgents.

It is to be feared that such individual measures might render international collaboration more difficult in the future and might also render more difficult the realization of the scheme of control envisaged by the London Committee. Such measures appear particularly premature when one considers that the Insurgents have not so far given their consent even in principle to the establishment of any sort of control while the Governments supporting them have not expressed clear and unconditional agreement either to the establishment of control or the discontinuance of dispatch to Spain of military contingents described as volunteers. In view of these considerations the Soviet Government although even at the present time they are not dispatching volunteer detachments consider it inexpedient to embark on unilateral measures.[16]

The replies of the Italian and German governments, delayed until January 25, were almost identical and except that they omitted the condition of a simultaneous ban on indirect intervention, they expressed a willingness to apply measures to stop volunteers going to Spain only "as soon as all other Governments have agreed to adopt analogous measures; there is an adequate system of supervision; and finally as soon as they have fixed through the London Committee a date for their simultaneous entry into force." They further proposed that all foreign combatants should be removed from Spain but did not make it conditional.[17] Great Britain, having failed in her attempt to bring about unilateral measures, concentrated her efforts on trying to effect a control scheme as soon as possible in order to meet the German and Italian conditions for adopting a prohibition on volunteers.[18]

Soviet Relations with England and France

As the preceding discussion indicates, the Soviet Union consistently coöperated with the English and French in the London committee from the beginning of November, 1936, except for the British proposal of unilateral action to prevent the recruitment of volunteers for Spain.

Following the example of the Soviet representative in the committee, the Soviet newspapers and leaders only occasionally attacked the work of the committee and the policies of England and France, although they persistently stressed that the Non-Intervention Agreement was being turned into a "farce" by Italian and German recognition of Franco and the dispatching of Nazi and Fascist troops to Spain.[19] Their partial abstention was, however, more in the nature of a truce while they waited for the democratic states actually to take a strong stand on Spain. The Soviet leaders were probably hoping that public opinion and the obstructionist tactics of Germany and Italy would impel the British government to resist actively the direct military intervention of Italy and Germany in Spain. The Kremlin had chosen to conduct itself with reserve in order to keep the Soviet Union on good terms with the British government and people.[20]

Outside the Non-Intervention Committee a few incidents did strain the period of truce. In the middle of November in a speech before the House of Commons, Foreign Secretary Anthony Eden declared: "So far as non-intervention is concerned, I say categorically that I think there are other Governments more to blame than those of Germany and Italy." The statement was aimed clearly at the USSR and the Soviet press immediately reciprocated; *Pravda* on November 20 retorted:

Mr. Eden's declaration exposes the complete hypocrisy of the so-called policy of nonintervention of the humanitarians on the London Committee, which is resulting in the virtual abetting of aggression.

In striving to support Italy and Germany Mr. Eden goes so far that he finds it possible to insinuate charges addressed to some "unknown third party," obviously borrowing his "reasoning" from the Fascist camp....

The Communists, as they had good reason to be, were extremely sensitive about their alleged intervention in Spain.

A few months later another altercation developed. On January 20, Foreign Minister Anthony Eden, debating foreign policy in the British House of Commons, inferred that Germany was not a real danger to peace. The Soviet press was unable to refrain from comment and on January 21 *Izvestiia* editorially denounced Eden.

Except for these two flare-ups, the attitude of the Soviet press from November, 1936, was not in general hostile, though it did not entirely support the British diplomatic maneuvers. An editorial in *Bolshevik* by N. Maiorsky was typical of this mildly critical attitude:

It is quite apparent that the significance of the Spanish problem has been widely recognized, and the anxiety of English and French political circles simultaneously increased.

Nevertheless, certain extremely characteristic facts should be noted. First, the exceptional haste with which both the Paris and London press have concluded that Italy has given up intervention in Spain, and that Germany is on the point of doing so, and second the extraordinary credulity shown by the press of these countries in accepting as true every promise made by Germany and Italy, or even a hint of such a promise. Actually there is no indication of the nature of the guarantee of non-intervention supposedly given by Italy, and intended to be given by Germany; nor has there been even a question raised as to whether the above negotiations would not be actually used for the development of intervention.[21]

Also by way of warning, the Soviet press daily reported the arrival of arms and troops in rebel Spain[22] and the danger of "Fascist pirates" to peaceful merchant shipping. The sinking of the Soviet ship *Komsomol* on December 14 was pointed to as only the beginning of "Fascist" excesses unless prohibitive measures were applied by the peace-loving powers.[23] Furthermore, the Soviet press tirelessly pointed out to France and England the strategic and economic threat of a Spain dominated by Germany and Italy.[24]

The Soviet policy of coöperation was put to its most difficult test by the signing of the Anglo-Italian accord published on January 4, 1937. The agreement recognized Italian *de facto* sovereignty over Abyssinia and was intended to maintain the *status quo* in the Mediterranean. While the Soviets avoided long tirades against the pact, they still subjected it to searching criticism. Their reaction was one of general scepticism: " 'He who dines with the devil should have a long spoon.' Does England have it in concluding an agreement with Italy? If not, the kettle in which the Anglo-Italian dish was cooked may prove to be empty for the English."[25]

The signing of the accord appeared particularly unfortunate to the Russians when the landing of 4,000 Italian troops in Cádiz was reported simultaneously with the announcement of the agreement. Obviously, the Italians considered the agreement a mere scrap of paper. The pact did in effect undermine the policy of nonintervention, as future events proved, by indirectly sanctioning Italian aggression and activities in Spain.

The Russians also doubted whether the Anglo-Italian accord would break up the amity between Mussolini and Hitler which had become very close as a result of their common intervention in Spain. The Italian press was quoted by the Communists as saying that the agreement had in no way affected Italian-German friendship.[26] Later in January this was apparently confirmed as Göring's visit to Mussolini was reported to have brought the countries even closer together.[27] Nazi-Fascist coöperation in respect to Spain also did not cease with the Anglo-Italian accord. For example, in response to the British note of January 10 urging each country unilaterally to prohibit the dispatch of volunteers to Spain, both Germany and Italy delayed their answers until January 25 and in substance sent identical notes. This unity of action clearly diminished the chances of Great Britain to detach Italy from Germany.

Thus it would appear from the Soviet press and from the various statements made by Soviet leaders both in and out of the London committee that the Soviet Union tried its best to get along with the British and not to antagonize them during this period. It was not an easy task and the overwrought Russians occasionally lashed out. In their support it must be said that the British Conservative government made almost no concessions to Soviet sensibilities. Great Britain did not consult Russia concerning any proposed *démarche,* in respect not only to the Spanish question but to all diplomatic questions at this time. The reasons for this attitude were basic to all British relationships with the Soviet Union prior to the Second World War. In the first place, both the Conservatives and Labourites were hostile to communism and the idea of world revolution, consequently they constantly mistrusted the motives of the Soviet government. This made it impossible for them to work closely with the Soviet Union. Furthermore, the British government did not envision any direct aggression on the part of the Soviet Union, even against British imperial possessions and satellites in Asia, and discounted her military strength. The extensive purges of the top military and party command in Russia seemed adequate proof of her weakness. The British government as a result did not feel the need to consult with Russia and generally treated her as a third-rate power not important to Britain's security. The British had also learned it was not really necessary to bother about the Soviet Union's attitude in the London committee because she was afraid of being isolated and, if pressured, could be counted on to back down. This was what had happened following the Soviet ultimatums on nonintervention during October of 1936. Finally, British foreign policy at this time was directed toward preserving the peace in Europe which meant—in the view of the Conservative government—conciliating Germany and keeping Germany and Italy apart. Thus they hesitated alienating Hitler and Mussolini by associating themselves closely with the Russians. The Nazis had incipiently professed anti-Communistic feelings and the British leaders thought that the Nazis would never make any agreement with a government closely associated with communism or the Soviet Union.

Regardless of the soundness of the British motives, the course they followed seems almost to have been contrived to alienate the Russians. The French, in an effort to maintain British friendship in the face of renewed German aggression, were forced, sometimes against their better judgment, to follow the British lead in ignoring the USSR.[28]

The Communist parties of Western Europe followed a slightly different line from that of the Soviet government and press. They continued to criticize the policy of neutrality in the Spanish conflict and specifically the policies of England and France.[29] For example, in the debate on the Spanish issue in the French Chamber of Deputies on December 4 and 5, 1936, the Communists bitterly attacked the attitude of Blum's government, and described the Italian and German activities in Spain as an attempt to encircle France and to plunder her African empire. In the final vote on the debate the Communists abstained (the vote supported Blum by a majority of 350 to 171). This refusal of the Communists to support the Popular Front government very much offended Blum and he considered it a serious breach of the Popular Front agreement.

The Communist parties of Europe never tired of admonishing that Nazi intervention in Spain was only the beginning. K. Gottwald in a speech to the Czechoslovakian Parliament on December 1, 1936, asked:

...And who under these circumstances can doubt that one fine day the "Third Empire" can organize a putsch in Czechoslovakia, under the pretext of saving Europe from Bolshevism, it can support the putschists, and under this transparent pretext it can carry out a military intervention in Czechoslovakia? If fascist Germany recognizes the Burgos "government" today then it may recognize tomorrow some "government" in Asch or Eger. And if today Madrid is reduced to ruins, is destroyed by German bombs, how can we be sure that tomorrow a similar fate may not strike Prague?[30]

This more outspoken and hostile attitude of the Western European Communist parties toward the policies of England and France was undoubtedly intended by the Soviet Union to pressure indirectly these governments into effective counteraction against German and Italian flagrant violations of the Non-Intervention Agreement.[31]

EXTENSION OF THE NON-INTERVENTION AGREEMENT

Toward the end of January Italy and Germany felt that in a few weeks they would have sufficient strength in Spain to insure the victory of Franco. The two powers together would have contributed almost 100,000 troops by the middle of February.[32] As a result, they could relax their delaying tactics in the Non-Intervention Committee and drop the various conditions they had imposed for adopting a ban on volunteers and a system of control. Their new policy was explained in a telegram dated January 26, 1937, from Foreign Minister von Neurath to the German embassy in London:

As far as control outside Spain is concerned, we and the Italians are pursuing the intention of putting through a control that is effective in every respect, to go into force some time after the middle of February, but not earlier than February 10....

Please keep in close touch with Grandi [The Italian Ambassador to the United Kingdom and representative on the Non-Intervention Committee] on all these questions.[33]

This new policy enabled the chairman's subcommittee, two days later, to work out a questionnaire to all the member governments concerning the banning of volunteers for Spain and the adoption of a system of supervision outside of Spanish territory, as had been discussed in the technical advisory subcommittee. This questionnaire brought in favorable answers from all the interested governments by February 10, and on February 16 a meeting of the full Non-Intervention Committee was held. It was resolved by the members that from midnight of February 20 the agreement would be extended "to cover the recruitment in, the transit through, or the departure from their respective countries of persons of non-Spanish nationality proposing to proceed to Spain or the Spanish Dependencies for the purpose of taking service in the present war." Further, the system of supervision outside Spanish territory, as prepared by the technical advisory subcommittee, "subject to the final adjustment of outstanding questions was to become effective March 6."

These new arrangements were acclaimed by the various members of the committee and the press reflected their enthusiasm. Only the Soviet Union's representative, at the committee's meeting on February 16, sounded a note of pessimism:

On behalf of my Government I welcome this agreement, and assure you that for their part the Soviet Government will be ready to assist the adoption of these measures—even at this eleventh hour. As an earnest of their goodwill in this matter they are prepared to modify their attitude in regard to some points in the scheme of control. But although at the present moment the situation seems a little brighter than it was, past experience even now should make us all cautious in estimating the prospects of success. Although most of the difficulties seem to be overcome, there are still some points which have to be satisfactorily cleared up before we can consider the scheme of control fairly launched.

In particular I would point out that the Committee does not yet know the attitude of Portugal to this scheme....

In conclusion I would like to underline that the success of last night's decisions is dependent upon two conditions: First that a satisfactory solution of the difficulties raised by the Portuguese attitude towards the scheme of control is found—a solution which maintains the complete efficacy of that scheme.

And secondly, that the whole-hearted co-operation of all the Powers, members of the Committee, is assured, on the basis, of course, of full equality among the members in shaping and carrying out the decision of the Committee.[34]

Soviet scepticism was not unfounded. Although the necessary legislation concerned the prohibition of volunteers to Spain was duly passed by the various states by February 20,[35] several additional problems had to be overcome, so the system of control did not go into effect until April 20, six weeks later.

The original concept of control by stationing observers on Spanish territory had been abandoned because of unfavorable response from the Spanish government and Franco's regime. After several preliminary notes, the Spanish government definitely replied on January 17 that they accepted in principle but with some modifications. The Franco regime in a note of January 19 had bluntly declared that in its existing form the plan was unacceptable. The subcommittee therefore was forced to revise the scheme completely. The new control proposal provided for the supervision of Spanish land frontiers by observers stationed on the non-Spanish side of the borders, for the embarkation of observing officers on ships of the participating countries bound for Spanish ports, and for the patrolling of the Spanish coast by warships belonging to the participating powers. Although all the powers had by February 15 agreed in principle to this new plan, the process of detailing the scheme was slow. Many of the impediments were technical, such as the difficulty of quickly recruiting a chief administrator and the necessary observers, over a thousand in number, the problem of setting up the administrative board and the apparatus to operate the observation plan, and the task of allocating financial responsibility among the various powers.

Three political obstacles, also, slowed up final agreement on the plan. First of all, Germany, allocated 16 per cent of the total cost, insisted on paying the bulk in reichsmarks. This was clearly unacceptable. Germany held out until March 8 when she agreed to pay the first installment in foreign currency. Second, the Portuguese refused to permit international supervision of their border with Spain. Great Britain, on the basis of her long friendship with Portugal, brought heavy pressure to bear on the Salazar government for the sake of completing the system of control. Finally, at the end of February, Portugal agreed that although she would still not allow international control, she would allow

British observers to supervise her border with Spain. The Soviet reaction to these delays by Germany and Portugal was clearly expressed in press comments on the resistance of the Portuguese toward accepting international control:

> ... There exists between the three Fascist Powers [Germany, Italy, and Portugal] which participate in the international committee, a definite division of duties. From the end of January Germany and Italy have tried to play the role of the members who came to their senses and who are peacefully inclined, but both these countries really favored, as before, the policy of delay and hindrance in the work of establishing control, and accordingly they have "hired" their "younger brother," Portugal, who so far and for almost three months has kept herself in the background, to cause delay. Germany and Italy meanwhile are continuing to send ammunition and troops to Franco and are expecting to bring the business to an end favorable to fascism on the battlefield. Such is the plan which was worked out between the two countries during the recent meeting of Göring and Mussolini.[36]

The Italian and German documents now available fully support the Soviet analysis.

The final political obstacle to completion of the control scheme was the attitude of the Soviet Union herself. The Soviet Union had originally proposed that the naval patrol of the Spanish coast be composed of a joint fleet so the various ships could keep watch on each other. The other powers, however, held to the view that the Spanish coast should be divided into sectors, each sector controlled by one power. The Soviet Union opposed this plan until the middle of February when she reluctantly conceded. But Soviet disagreement did not end here. She then, as one of the great powers, insisted on the right to patrol her own sector. The other powers accepted the demand and assigned her a zone on the Bay of Biscay. But the Soviet Union wanted one on the Mediterranean coast, closer to her Black Sea bases.[37] This, of course, was unacceptable since it would permit her to smuggle goods to the Loyalist troops. The Soviet Union continued to object to her sector until February 26. Then Maisky, the Soviet representative on the committee, on that date wrote a letter to the chairman:

> Now, when ... the Sub-Committee has finally recognized the right of the Soviet Union to take part in the naval control, I have received instructions from my Government to state that at present they do not claim to make actual use of this right, as they are not interested, politically or otherwise, in the presence of their naval forces in the Mediterranean Sea or in the Atlantic Ocean, at a great distance from their own naval bases.[38]

It is not clear even today why the Soviet Union put this obstacle in the way of settling the final organization of the control scheme. It is doubtful, though, whether the Soviet position was the important factor in delaying the inauguration of the control scheme. Technical difficulties and the problem of the German financial contribution were already holding up implementation. Nevertheless, her resistance was used to good advantage by the Germans to fend off the blame for the delay. The democratic states felt, furthermore, that from the point of view of stopping intervention immediately, the Soviet position was untenable. In conclusion, the Soviet move was considered by the other members to be nothing more than a tactic to hold up agreement, perhaps to give the Communists time to send more troops and matériel. The evidence, however, instead of supporting the contention that the USSR wanted to build up her forces in Spain, shows that Soviet aid to Spain began to fall off during the spring of 1937.

Several other possible explanations for the Soviet obstruction present themselves. First, the Russians may have done it as a matter of prestige and Maisky's note to the committee strongly suggests this. The Soviet Union did not want to be relegated to the position of a lesser power and therefore asserted her right to participate in the patrol as a great power, her rank, not the patrol, being of prime importance. The Soviet Union at this time was very sensitive about her status and resented the attempts, particularly by the British, to ignore her. Secondly, Russia may have wanted to use her position as a bargaining point. She would abandon her position on the naval patrol in exchange for Portuguese and German coöperation in the scheme.

Finally, the Russians may have wanted to defeat the revised control plan because they felt it would be ineffective. They rejected, however, definitive action because they did not want to bear the responsibility of destroying the scheme. Yet the Soviet Union did not even hold for long to her demand for a sector on the Mediterranean coast. Nevertheless she shared the opinion of many that the scheme had too many loopholes which would permit continued Italian and German intervention.[39] There was no air control; this would allow Italy and Germany to fly planes directly to Spain, a method closed to the Soviet Union because of distance. Secondly, the plan still did not provide for sanctions against a power violating the agreement. The procedure simply provided that, were an observer to discover that the ship on which he was embarked unloaded war material, he was to report in confidence to the London Board. The board then was to inform the government whose nationals were guilty of violating the agreement, and that government was responsible for the punishment of the guilty parties. That is all. No provision was made for the punishment of violations by governments, who were clearly the guilty parties. Nor did the scheme cover Spain or other nations who were not members of the committee, thus opening the way to nominal transfer of ships to Spanish registry to circumvent control. In addition numerous reports of more landings of Italian troops and German material continued even after February 20, when the ban on volunteers had gone into effect. Almost daily the Soviet newspapers carried such reports, mainly quoted from the foreign press. In conclusion it can be said that Russia had good reason for desiring the abandonment of the control scheme, but did not want the responsibility for its defeat.

In spite of the Soviet Union's scepticism, her representatives on the committee coöperated in every way to work out the details of the plan. Mr. Hemming, secretary of the Non-Intervention Committee, in a conversation with the author declared that none of the representatives were more helpful to him at this time than the Russians. Furthermore, a reading of the minutes of the technical advisory subcommittees during this period clearly reveals that the Soviet representative was first in supplying information, in working out details, and in efforts to make the scheme as foolproof as possible.[40] It would seem that the Soviet Union was trying to make the best of an unfortunate situation. Realizing it was politically injudicious for her to block the inauguration of the scheme, she elected instead to make it as effective as possible.

The final plan of control was adopted by the full committee on March 8, 1937. After this date the real organization commenced. On March 12 the Non-Intervention Board was appointed to administer the plan. But it took time to hire the observers and disperse them as necessary. Further delay was also caused by the period necessary for the member countries to pass legislation making it obligatory for all merchant ships in their registry to comply with the provisions of the scheme and call at specific ports to take on official observers. As a result, the system of supervision was not effected until April 20, and then merely on a skeleton basis.

By way of concluding this episode of the Non-Intervention Committee, it seems appropriate to amplify the reasons for the Soviet Union's agreement at all to a system of control, especially one which had so many loopholes tending to favor Italy and Germany. From the discussion thus far, the Soviet leaders considered the Spanish Civil War in relation to collective security against "fascism" and not as a field for Communist aggression. They would have been quite willing to withdraw their military support to the Loyalists on the certainty that Italian and German aid would also stop. But this does not explain why they would permit an ineffective system of control that would allow Germany and Italy to continue sending aid, even if in lesser amounts.

Soviet aid to the Loyalists, after reaching a maximum in December of 1936 in order to save Madrid, gradually diminished through 1937. It is significant that during the period of the operation of the control scheme not one Soviet ship called at a control port to pick up an observer in order to carry nonmilitary goods legally to Spain, and no violations against the observation scheme by Soviet ships were reported out of a total of 111 offenses alleged.[41] There are several possible reasons for the drastic reduction of Soviet aid during 1937. Perhaps Russia felt she could not spare any more military equipment at the expense of her own sadly deficient defenses. It is also very likely she had never considered aid to the Loyalists over the long run, that her support was merely to fill in the gap until France and Great Britain became fully aware of the situation and were in a position to give assistance to the Loyalists, or to take collective measures to halt Italian and German intervention. Finally the Soviet military authorities, as many others, may have predicted Franco would with the determined aid of Germany and Italy win very soon, and victory for the Loyalists could be purchased only at a great cost, if at all. As a result there was no point in wasting resources on the Loyalist cause. Predictions of a quick victory, however, proved wrong. The Loyalists, with the support of the majority of the Spanish people but with much less outside aid, managed to put up a fight until 1939. It is possible that constant large-scale assistance to the Loyalists might have brought them victory, particularly if Hitler and Mussolini had decided Spain was not worth the cost. Even as it was, Hitler and Mussolini grumbled unhappily over the expense involved and in the end doubted its merit.[42] Regardless of the reason, the Russians decreased their aid to the Loyalists during 1937 and only played a delaying game in Spain.[43] As a result they were willing to agree to the control scheme because it did not interfere with their plans in respect to Spain and would not be a source of future embarrassment as the original agreement had been. Finally, Soviet refusal to support the scheme would have in itself served no purpose. No matter how ineffective its operation, it was better than no control at all.[44] Russian obstinacy would have won nothing more than enmity of the English and French governments whose friendship the Soviet leaders had been seeking.

CHAPTER VIII

OTHER ISSUES: MARCH AND APRIL, 1937

QUESTION OF THE WITHDRAWAL OF VOLUNTEERS

GERMANY AND ITALY were greatly encouraged by the capture of Málaga by Nationalist troops on February 8, 1937. It was a severe defeat for the Loyalist forces and cost them much in equipment and men. Thus during February Italy and Germany gave their full coöperation to the Non-Intervention Committee for setting up a system of control, thinking Franco's victory was clearly in sight. But by the middle of March the course of battle turned. The Italian forces to the northeast of Madrid suffered a serious defeat at Guadalajara where over four hundred Italians were killed and almost two thousand wounded.[1] This defeat terminated the affable attitude of Germany and Italy in the London committee.

With final approval of the control scheme in sight, Lord Plymouth on behalf of his government on March 1 introduced a new issue, a plan to withdraw foreign nationals fighting in Spain. He was supported by the French and Soviet representatives.[2] Germany, Italy, and Portugal, however, tied consideration of this problem to a discussion of prohibiting indirect intervention such as financial assistance, obviously to impede any agreement as long as possible—a tactic which had in January successfully delayed consideration of extending the agreement to a ban on volunteers. In order to keep things moving, the chairman's subcommittee on March 8 accepted the German-Italian conditions. On March 15, however, Maisky sent a letter to the secretary of the committee introducing a Soviet exception to the consideration of indirect intervention:

As regards ... the question of Spanish capital assets, and especially with the question of Spanish gold, the Government of the U.S.S.R. maintains: . . . .
* * *

(b) ... the adoption or even consideration of any measures affecting assets belonging to the Spanish State would be an infringement of the sovereignty of a friendly State, incompatible with the established and universally recognized principles of international law and with the comity of nations.

For the reasons stated above the Government of the U.S.S.R. cannot see its way to agree to any discussion affecting the assets of the Spanish Government.[3]

The Soviet Union wanted to avoid discussing the question of the gold assets of the Spanish government because a large portion of it had

---

[1] For notes to chap. viii, see pp. 155–157.

[71]

recently been shipped to the USSR.[4] Italy and Germany sought to use this new Soviet condition to escape responsibility for their own planned procrastination. Not wanting to repeat earlier painful experiences along this line, the Soviet Union at the next meeting of the subcommittee, March 23, decided that her position was not worth defending and withdrew her objection to discussion of the Spanish gold reserves. The Russians probably concluded that the Italian defeat at Guadalajara would make the Italian attitude toward the withdrawal more intransigent than ever, and thus enable Russia to attribute the delay and failure to Italy. Furthermore, haggling over the Spanish gold problem was obscuring the main issue of the war, that is, the continuous flow of Italian and German munitions and troops into rebel Spain, in spite of agreements to the contrary.[5]

The Soviet Union considered this period to be a time of serious crisis and feared England and France were deceived by the February 20 interdiction on foreign volunteers entering Spain and by the impending establishment of the control scheme. The Soviets were certain Germany and Italy were merely giving them lip service, fully recognizing the important loopholes in the control scheme. During the months of March and April the Soviet press abounded in reports of continued landings of Italian troops in Spain. They also delineated in detail the battles in which Italian troops and German planes were to be found en masse. Ambassador Maisky, in a public speech on March 13, declared:

> We in the Soviet Union believe that Europe at the present time has arrived at a turning point where it has to make a final choice. There are two possible ways of advance: the first is the way of reinvigorating the League, of strengthening collective security, the way of active organization of active resistance to the aggressor on the part of the peaceful nations.
>
> The other is the way of so-called "localization of war," the way of constant retreat before the aggressor, the way of submission in the face of the aggressor in the ridiculous hope that perhaps, after all, this ravenous wolf will not devour Red Riding Hood.[6]

Repeated Soviet warnings throughout March, both inside and outside the committee, were unable to stir France and England. They did not deny the intervention or its danger, but rejoined that the way to stop intervention was not by counter-intervention or openly accusing Italy and Germany of aggression, which would break up the committee and perhaps lead to a general war, but by bringing about an agreement on the withdrawal of volunteers. The Russians felt such an agreement would inevitably come too late—no agreement could be expected from

Italy and Germany unless they were sure of victory. The Nazi-Fascist bluff had to be called immediately. Litvinov was reported by United States Ambassador Davies to have analyzed the situation as follows:

He [Litvinov] emphasized strongly that if the democratic governments would now serve firm notice upon Italy that such action would not be tolerated, Mussolini would not take such action, for he said Italy did not want European war, that international conditions, economic and political, in Italy were not good and that Italy could not stand a European war. When I suggested that perhaps the democratic countries, including England, did not wish to hazard a firm position until they were prepared adequately, he stated that neither Germany nor Italy was prepared adequately. To my expressions of surprise that Germany was not prepared from a military point of view, he stated again that their information was positive that Germany was not ready, even in a military sense.[7]

Captured German documents now verify Litvinov's analysis of the situation.

In spite of the yielding policies of Great Britain in the Non-Intervention Committee, the Soviet leaders probably had not yet concluded that the British were hopelessly wedded to the principle of appeasement to stop the Nazi threat. This is indicated by a dispatch of Ambassador Davies from Moscow on March 18, 1937: "Aside from the Spanish situation, the universal opinion is that England is 'stalling' for time in order to rearm; and that she will not again hazard her fingers being burned, as in Ethiopia. It is generally considered that this will require a year and a half or two years."[8]

A break to the Soviet advantage resulted from the meeting of the chairman's subcommittee on March 23. One of the items on the agenda was Lord Plymouth's suggestion that the matter of foreign volunteers be referred to a technical subcommittee for expert examination. Count Grandi, the Italian representative, countered that this was not a technical problem but a general one. The Italians at this time were smarting under the disgrace of their troops' defeat at Guadalajara. Maisky, baiting Count Grandi, declared that this position was in sharp contrast to Italy's previously declared policy. Grandi retorted with the very startling statement that he personally hoped no Italian volunteer would leave Spain until the end of the war.[9] Rather then let the issue drop, the Italian press took up the theme and stated emphatically that Italy would never consent to the withdrawal of her volunteers until General Franco had triumphed. The *Tribuna* declared that "the volunteers must remain in Spain to face the most nefarious coalition ever formed against national and social order. They must remain to accomplish the mission to which they have dedicated themselves in an impulse of noble and proud generosity."[10]

The next day at the plenary session of the committee the Soviet Union pursued her advantage and formally reported Italian violations of the Non-Intervention Agreement, primarily in respect to volunteers. Maisky in part declared: "According to the most reliable information at our disposal, the number of Italians in Spain, at the middle of February, was not less than 60,000. We have the best reasons for believing that since that time this number has considerably increased."[11] As a basis for his statement, Maisky relied on the evidence cited in the note of the Spanish government to Great Britain on March 13. The Soviet Union at the same time proposed that a special commission be sent to investigate the allegations that Italian troops were being landed in Spain after February 20.

The Soviet proposal threw the committee into consternation. Lord Plymouth as well as the French representative, Charles Corbin, were exasperated and refused to discuss it. Lord Plymouth claimed the only item on the agenda of the meeting was the appointment of administrators and he, as chairman, had not received prior notice of the Soviet proposal. He tendered that the matter be turned over to the subcommittee for disposal. This motion was accepted by the committee. The German representative, Joachim von Ribbentrop, availed himself of the annoyance of the British and French representatives to put the Soviet Union in as unfavorable a light as possible. From a reading of the stenographic minutes of the meetings, the Soviet Union had again blundered.[12] Two factors worked against Russia. First, she had not bothered to follow the established form and had presented her proposal without regard for diplomatic formalities. Second, and more important, the western democracies were disconcerted by and even dreaded any action that might upset the frail bonds of the committee by furnishing Germany and Italy with a pretext for leaving.[13] They were willing to concede, to appease, and to accept half-truths to keep Germany and Italy in the committee, which they felt to be the last barrier to a complete breakdown of diplomacy in Europe.

Under pressure from England and France the crisis gradually subsided. The Italian government on March 27 backed down and disclaimed any intention of violating the Non-Intervention Agreement or any plan of sending more troops to Spain, and gave the British government assurances to this effect. On the other side the Soviet Union was prevailed upon not to press her demand for a special commission to establish the truth of her accusations against Italy.[14]

In the balance the Soviet Union failed again to halt the temporizing attitude of France and England toward Hitler and Mussolini.[15] It is true that Italy also retreated. Nevertheless, this was a small concession since Italy still had no intention of permitting an agreement on the withdrawal of volunteers until her defeat at Guadalajara had been fully avenged and her prestige recovered. In this aim she had the complete coöperation of the Germans.[16] Thus the outlook for the talks on withdrawal was bleak. Despite strenuous efforts by the British government through direct conversations with the interested governments to bring about a truce as the first step in the withdrawal of volunteers, Italy and Germany were able to defer and defeat the proposals.

The League Again Bypasses the Spanish Appeal

While the question of withdrawal of foreign volunteers was being discussed in a special subcommittee of the Non-Intervention Committee in London, Spain also brought it to the attention of the League Council at its regular session at the end of May. Both England and France again wanted to avoid discussing the issue in the League, but could not stop the Spanish government from putting the matter on the agenda although they attempted to modify its demands.[17] The question came up before the Council on May 28 and Julio Alvarez del Vayo presented the Loyalist case. To verify its plea the Spanish government submitted to the Council a white book containing evidence of Italian and German intervention on behalf of Franco.

Maxim Litvinov, Soviet commissar of foreign affairs, in his speech in the Council put the Soviet Union squarely behind the Spanish government:

... I venture to remind you of these simple indisputable facts because some people are beginning to forget them. They are beginning to forget that in the present case there can be no talk of sides having equal rights. Foreign governments have the right to enter into relations with the Spanish Government, conclude with them any commercial transactions, including the sale of munitions, without violating any international principles and obligations. But relations with mutinous generals, and supplying them with war material even more, constitute a classic example of intervention in the internal affairs of another state.

* * *

The circumstances of the case fully justify the appeal of the Spanish Government to the League of Nations. We know that in some countries this appeal is criticized and even condemned. There are some people who consider themselves supporters of the League of Nations and who think that the League of Nations can be kept alive only on condition that nothing will be asked the League and nothing expected, and that any appeal to the League in any serious international affair is an attempt upon the existence of the League. These people would like to change the League into a "universal" mummy and admire its inertness and imperturbable calm.[18]

But without the support of England and France the Spanish government could not hope for a decisive resolution by the Council. The attitude of these countries was to emphasize not the extent of continued intervention in Spain but rather the accomplishments of the London committee since the last meeting of the Council in December.[19] British Foreign Minister Anthony Eden declared that "it would be impossible to deny that real progress has been made since that date, and in these days, when the possibilities of international collaboration are so frequently decried, it is well to recall this fact." Eden concluded his speech to the Council by outlining the stand the Council should take toward this question:

What, then, must be the main purpose of this meeting of the Council? Surely to uphold and endorse the work of the Non-Intervention Committee, to emphasize our wish for the early withdrawal of all foreign nationals from Spain, and ourselves to determine to do all in our power to facilitate this result both by constructive cooperation and by resisting the temptation to indulge in polemics or provocation.[20]

The resolution passed the next day closely followed the directive of the British foreign minister. Decisive action was out of the question, but probably it was not expected by the Spanish government.

ILLEGAL SEIZURES

At the instigation of Denmark, Norway, and Sweden, the matter of constant interference with neutral warships and merchant vessels by both parties in the Civil War, but particularly by the rebels, was brought before the Non-Intervention Committee at the end of April, 1937. They suggested a patrol system, under the Non-Intervention Committee, that would extend its activities to protect merchant ships who had control observers on board. Denmark reported that 26 Danish ships had been seized by the Nationalists outside the territorial waters of Spain. Fifteen of these ships had their cargoes confiscated. Norway reported 28 ships seized, of which 16 had their cargoes confiscated. The Netherlands reported confiscation of cargo from 18 of her vessels. The Soviet Union at the same time presented the following account:

During this period [October 30 to April 10, 1937] 84 Soviet ships have been detained, 74 of them in the Straits of Gibraltar, and subjected to inconvenience and trouble of one sort or another by the measures adopted by General Franco. One, the *Komsomol*, was sunk, and her crew interned. Another, the *Smidovich*, was detained at Port Ferrol, and is still detained, while her crew was also interned. But the most remarkable, the most outrageous aspect of all this is that out of these 84 ships which have been held up, only one, the *Smidovich*, was bound for Spain. All the others were simply passing through the Straits of Gibraltar or Spanish waters on their way to ports of other countries.[21]

It is surprising that the Soviet Union at the time of these incidents did not protest nor did she bring the matter before the London committee.[22] Her only actions were attempts to recover from the Nationalists the *Smidovich* and the equipment saved from the sinking of the *Komsomol*. Because the Soviet Union did not recognize the Franco regime, she was unable to make direct representations to it. Surprisingly enough, her main contact with the rebels was through "the friendly mediation of the Italian Ambassador in Moscow."[23]

Methods of preventing further illegal seizures were discussed in the chairman's subcommittee on April 30. The members reached no agreement on the course of action which should be taken. Great Britain in particular objected to extending the duties of the naval patrol to cover this aspect because her fleet was already overburdened with the patrol and protection of British shipping. The equivocal attitude of the British even toward her own merchantmen manifested itself in relation to Franco's attempted blockade of Bilbao, the last stronghold of the Loyalists on the north coast and then under attack by Nationalist troops. Since there had been no recognition of belligerency by foreign states or the Spanish government, a blockade constituted a violation of international law. Nevertheless the British cabinet, apprehensive of the crises that British ships might induce if they endeavored to enter the harbor at Bilbao, warned British shippers not to make the attempt, denied convoy services to that area and refused to lend the support of the British government in the event of seizure or attack—even though the government had declared the Nationalist blockade illegal. The British merchantmen, however, found the blockade ineffective and an easy matter to run and, as a result, the British government subsequently retracted in part and permitted naval protection up to the three-mile limit. This was another example of the British policy of bowing to force, or threats of force, by Hitler, Mussolini, and Franco in order to prevent a crisis and possible war.

The Non-Intervention Committee on May 5, in the absence of agreement on methods to protect shipping in Spanish waters, decided to send a questionnaire to its members to find out the extent of interference and their proposals for remedying the situation. The Soviet position was that although she would go along with the majority, the questionnaire was as much a waste of time as the previous ones had been. Franco's piracy was well known and several plans had already been presented to stop it. Consequently, the next step was to work out a solution on the basis of these proposals and not delay with questionnaires. For her part the Soviet Union proposed a composite fleet to patrol the Spanish waters, which she felt "might have a very salutary effect on our 20th century pirates."[24]

ATTEMPTS TO HUMANIZE THE CONFLICT

Another matter before the committee at this time was an appeal to both sides to abstain from the bombardment of open towns and generally to humanize the war. The instigation for this appeal was the bombing of Guernica in the Basque province by German planes. On April 26, 1937, German airplanes first bombed the town by relays, machine-gunned the inhabitants as they tried to escape, and then dropped more bombs, incendiary as well as high-explosive.[25] Shocked by such brutality, the United Kingdom at the beginning of May proposed that an appeal be sent to both sides to refrain from the bombing of open towns. The German government supported by Italy and Portugal sought to broaden the entreaty to a general humanization of war. An appeal directed exclusively against the bombing of open towns would, the Germans feared, be a censure against themselves and the Nationalists for the bombing of Guernica and other cities. A broader petition would implicate the Loyalists as well and would obscure the whole issue in a fog of pious platitudes that both sides would tend to disregard. The Soviet government strongly objected to the new draft embodying the German proposals. Discussing the new draft, the Soviet representative declared:

> In the present draft of the appeal the original object of the British suggestion is completely obscured and replaced by generalities introduced at the insistence of certain representatives who seem unwilling to deal with definite objects likely to produce concrete results, and who prefer to talk about "humanizing" the war in general, thereby side-tracking the immediate and pressing purpose of the original British suggestion.[26]

The other states for the sake of compromise were quite willing to accept the German proposal for broadening the appeal and believed the Soviet Union's objection to be merely an obstructive tactic. Lord Plymouth caustically remarked, "The Soviet Representative likes to make the most of the difficulties: I like to make as little as possible of them."[27] The committee ignored the Soviet protests and went ahead with the revised draft. The Soviet government was forced to concur or be left out.

CHAPTER IX

DEADLOCK: SUMMER, 1937

The "Deutschland" and "Leipzig" Incidents

Discussion on humanizing the war and on methods to end illegal seizure of merchant cargo in Spanish waters was interrupted by more serious problems that threatened to destroy the entire nonintervention system. On May 24 and 26, Loyalist planes bombed the port of Palma on Majorca with resultant danger to British, German, and Italian ships in the harbor. On May 24 the Italian naval auxiliary vessel *Barletta* was hit, six officers were killed and others wounded. The Italian government, following the prescribed pattern, reported the incident to the Non-Intervention Committee. The matter was discussed by the committee on May 28.

This incident was soon overshadowed by a Loyalist air attack on the armored vessel *Deutschland* on May 29. The official German account related that the *Deutschland* was peacefully at anchor at the roadstead of Iviza and was suddenly attacked by two planes of the "Red Valencia" government. The *Deutschland* was unable to return the fire. Thirty-one German seamen were killed and seventy-four wounded. The Spanish government's version of the event differed greatly. The Spanish reports declared the German naval commander in the area and the authorities at Valencia had exchanged communications, in which the German commander had declared Republican aircraft would be fired upon if seen flying over German warships engaged in the naval patrol. The Spanish government answered that the German ships would be in no danger as long as they carried on their patrolling duties at the stipulated distance of ten miles from shore, but their safety could not be guaranteed if they entered roadsteads or ports that were known centers of rebel activity. In the case of the *Deutschland,* Loyalist reconnaissance planes were fired on and they retaliated.

The German government did not follow the example of Italy and report the incident to the Non-Intervention Committee to be handled jointly by all member governments. In the early morning hours of May 31 a German cruiser and four destroyers fired 200 shots at the town of Almería, inflicting heavy damage and killing nineteen persons. Only then did the German government notify the Non-Intervention Committee of the incident and her act of retaliation. At the same time she announced her withdrawal from the committee until measures were adopted which would "serve to prevent new criminal attacks." Italy at the same time announced her temporary withdrawal.

Of the members of the London committee the Soviet government was, of course, the most outspoken against the German action. The Russians accepted the Spanish government's version of the events without a question. They sought to make use of the situation to turn the wrath of the committee against Germany and Italy. The Soviet representative at the meeting of the chairman's subcommittee on May 31 declared Berlin had taken upon itself the offices of prosecutor, judge, and executioner. The bombardment of Almería had dissipated the chances of a peaceful settlement of the *Deutschland* incident, and the Germans had destroyed their own case by what constituted a flagrant breach of the Non-Intervention Agreement.

Later the Soviet Union expanded its scope of attack. In a letter to the committee on June 8, the Soviet government declared:

...I have the honour to enquire whether the German Government has at any time since the inauguration of the Naval Observation Scheme informed the Non-Intervention Committee that the "Deutschland" has been charged with the duty of performing naval observation functions in Spanish waters. If the German Government has not done so, and there is every reason to believe this to be the case, then what proof is there that the "Deutschland" was taking part in naval observation and was not in Spanish waters for other purposes? . . .

But even should the "Deutschland" at any time have performed naval observation functions, there can be no doubt whatsoever that she was not doing so when she was near the Balearic Islands. . . . Moreover, according to the scheme approved by the main Committee on March 8th, naval observation is not to be exercised actually in port, or in close proximity to the coast.[1]

It must therefore be considered as definitely established that the bombardment of the "Deutschland" did not take place while she was performing naval observations— even if she has ever been nominated for such purposes.[2]

The French government was also upset by the provocative acts of the Germans. The French representative on the committee, Charles Corbin, said France had endured two similar trials—the shooting down of a French air liner and the bombing of Cerbère at the eastern extremity of the Franco-Spanish frontier—but had refrained from retaliatory measures. He deplored reprisals as a breach of the nonintervention principle; it was the committee's responsibility to satisfy grievances.

Although Great Britain was shocked at the German excesses, she was more alarmed that Germany and Italy had withdrawn from the naval control scheme and might permanently quit the Non-Intervention Committee. The committee had emerged as the main instrument of the

---

[1] For notes to chap. ix, see pp. 157–160.

British government's foreign policy and they felt it to be the only stabilizing factor against a general war. Consequently, their main concern was not how to censure the Germans, but how to bring them back into the committee. The thought appears to have crossed the minds of some government leaders in England and France that the *Deutschland* incident may have been instigated by the Soviet government for the purpose of breaking up the Non-Intervention Agreement. The United States ambassador in the United Kingdom reported to the secretary of state on June 1, 1937:

> ... I mentioned to Eden it was an ominous coincidence that on several occasions when the situation seemed to be improving some untoward incident has occurred to upset the situation and increase its hazards and dangers. Eden replied that this was true and that it looked as if the Soviet Government wanted the British to pull its chestnuts out of the fire and would not be disturbed if Germany was at war with England and France leaving Russia with a comparatively free hand on the other side.[3]

The extensive Communist influence at this time over the Loyalist government and particularly over the air force supports this supposition.[4]

Immediately after the incident and after consultation with the chairman's subcommittee on May 31, France and England applied directly to Germany and Italy to ascertain what guarantees would be sufficient to satisfy them and bring them back into the naval patrol scheme and Non-Intervention Committee. As the talks of the four powers progressed, the USSR objected because she and others were not a party to the negotiations.[5] The Soviet Union's suspicions were always aroused by any talks among the four western powers in fear that a four-power pact aimed against herself might result.[6] She was very uneasy over these present negotiations because she knew strong elements in both the French and British governments wanted agreements with Germany and Italy.[7] But because the Soviet Union in the committee had not objected to the suggestion that France and England negotiate directly with Germany and Italy, she was unable to justify her complaints.[8]

The conversations were successful; on June 12, a compromise agreement was arrived at between England and France, and Germany and Italy. Action in self-defense was considered permissible, but not action in retaliation. However, undue delay by the four powers—Italy, Germany, Great Britain, and France—to agree on collective action concerning hostilities committed against their naval patrol forces would create a new situation in which each of the powers might reserve the right to determine its own attitude.[9] Germany and Italy returned to the committee and took up their patrol duties off the coast of Spain.

The Soviet Union's answer to this four-power agreement was to argue again that the committee had never sanctioned the talks. Her note to the committee on June 16 stated in conclusion:

4. In connection with the method used to deal with the incident under discussion, it is essential to stress that naval observation has been created at the decision of the Non-Intervention Committee, which thereby assumed a certain moral responsibility, and cannot, therefore, be uninterested in the circumstances in which naval observation is carried out, or in the relations existing between the fighting forces in Spain and the naval observation vessels. Apart from that, participation in naval observation is not solely the duty of only four Powers, insofar as the Non-Intervention Committee has adopted the principle that other members may, at any time, if they so desire, take part in the naval observation. Consequently, it is not a question of guarantees for four specific Powers which, incidentally, are acting in this respect as agents of the Non-Intervention Committee, but for naval observation vessels of all Powers who are, or may be, participating in naval observation. . . .

5. In view of the fact that the proposals adopted by the four naval Powers were elaborated without the participation of, and even without consultation with other members of the Non-Intervention Committee, the Soviet Government is compelled to disclaim any responsibility for the proposals in question, as well as for any developments which may result therefrom.[10]

The Soviet protest met with little sympathy from the other members of the committee and was ignored. Furthermore, a new incident turned attention from the Russian objections.

Germany alleged in a communiqué on June 19 that on June 15 and 18 the cruiser *Leipzig* was subject to torpedo attacks, though the ship was not hit. Germany asked for consultations among the four powers to consider collective action against the Loyalist government. The Spanish government denied categorically its submarines had attacked the *Lepizig* on either day and declared all her submarines were in port on both days. Somewhat skeptical, both France and England in discussions with Germany and Italy suggested that further investigations were desirable. They were acting in part upon various experiences in the First World War when reports of submarine attacks, made in perfect good faith, had subsequently proved to have no foundation in fact. Nevertheless, the Germans, supported by the Italians, demanded immediate action. On June 22, negotiations among the four naval patrol powers broke down. Germany decided to refrain from any new retaliatory measures against Spain but did show her objections by withdrawing definitively from the naval control scheme. She did not leave the Non-Intervention Committee—much to the relief of the western democracies. The Italian government followed the example of Germany and withdrew from the naval patrol.

A Fascist Victory

Just prior to the *Leipzig* crisis, the British government had resolved to take a firmer stand in the Non-Intervention Committee.[11] It had become blatantly clear that Italy and Germany were purposely delaying any agreement on the withdrawal of volunteers, and that significant amounts of aid were still going to both parties in Spain. As a result, Lord Plymouth at the next meeting of the chairman's subcommittee on June 21 warned:

... His Majesty's Government ... feels the keenest disappointment that despite the agreements entered into and the elaborate organisations set up, arms and war material continue to reach both sides in Spain. In the view of His Majesty's Government this state of affairs cannot be allowed to continue if the existence of the Non-Intervention Committee is to be justified and its previous efforts not wasted.

His Majesty's Government therefore looks to all the other Governments represented on the Committee to do what they can to improve without delay the present position. ...

If there is no early evidence that such co-operation will be forthcoming, His Majesty's Government will feel bound to take this fact into account in giving further consideration to the situation.[12]

Although a stronger statement than was usual from the British government, it was by no means an ultimatum and was ignored by Germany and Italy. The Soviet press was heartened by the growing impatience of the British government, but "the alarm of the Chamberlain government is not hard to understand. Fascist intervention has reached such a degree that it cannot be practically considered otherwise than open war against the Spanish Republic."[13] Such open aggression, they concluded, could not be stopped by mild phrases alone.

The ineffectiveness of the British plea was obvious when on June 23 Germany, followed by Italy, withdrew from the patrol scheme. It might be said that Germany by the *Leipzig* incident called the British bluff and the British government, instead of reconsidering the whole non-intervention scheme as she had promised, sought only to patch it as best she could. England and France were clearly not able or willing to take decisive action to end the Spanish problem.[14] Thus rather than bring the Spanish issue to a showdown, as urged by Russia, the British and French governments side-stepped and on June 25 suggested to the committee that they should take over the duty of patrolling the German and Italian zones as well as the zones originally allocated to them. The German and Italian representatives objected on the grounds that it did not give the necessary equilibrium to insure absolute impartiality of control. They alleged that aid was being sent to the Loyalists by French coastal shippers. In answer the subcommittee asked Italy and Germany to present their own plan since they had thrown out the British and French suggestion.

Italy and Germany met the challenge and presented their plan to the subcommittee on July 2: (1) belligerent rights to the two parties in Spain should be granted and (2) "with the exception of the patrol system, which, as already pointed out has proved an entire failure and cannot therefore be continued, the present supervision system already approved by the Committee should still be maintained. The German and the Italian Governments accordingly suggest that the observation of the land frontiers of Spain, as well as the system of supervision both in the ports and with the observers embarked on board the ships flying the flag of the non-intervention countries, should be maintained."[15] It was not surprising that Italy and Germany tied their proposed scheme to the granting of belligerent rights. The recognition of belligerency would confer on both sides the right of visit and search on the high seas. The Nationalists with their greater naval strength would have been at an advantage. Since the war on land had reached a temporary stalemate, the Nationalists were anxious to extend their military activities against Loyalist shipping to the point where they could legitimately and effectively isolate the Republicans from all outside help.

A debate now ensued in the committee as to which plan should be adopted. Only three of the powers, Portugal, Italy, and Germany, backed the German-Italian plan, while all the other powers supported the British plan. The Soviet Union, as was to be expected, was the most adamant against the German-Italian proposal. During the debate on the question by the full committee on July 9, the Soviet representative took the opportunity to present again the Soviet case against Germany and Italy. He pointed particularly to the various frank admissions by Italian and German newspapers and leaders of their intervention in Spain. For example, he quoted from Hitler's speech at Würzburg on June 27, "Germany needs to import iron ore. That is why we want a Nationalist Government in Spain, so that we may be able to buy Spanish ore"; then quoting from the *Popolo d'Italia* of June 4: "One day the veil will be lifted on events in Spain. The world will know then in the most clear way that the legionaries of fascism have written on the Iberian land a new page of history and glory." In arguing specifically against the German-Italian proposal, the Soviet representative declared:

To-day I am in a position to state the considered view of the Soviet Government. They believe that complete naval control off the Spanish coasts is an essential element of the non-intervention scheme, and without it the very basis on which the non-intervention system was built up, including the observation of land frontiers, must inevitably go.

They consider further that the granting of belligerent rights to General Franco is a very complicated problem which raises the gravest issues.

In the first place this problem should be considered in its legal aspect. To grant belligerent rights to General Franco would mean putting the legitimate Government of the Spanish Republic and the rebellious General, who, in defiance of his oath, took up arms against his Government, on the same legal basis. Such an action would obviously be contrary to international law, to international custom and tradition, and consequently cannot be accepted.

* * *

In the second place, the German-Italian proposals should be considered from the military point of view, as to their effect on the course of the Spanish War.

In the opinion of my Government the demands advanced by Germany and Italy, if accepted, must inevitably result in the complete upsetting of the balance in favor of General Franco, and therefore such an absolutely one-sided proposal cannot be supported.[16]

The French government strongly supported the Soviet government's position except for the contention that it was illegal to recognize the belligerent rights of both parties under international law, for which no precedent could be found in current practice.[17] The British, fearful of breaking up the committee, were much more willing to appease.

On the suggestion of the Netherlands representative, the committee at the conclusion of the meeting on July 9 agreed to ask the British government, as the most impartial great power member of the committee, to see if it could not work out a compromise between the two plans in dispute. The Soviet Union accepted this proposal, but with misgivings:

Although I must express some scepticism about the possibility of finding an equitable solution which would satisfy all parties concerned, still I do not object to the proposal put forward by the Netherlands Representative. At the same time, I must say in all friendliness that we cannot go on like this indefinitely. We have already had a full week for reflection, a full week in which to try to find a compromise. So far no compromise acceptable to all parties has been produced from any quarter. I do not wonder. The gulf between the two sets of proposals is so wide it could hardly be bridged in any satisfactory way. Meanwhile the situation in Spain and off the coast of Spain is extremely tense and so fraught with possibilities of danger; naval control is disorganised; the Portuguese frontier is open; only the French frontier remains closed. . . .[18]

The situation was certainly fraught with danger, as Soviet Ambassador Maisky declared. There were many rumors of war and the likelihood of a break-up of the whole nonintervention scheme. Consequently, the British moved quickly to find a compromise and were able to offer a proposal to the powers as early as July 14, to be considered by the whole committee on July 16. The new British proposal set up a program to be carried out by the following stages:

1. Establishment of [Non-Intervention] officers in Spanish ports, and withdrawal of naval patrol, as soon as possible;

2. Establishment of commissions to make arrangements for and supervise the withdrawal of foreign nationals, and extension of the Non-Intervention Agreement to follow (1) as quickly as possible;

3. Recognition of belligerent rights to become effective when the Non-Intervention Committee place on record their opinion that the arrangements for the withdrawal of foreign nationals are working satisfactorily and that this withdrawal has in fact made substantial progress.[19]

In the meeting of the committee on July 16, all members agreed that the British proposals should serve as the basis for future discussion and accepted the British plan in principle. The Soviet Union modified her acceptance, stating "the British proposals require certain important modifications which will be put forward by the Soviet Government at a later stage when the British plan is submitted to the sub-committee for closer examination."[20] The Italian and German governments made similar reservations.

The Soviet Union had gone along thus far with the compromises so as not to be left isolated during this time of war scare nor to be accused of causing the failure of the nonintervention schemes. Nonetheless, from the reports in the Soviet press obviously she was in some despair throughout this period over the policies of Great Britain. The British habit of compromising compromises was rapidly shifting the Non-Intervention Committee exactly into the innocuous position Hitler and Mussolini wanted it to assume. Repeatedly, editorials in the Soviet press attacked the appeasement policy of the British and urged them to make a definite stand.[21]

In addition it was soon clear that the German and Italian agreement in principle was deceptive and they intended to prevent a final solution by haggling over details.[22] For example, at the meeting of the chairman's subcommittee on July 20 the Italian ambassador supported by the German representative was able to halt the deliberations by a prolonged discussion over procedure. They insisted the next item for discussion was the restoration of control over land frontiers whereas the other members argued that the next matter should be the withdrawal of volunteers. The meeting ended in deadlock and the next few days' diplomatic conversations were unable to break it. The plenary meeting of the committee on July 26 was able to decide only that the governments should submit their views on the British plan in writing.

At this point the Soviet Union made known her objections to the British plan, enabling Italy and Germany again to throw the onus of obstruction on the USSR. In a note dated July 29 to the committee the Soviet government supported the first two parts of the British plan except for minor changes insuring the full coöperation of all parties. But in respect to belligerent rights the Soviet government had this to say:

3. . . . A change in attitude towards Franco, and more so the granting to him of any rights legalising his rebellion represents an act of open interference in Spanish affairs in favor of the rebels, and at the same time a change of the whole foundation on which the obligations of Non-Intervention were undertaken and the Non-Intervention Committee in London created. Even consent in principle only to grant Franco, in case he fulfills certain conditions, belligerent rights, would in itself amount to a change of attitude towards Franco as the leader of the rebels which would preserve its significance even in case Franco does not fulfil the conditions put to him.

Apart from that, the Soviet Government has no doubts whatever that Franco will either refuse to agree to the withdrawal of foreign nationals, or having given his consent to the withdrawal will not loyally carry out their evacuation. The Soviet Government has also doubts as to the loyal and complete recall of the so-called volunteers, but actually military formations, by certain members of the London Non-Intervention Committee. Thus the conditions to which the granting of belligerent rights in the British proposals is made subject will not be fulfilled, whereas, the granting in principle of belligerent rights to Franco will remain. The Soviet Government cannot give its consent to this.

If and when the complete and loyal evacuation from Spain of all foreign nationals engaged in the conflict there is effected, then a new situation will arise, likely to allow a return to the examination of those points of the British proposals which in the opinion of the Soviet Government could not and should not be settled at the present time.[23]

It is not clear why the Soviet Union risked this opportunity for Italy and Germany to extricate themselves so easily from the role of obstructionist. The Soviet Union may have feared the British would make still another compromise to accommodate Hitler and Mussolini and thus she resorted to the only tactic left to her, the introduction of her own conditions for acceptance of the British plan. In this way perhaps she hoped to keep the British and the French from capitulating entirely, although such a move was bound to make her lose even more prestige. The conservative English and French press immediately heaped abuse

on the USSR for her obstruction and put the failure of the nonintervention system at her door.[24] It must be said in behalf of the Soviet Union
that her predictions concerning the procrastination of Italy and Germany toward the various nonintervention schemes were completely
fulfilled.

The intransigent attitude of the Soviet Union now made the deadlock
appear more insoluble than ever.[25] At the meeting of the chairman's
subcommittee on August 6 the Soviet representative futilely attempted
to put the odium for failure back on Germany and Italy by asking their
representatives point-blank if they would agree "unconditionally to the
withdrawal of all foreign nationals fighting in Spain on either side."
The Italian and German representatives side-stepped the issue successfully and avoided answering. With neither side giving ground, the
lengthy discussions in the subcommittee on August 6 came to naught,
and the members tacitly agreed that further discussion was useless. As
a result no meetings of the committee or the subcommittee were held
until the end of August. During August and September the powers
were busy dealing with the renewed aggression against China by Japan
and with attacks on shipping in the Mediterranean.

The events of the spring and summer of 1937 undoubtedly clarified
the policy of the British and French toward the Spanish crisis. The
Italian and German intervention on the side of the rebels had long been
an open secret. Not only did England and France know the fact of intervention but also exact figures on the amount of equipment and troops
being sent to the Nationalists.[26] It was also common knowledge that
Hitler and Mussolini were committed to "see Franco through" to a
decisive victory in Spain.[27] The intervention of the Soviet Union on the
side of the Loyalists was equally obvious, but the commitment of Russia
to the Spanish government was less certain. These public facts alone
proved that France and particularly Britain no longer had any real
intent to end intervention. Their sole purposes in the now misnamed
Non-Intervention Committee were to keep the war from spreading to
the rest of Europe and to prevent Spain from being used by Germany
and Italy as a permanent military base, although the democracies had
come to accept the temporary occupation of Spain by German and
Italian troops. Evidence that British government circles preferred a
Nationalist victory to a Loyalist victory increased. The documents now
available prove this. For example, Foreign Minister Delbos of France
reported to United States Ambassador Bullitt on August 1, 1937, "Eden
had told him frankly that he would prefer to see Franco win and that

he believed that Great Britain could make an agreement with Franco which would ensure the departure of Germans and Italians from Spain."[28] Finally, the French clearly had lost all initiative in respect to European politics. In the same interview with Ambassador Bullitt, Premier Chautemps "pointed out that France was in a peculiarly unfortunate position diplomatically to take steps. England was engaged in negotiations of one sort and another with Germany and Italy and Spain counting on the readiness of France to support England at all points. France on the other hand was engaged in no negotiations with either Germany or Italy or Franco and had no control over the course of events."[29] Under these circumstances it is feasible that already by the summer of 1937 the Soviet Union seriously doubted the possibilities of an alliance with the western democracies, and her renewed obstruction in the Non-Intervention Committee was not designed to arouse the democracies to collective action, as she had attempted previously, but to delay appeasement.[30] The Nyon Conference at the end of the summer, however, momentarily offered renewed hope to Russia for a positive western alliance against Nazi-Fascist aggression.

CHAPTER X

THE NYON CONFERENCE: SEPTEMBER, 1937

DURING THE month of August, 1937, the indiscriminate attacks on merchant shipping by unidentified warships, aircraft, and submarines in the Mediterranean reached a new height. Most of the previous assaults had been directed against Spanish merchant ships, but in August these hostile acts were extended to all ships regardless of flag or destination. Furthermore, attacks occurred throughout the length of the Mediterranean Sea. During the second week of August alone, ten ships were assailed of which four were sunk. Similar incidences continued throughout August. In this offensive by "unknown pirates" two Russian ships were sunk, one off Algiers and the other in the eastern Mediterranean. The origin of this foul play was at the time unproved though the evidence pointed toward Italy.[1] A couple of Italian ships were fired upon, but most of the victims were merchantmen of the Spanish government, the Soviet Union, and the democratic powers.

This offensive by sea appears to have been a part of the more open and flagrant intervention of the Italian government in Spain. Statements at this time by Italian officials, including Mussolini, made it clear to the world that Italy would not tolerate the establishment of a Communist state in the Mediterranean and Italian legions were in Spain to prevent any such possibility.[2] Such statements by high officials in the Italian government might legitimately have been considered an official denouncement of the nonintervention pact by Italy. The Soviet Union was of such mind but the democratic powers still clung to the straw of nonintervention.

Although France and Great Britain were inclined to overlook Mussolini's provocative remarks confessing aggression in Spain, they took a very different view of the attacking and sinking of their own merchant ships. This was a direct and immediate assault on their security. The British government might ignore the imperialist designs and aggressions of other powers as long as it involved only foreigners, but when innocent British merchantmen were being sunk and when later the British destroyer *Havock* was attacked, the British people and government were thoroughly aroused. As the traditional defender of the sea lanes essential to her livelihood, Great Britain could not allow such piratic attacks to continue with impunity. Although all the democratic

---

[1] For notes to chap. x, see pp. 160–162.

powers of Western Europe were determined to stop the sinkings of their ships, none were willing to go as far as the Spanish government, who on August 21 appealed to the League Council under article 11 of the Covenant and sent notes to European governments on August 22 accusing Italian submarines and destroyers as the attackers. The Italian and German documents now available prove absolutely that Italy was carrying on these unprovoked attacks.[3] The Soviet Union alone endorsed the Loyalist condemnation of Italy. England and France refused to name the guilty party, though there is good reason to believe the British government in particular had sufficient evidence to conclude definitely it was Italy.[4] Britain and France decided, rather, that accusations were of no value and measures should be taken only to forestall future acts of piracy. The French government suggested that a special meeting of the foreign ministers of the interested parties be held to decide what action should be taken. Just a few hours before the British Cabinet on September 2 met to consider the French proposal, the British destroyer *Havock* was attacked. This assured the enthusiastic endorsement by the British government. Since the League assembly was to open on September 13 in Geneva, the conference was planned for nearby Nyon. Geneva was rejected in order to avoid embarrassment to the Italians and Germans—no longer members of the League. The Soviet press also claimed the League was shunned in order to eliminate Spain. "By the exclusion of Spain from the number of participants in the conference for the struggle against piracy, Great Britain and France were already making one concession to the Fascist aggressors."[5] On September 6 a joint Anglo-French invitation for a meeting beginning September 10 was sent to ten powers; Germany and the riparian states of the Mediterranean and Black seas, excluding Spain. In response the Soviet Union decided on a maneuver of her own.

During the summer of 1937 the Soviet Union had become increasingly apprehensive concerning the British efforts to compromise and negotiate with Italy over Spain and other issues. The Soviet press carried frequent editorials denouncing these bilateral talks which appeared to Soviet eyes to be an incipient *rapprochement* between fascism and the West.[6] Gabriel Péri, a French Communist, summed up the Communist mistrust in an editorial in *Inprecorr* called "Towards a New Four-Power Pact."

In any case, neither attacks nor slanders hindered Great Britain, after the bombardment of Almería, from carrying on with her project. The negotiations which were commenced after March 31, and which led to the temporary agreement of

June 12, were four-power negotiations. The Italian press took pains to emphasize the new character of these negotiations, from which it deduced, and not without reason, that this was a case of prelude to the resuscitation of the Four-Power Pact.

Also, after the crisis of non-intervention on June 23, Great Britain did not abandon its plans. On the contrary, the Eden plan and the intrigues of Lord Plymouth have only one aim: not to jeopardize the Italo-British bargaining. Britain has already informed Italy that on the basis of the promise of evacuation of the Balearics, Italy would have a free hand in Spain....[7]

That this fear of the Soviet Union was perhaps not groundless is seen from a report of the American embassy in Berlin to the secretary of state on August 4, 1937:

The Germans see the Anglo-Italian negotiations as a move to isolate Russia. Russian diplomats in Berlin declare, however, that it is really a move to win Italy over from the Axis. The consensus of opinion is that it is really a move to isolate Russia and that the British are attempting to formulate a four-power pact of Germany, Italy, France and England.[8]

Furthermore, certain groups among the British Conservatives hoped the Soviet Union and Italy and Germany might become embroiled, leaving the democracies free. Sir Winston Churchill had had the following to say during January of the same year:

When I read of large numbers of German Nazis and Italian fascists traveling to the Spanish arena to slay large numbers of Russian Bolsheviks and French Communists, I deplore these savage excursions. But when I search my heart I cannot feel, that if all these armed tourists to Spain were to transfix each other with the simultaneous efficiency of Ivan and the Bulbil Amir till there was no one left, except the press representatives to tell the tale, the interests and safety of Britain would be in any way endangered.[9]

Probably a good many Englishmen, had they been as forthright as Sir Winston, would have said the same thing. They would have been quite willing to bargain with Hitler and Mussolini at the expense of Communist Russia. There is no evidence, however, to prove that the British government was actually plotting to turn Germany against Russia.

The Soviet Union saw the Nyon Conference as a chance to prevent the "pending four-power pact." On September 7, 1937, the Soviet Union sent a very inflammatory note to Italy accusing her of sinking two Soviet merchantmen on August 30 and September 1 and demanding compensation and punishment of the perpetrators. The note was written in expressly undiplomatic terms.[10] The Soviet Union had several reasons for sending such a note. She was probably genuinely aroused by the sinking of two merchant ships in time of peace and felt that her honor demanded immediate recompense. The evidence publicly available pointed to Italy, and in addition the USSR may have had intelligence reports confirming Italy as the culprit. Secondly, Russia wanted to demonstrate to Hitler and Mussolini that she was not an appeaser and would not allow open attacks on herself with impunity. Finally, Russia undoubtedly hoped the note at this particular time would keep Italy away from the Nyon Conference.[11] Russia could easily blame Italy, should the conference be a failure, for her refusal as a Mediterranean power to attend. On the other hand, if the conference were successful England and France might awaken to the advantage of collective action as a means to stop Mussolini and Hitler.

Italy, followed by Germany, fell into the Soviet trap.[12] The Italian government in its reply to the Soviet Union absolutely denied any responsibility, as was expected, and on September 9 both Germany and Italy refused to attend the Nyon Conference as long as the Soviet Union was present. Very likely Italy and Germany looked upon the Soviet note less as an insult (criminations back and forth had become everyday matters even on the diplomatic level) than as another of the frequent *faux pas* of Soviet diplomacy. Using the Soviet note as a pretext, they hoped to break up the Nyon Conference.

This time, however, the Soviets had analyzed the democratic attitude correctly and the German-Italian plan misfired. Italy and Germany in their note refusing to come to Nyon, suggested, as an alternative, consideration of the problem by the London committee. The French and British governments, not wanting mere procrastination over this issue, openly acknowledged the committee for what the Soviet Union had always said it was, a legal camouflage permitting Germany and Italy to cover up by delay their direct intervention in Spain. This matter was too important to England and France to be lost in the labyrinth of squabbles in the London committee. Consequently, the urgency of the matter decided them to meet in Nyon without Germany and Italy.[13]

The Soviets, in spite of their successful "ambush" of Germany and Italy, were still skeptical as to the outcome of the conference. For the last year or more they had been witnessing the degeneration of British and French foreign policy vis-à-vis the dictators, and even though France and England had decided to meet at Nyon without Germany and Italy, no changes occurred in the composition of their governments or policy statements which would indicate a reversal in the strategy of appeasement. *Izvestiia* on September 8 characterized this misgiving of the Russians:

...All in all preparations for the Conference ... are suspiciously reminiscent of the well-known tiresome noise around the London Non-Intervention Committee.

If the Nyon Conference takes the same direction as the London committee then a diplomatic torpedo will have been added to the Italian torpedoes blowing up the cause of peace.

This incident perhaps shows that fundamentally neither Stalin, nor Hitler and Mussolini by this time considered the democracies capable of acting resolutely. This characterization of the democracies as "spineless" was to become an important factor in determining the policies of the Communists, Nazis, and Fascists jockeying for allies and settlements just before the Second World War in 1939.

The foreign ministers of France, England, Greece, Yugoslavia, Turkey, Egypt, Rumania, Bulgaria, and Russia met in Nyon on September 10. They immediately got down to the problem of deciding adequate techniques to stop further piracy. Only the Soviet Union proferred a political statement aimed at Italy.[14] The French and the British representatives on the first day presented a plan for dividing the Mediterranean into zones for patrolling and counterattacking any unidentified submarines in the area where a merchant ship suffered an attack. The USSR and the smaller powers, however, were reluctant to undertake such a task because of their lack of naval forces and their fear of reprisals by a stronger power. Consequently, England and France on the second day agreed to assume full responsibility for patrolling; on this basis a detailed plan was worked out the very same day. The text was then referred back to the governments who gave it their immediate approval and the accord was signed on September 14. In a little over four days an agreement had been drawn up and signed— almost a record in international diplomacy during this period. The strong desire of all the participating governments to end the piracy and the absence of Italy and Germany made this possible. On September 17 a supplementary agreement on aircraft was signed. The effect of the agreement was immediate. The submarine attacks on shipping immediately ceased. Air attacks were reduced but not stopped, because it was much harder to bring unidentified aircraft to heel than submarines.

The Soviet Union throughout assumed a coöperative attitude toward the negotiations, even though she had not been entirely satisfied with the arrangements for the conference. The Soviet Union had regretted the omission of the Spanish government,[15] and in his opening statement Litvinov declared:

However, I must express my regret that a Mediterranean state which has suffered most from piracy and against which this piracy is directed, is not present here, namely, Republican Spain. It is not yet too late to fill this gap and thereby raise the prestige of the conference itself.[16]

The Soviet Union also protested the omission of the commercial vessels of the Spanish government in the protection scheme. The conference passed over both of these objections. But in neither of the above instances did the Soviet press the issue to the point of blocking agreement. It is interesting to note that France originally favored asking the Republican government of Spain, but bowed to the wishes of England who wanted to make it as much as possible a nonpolitical conference.[17]

In one aspect the Soviet delegation was successful. The agreement expressly stipulated that neither of the warring parties enjoyed belligerent rights.[18] It was this point that the Communist press stressed in editorials as the great victory of the USSR.[19]

In conclusion, the Soviet Union although not entirely satisfied with the Nyon Conference was nevertheless pleased because it was a step toward collective security, and because the revival of a four-power pact had been averted, at least temporarily. At the signing of the Nyon Agreement, Litvinov summed up the attitude of the USSR:

We, on our part, wish to travel a few stations further along the road we have followed together here. But the history of the Disarmament Conference and other international conferences has already shown that the youthful Soviet Union, full of strength, energy, courage, and belief in the correctness of her international conception is always prepared to advance more quickly on the path of defending peace and is more determined to act than other states.

* * *

At a time when aggression, international lawlessness, and adventurist impudence have been accustomed to success, any action combating these phenomena which takes the form not merely of discussion, protests, and declarations, but of practical steps, must be particularly welcomed, while today we have before us an international agreement with very material backing.

Moreover, this agreement represents a partial realization of the idea of collective security and likewise of the idea of regional agreements. . . .[20]

The Soviet Union was also elated that the success of the Nyon arrangement was achieved largely because Germany and Italy did not participate. Litvinov in his speech to the League a few days later drew the following conclusion:

What is wanted is not universality, but that those who take part in any international organisation or conference, whatever the differences between their national interests, should be united by a common universal idea binding them together, such as the idea of peace, the idea of respecting the integrity and independence of all peoples, the idea of outlawing force as an instrument of national policy, the idea which lies at the foundation of the Covenant of the League of Nations and the Pact of Paris.[21]

No doubt the Soviet Union hoped that the Western powers had benefited by this lesson and would willingly revamp the Non-Intervention Committee to allow Germany and Italy to quit the committee, as they had threatened, and to turn the remaining members into an effective organization of collective action against German-Italian intervention in Spain.

The democratic powers, however, had no intention of traveling a few more stations with the Soviets and in fact were sorry they had come along as far as they had. In an effort to retreat from their strong stand at Nyon, they began immediately to negotiate with Italy to bring her into the control scheme. Italy, very much alarmed at the progress made in the absence of German and Italian diplomats, without hesitation accepted the invitation to share patrol duties. Naval conversations were opened in Paris on September 21, and Italian participation became effective on November 11.

CHAPTER XI

NEW EFFORTS AT COMPROMISE: FALL, 1937

SPAIN AGAIN PLEADS IN THE LEAGUE

IN AUGUST OF 1937, Spain for the fourth time within a year brought
to the attention of the League the continued intervention of Italy and
Germany on the side of the Nationalists. As in the previous instances,
Spain used the League to keep her case and its urgency before world
public opinion. The Spanish government in its note to the League secretariat did not ask for a special meeting since the Council was soon to
hold its regular meeting.

When the Council met in regular session on September 16, Premier
Juan Negrín presented the Spanish case. The main body of Negrín's
protest was that, since Spain had not been invited to the Nyon Conference and because her merchant shipping was not protected by the
agreements, she was exposed to aggression and continued attacks by
Italy. He also urged the Council to abandon "fiction and make-believe"
and declare the attacks to have been perpetrated by Italian warships.
Only the Soviet Union backed his arguments. Litvinov concluded his
comments on the Spanish case by saying "Nyon has done something, but
it does not follow that the League of Nations, which is called upon to
protect its Members from every kind of aggression, has no say in the
matter. I hope—and I feel confident—that the Council will say its
word on the appeal made by a Member of the League,—a Member of the
Council itself."[1]

The other members of the Council refused to support the Spanish
requests and merely praised the effectiveness of the Nyon agreements.
The resolution passed by the Council on October 4, after Spain had
been given a further chance of a hearing before the Assembly, merely
supported the Nyon agreements and declared the attacks were contrary "to the elementary dictates of humanity underlying the established rules of international law."[2] The resolution mentioned nothing
about including Spain in the agreements. Nevertheless, the Spanish
and Russian representatives accepted the resolution as they could gain
nothing by obstruction. Spain did, however, reserve the right to reopen
the case at any time.

In the League Assembly the Spanish plea fared somewhat better. As
in the Council, Negrín urged the Assembly to recognize the failure of

---

[1] For notes to chap. xi, see pp. 162–166.

the policy of nonintervention and name Italy and Germany as aggressors against the legitimate Spanish government. Again the main support of the Spanish argument came from Litvinov who took the opportunity to restate the Soviet policy of collective security.[3] He tied the events in Spain to the outbreak of aggression in China by the Japanese and to the growing tendency of the Nazis and Fascists to trample on the weak. He said that the USSR was particularly alarmed about the role of the League in these matters:

> We would search in vain for an echo of these events [in Spain and China] in the report of the League Secretariat to the present session. The League of Nations, whose purpose is to guarantee the integrity of the States which are members of it, to preserve peace and international order, to see that international treaties are observed inviolate and international law is respected, stands aloof from these events, without reacting to them. What is worse, there is a growing opinion that the main thing is to shield and isolate the League of Nations like some blushing damsel, lest the odour of these shocking events should reach it.[4]

If Russia and Spain hoped they would gain the support of the smaller nations in the Assembly, they were unrewarded. The debate consisted of a series of platitudes without any nation, great or small, concretely suggesting a future program of action either to the League or the London committee. In contrast to previous debates on Spain, at least there was frank admission that nonintervention had been a failure and the prospects of ending foreign interference were not good. While most of the states were sympathetic to the Spanish government, though not overtly so, they offered little hope and clung to the Non-Intervention Agreement as the only possibility of stopping a general war. Anthony Eden expressed the opinion of most members when he declared, "Let us not, however, conceal from ourselves this patent fact: if the policy of non-intervention is abandoned, Europe will be swept into deeper and more dangerous waters. A leaky dam may yet serve its purpose."

Litvinov and Alvarez del Vayo in committee tried to press a resolution condemning Italy and Germany, ending the Non-Intervention Agreement and providing for League action against the aggressors. France and England argued for a resolution that merely asked the powers to back up their commitments to the Non-Intervention Agreement and warned nonintervention might have to be abandoned if the situation did not improve. France and England, although they were discouraged with the course of the London committee, still had no idea of ending it. In fact during the last two weeks of September, while the debate on Spain was proceeding in the League, they sought to reopen direct conversations with Italy as a means to settle the Spanish problem and to conclude a general agreement on the status of the Mediterranean.

On September 22 Foreign Minister Delbos of France carried on conversations with the Italian representative in Geneva, Bova-Scoppa. Bova-Scoppa reassured the French that Mussolini had no territorial ambitions in Spain and would withdraw his forces at the end of the war. Buoyed by this beginning, France and England were hopeful of working out a compromise with Italy. They had become particularly anxious about Italy because of the growing amity between Hitler and Mussolini, which appeared to be reaching a new climax with the latter's visit to Germany beginning September 23.

The resolution finally negotiated in committee favored chiefly the views of France and England over Spain and Russia. Two paragraphs, however, distinguished it from the League's usual innocuous resolution on Spain:

[Paragraph] 4; the Assembly:
Regrets that not merely has the London Non-Intervention Committee failed, despite the efforts of the majority of its Members, of which the Assembly expresses its appreciation, to secure the withdrawal of non-Spanish combatants taking part in the struggle in Spain, but that it must today be recognised that there are veritable foreign army corps on Spanish soil, which represents foreign intervention in Spanish affairs.

[Paragraph] 7:
Appeals to the Governments, which must all be animated by the desire to see peace maintained in Europe, to undertake a new and earnest effort in this direction [securing the immediate withdrawal of non-Spanish combatants] ;

And notes that, if such a result cannot be obtained in the near future, the Members of the League which are parties to the Non-Intervention Agreement will consider ending the policy of non-intervention.[5]

Litvinov was thankful for the stronger note struck by the resolution but was apprehensive about paragraph 7:

What does "the near future" mean? There is no precise definition of these words. . . . The action of certain Powers justifies the apprehension that in the present case the approach to those Powers may be met again by proposals for certain conditions and by other dilatory methods, of which those Powers have shown themselves to be past masters, and in the result "the near future" may pass on into eternity.[6]

The resolution was debated by the full Assembly on October 2. In the final vote Portugal and Albania voted against the resolution and fourteen states abstained. Although the resolution failed to pass, the fact that the major European powers in the League voted for it, as did twenty-nine other states, imbued it with strong moral force.

From the foregoing discussion it might be assumed that the Soviet leaders found some encouragement for the policy of collective security in the resolution, but actually they were dubious as to its real significance, particularly at a time when both France and England were trying to woo Mussolini.

> The resolution passed by the political committee of the League of Nations in spite of all its "elasticity" could play a significant role, if it were not for the parallel activities of some of the powers whose representatives spoke for it in Geneva. As is well known, on the suggestion of England, Anglo–Franco–Italian negotiations have already begun, the participants of which are obviously sounding out the possibility of a bargain at the expense of the interests of the Spanish people. . . .[7]

Clearly, from the comments of the Soviet representative in the League debates and the Soviet press, the Soviet leaders had become more and more discouraged with the League and with their attempts to ally with England and France against Hitler and Mussolini.[8] Resolutions, no matter how strong, they felt, were worthless in opposition to blatant aggression by Italy and Germany in Spain. Words without concerted action to enforce them were no deterrent. The months of failure in the London committee verified England and France were not ready to act. Unquestionably, by this time disillusionment concerning collective measures had gone far. It is difficult to say when disappointment submerged hope in the minds of the Soviet leaders. But by the fall of 1937 Russia was unwilling to become more deeply involved in Spain on behalf of collective security. Although Russia abided by Spain diplomatically, she was reducing the flow of arms to the Loyalist government[9] and was making little effort to coöperate with England and France in the Non-Intervention Committee.

THE NON-INTERVENTION COMMITTEE TRIES AGAIN

By the middle of September, 1937, no one could deceive himself that the Non-Intervention Agreement had ever been taken seriously by Hitler and Mussolini. Italian intervention on behalf of Franco had been admitted by Mussolini for several months. On August 27 Mussolini had sent an open telegram to Franco celebrating the fall of Santander to rebel troops:

> I am particularly glad that during ten days of hard fighting the Italian legionary troops have made a valiant contribution to the splendid victory of Santander, and that that contribution finds today, in your telegram, the recognition to which they aspire. This comradeship of arms—now so close—is a guarantee of the final victory which will liberate Spain and the Mediterranean from all threats to the civilization we share.[10]

In addition the systems of control, over which so many long hours of negotiation had been spent, faded away within a few months. The chairman and the secretary of the Non-Intervention Board on August 25 reported to the committee on the operation of the observation scheme and offered suggestions as to the best methods for improving it. The report stated that, since the scheme began on April 19, 19 per cent of the ships that called at Spanish ports flew the Spanish flag and 1 per cent were non-European. These ships did not come under the control scheme at all. Although the naval patrol reported only four ships had violated the scheme, information from insurance companies and shipping agencies indicated that forty-two ships should have taken observers on board, although at the time the ships may have deceived the naval patrol by flying the flags of nonmembers of the Non-Intervention Agreement. Consequently, the only conclusion to be drawn was that the naval patrol had been a failure in detecting violations and the report suggested it be abandoned.[11] As a result, when the Nyon agreements came into effect, the British and French governments acted bilaterally on the advice of the report and notified the chairman of the London committee on September 16 that they were withdrawing their ships from the patrol scheme for use under the Nyon agreements.[12] The work of the frontier observation scheme was even less fruitful than the naval patrol since it had not functioned at all during the summer of 1937. In June the Portuguese had suspended control of their frontier and the French, not wishing that theirs should be the only border under surveillance, likewise suspended international supervision on July 13. The French government, nevertheless, unilaterally kept the border closed to arms and to volunteers crossing to fight in Spain. The only international regulation still in operation was the scheme of taking neutral observers on ships traveling to Spain and this was not working successfully, as evidenced by the board's report that forty-two ships had violated the agreement. In spite of its deficiencies, however, the board suggested that the scheme for observers on ships be maintained with some minor changes. In place of the naval patrol, it proposed stationing additional observers in all Spanish ports.

The board asked the members of the London committee to comment on its plan by September 21. Neither Italy, Germany nor the Soviet Union replied in time, and only the Soviet government later raised serious objections to the plan:

... With the abolition of the [naval] patrol any possibility of such supervision disappears, and the observance of the undertaking to take observers on board the ships depends solely on the good will of all the interested countries—on which, as the experience of the past 14 months has shown, no reliance can be placed.... In effect, this means that we return to the situation prevailing before the introduction of control and before the declaration by the Soviet Government made in the Committee on October 7 last year. In these conditions the Soviet Government sees no useful purpose in the maintenance of the system of observers on ships, which does not in any way ensure the observance of the Non-Intervention Agreement.[13]

By reference to her earlier declaration, the USSR indirectly renewed her threat to break up the Non-Intervention Agreement. On October 7 the Soviet representative further notified the committee his government would no longer pay its contribution toward the maintenance of the observer scheme.[14]

With the collapse of the control schemes, it is not surprising that the problem of withdrawing foreign volunteers remained deadlocked throughout the summer of 1937. Except for one brief meeting to hear the board's report, neither the Non-Intervention Committee nor the chairman's subcommittee had met for over two months. In the interval the French and British governments had tried to negotiate an agreement on volunteers directly with Italy—as part of a general settlement of issues in the Mediterranean—but without results.[15] As mentioned previously, some optimism was generated by the friendly talks between Foreign Minister Delbos and Bova-Scoppa, the Italian representative in Geneva, on September 22 and 23.[16] Mussolini's subsequent visit to Berlin, however, seems to have altered his attitude toward a separate agreement with England and France. All further attempts by the French and British governments to open direct negotiations with Mussolini were rebuffed with the remark that such matters should be taken up in the London committee. In addition there were continued rumors of more Italian troops being sent to Spain[17] and of a proposed Italian assault on the island of Minorca, the last major Mediterranean island held by Republican forces and an excellent site for a naval base. In desperation the French appeared ready at this point to abandon the Non-Intervention Agreement, but under strong pressure from England they were dissuaded from this action. The British government as an alternative urged that the matter be taken up again in the Non-Intervention Committee.

The Soviet Union had already indicated she favored the French move to end nonintervention, but her influence at this time on French policy was nil. French governing circles since the beginning of the Spanish conflict had tied their foreign policy unalterably to that of the British government.[18] Although the Soviet Union was disappointed that England and France still clung to the fiasco of nonintervention,[19] she was nonetheless heartened that matters were again turned over to the Non-Intervention Committee where she could have at least some influence on the outcome of negotiations. The Soviet press had shown great concern over the attempts by England and France to negotiate directly with Italy, and had sought to discredit the democratic efforts as improbable and foolish.[20]

At the meeting of the chairman's subcommittee on October 16, consultations concerning the withdrawal of foreign volunteers were renewed. From the statements of both the French and British representatives, it was clear their two governments were thoroughly disheartened by the state of affairs in the Non-Intervention Committee yet wanted to give it another chance.[21] Although at the moment, they admitted, Italy was the obstructer, they put by no means all the blame on Italy and Germany. An editorial in the London *Times* on October 15, the day before the meeting, probably expressed quite accurately the feelings of the British government circles:

... Foreign intervention has been largely responsible for provoking and prolonging the civil war. Much of the resentment which caused the revolt against the Government was directed against the influence of the Comintern agents, whose activities were as notorious as they were destructive. This Russian interference in Spanish affairs, none the less harmful for being unofficial and subterranean, provoked Italy and Germany to send help to the other side, which in turn led Russia to send more men and more munitions, and launched a competition in intervention with which the Non-Intervention Committee proved quite unable to cope.

The British government by way of forcing an early settlement of the issues resorted to the tactic of threat.[22] At the October 16 meeting of the chairman's subcommittee Lord Plymouth concluded his introductory account by saying: "Lastly, I feel it my duty to inform the Committee that, should it not be possible to secure such agreement within a very short space of time the United Kingdom Government must reserve to themselves the right to resume full liberty of action."[23] The British government had similarly threatened the committee in June without effect,[24] so Mussolini and Hitler did not take this warning seriously. The government leaders of Britain and France, furthermore, were soon stating openly that they did not earnestly contemplate abandonment of the nonintervention policy. For example, Yvon Delbos on November 19, 1937, declared before the Chamber of Deputies: "But instead of proclaiming the end of non-intervention, we have wished in the interest of peace, which stands foremost in our thoughts, to make a supreme effort in order to make that policy a reality."[25] Nevertheless, France without consulting the British government[26] unofficially opened the French frontier to Barcelona for the transshipment of arms.[27]

Not wanting to break up the nonintervention scheme at this moment, the Italians and Germans decided to end their obstructionist tactics in the committee and to work for an agreement on the withdrawal of foreign volunteers.[28] In the chairman's subcommittee on October 19, 1937, they accepted the British plan of July 28 as a basis for negotiations. Several reasons convinced Italy, in particular, to alter her course. Most important, the war in Spain was going in favor of Franco. The campaign by the rebels to take the northern provinces was proceeding as planned and Mussolini felt confident that by the time any scheme could be worked out on volunteers, Franco's victory would be assured. The many technical problems of such a scheme would require detailed negotiations that, at a minimum, would take a couple of months, thereby allowing Franco the necessary time to consolidate his victories.[29] Germany and Italy also counted on Russian obstruction in the committee and their ability to throw the responsibility for failure on the Russians, if need be. Finally, they knew if the committee reached an agreement when Franco could still not spare the Italian divisions, he himself would prevent indefinitely the final settlement.

Italy and Germany were immediately rewarded for their coöperation by Russian obstructionism. The Soviet delegate in the meeting of the chairman's subcommittee on October 19 declared his government still insisted that belligerent rights should not be granted until all the foreign volunteers had left Spain. He further stated that the Non-Intervention Agreement had completely failed and that without an adequate system of naval patrol there could be no hope of enforcing any agreements made by the committee. In conclusion he declared:

... [The Soviet Government] cannot take upon itself in the slightest degree the responsibility for such a policy [the continuation of the so-called policy of non-intervention] which has already proved to a sufficient extent its worthlessness, and which at the same time has detrimentally and iniquitously reacted upon the interests of the Spanish people and its legitimate Government. If the French, British and other Governments consider it necessary to continue this policy and still entertain some belief in the possibility of its success, the Soviet Government does not intend to create for these other Governments any difficulties with regard to such a policy, but declines any responsibility for same.[30]

Thus is was a policy of noncoöperation, nonresponsibility, and non-obstruction which the Russians hoped to follow during this period in the committee.

Although the attitude of the Soviets was intended not to disrupt the decisions of the committee, Italy and Germany were able to cast aspersions on the Soviet Union as the only country primarily responsible for preventing the committee from functioning.[31] In spite of the diplomatic disfavor created by this policy of noncoöperation, the Soviet Union still refused to take part in the British compromise plan of July to recognize the belligerency of the two parties when the arrangements for withdrawal were in successful operation and a substantial number of volunteers had been withdrawn. She yielded only one minor concession during the subcommittee meeting on October 26, 1937:

> If and when the Soviet Government has the conviction that the bulk of foreign combatants has been actually withdrawn, that new reinforcements for the rebels have ceased to arrive, and that there can be detected therefore a sincere desire on the part of the respective governments to stop all interference in Spanish affairs, then it might perhaps consent to consider the question of granting belligerent rights, but the Soviet Government reserves the right itself to judge as to the moment for such a consideration.[32]

But beyond this the Soviet Union refused to compromise.[33] She equated any further concessions with being a party to "Fascist" intervention in Spain.

The importance of these negotiations to England and France, as the last desperate chance to remove the troops of Italy and Germany from this vital area and prevent Europe from splitting into two armed camps, was evident; at four of the meetings of the chairman's subcommittee, Anthony Eden himself took on the job of chairman. Consequently, the Soviet attitude perturbed them and they joined with Italy and Germany in blaming Russia for the breakdown of the nonintervention schemes.[34] The British and French ambassadors in Moscow brought as much influence as possible to bear on the Soviet government to change its position.[35] They succeeded merely in keeping the Kremlin to its word not to obstruct. Now that Hitler and Mussolini exhibited a more affable demeanor, England and France were determined that the Soviet attitude would not stop the committee from adopting the British compromise plan.[36]

At first Italy and Germany tried to utilize the Soviet position as an obstructive tactic of their own. They tied their own approval of the plan to the unanimous agreement by all the members of the committee. Therefore, when the Soviet Union decided to abstain on the point of the committee's resolution concerning recognition of belligerency, the Italian and German representatives declared that their governments could not accept the committee's official approval of the resolution, because the previous rule was unanimity. However, under heavy pressure from France and England to reconsider, Italy and Germany changed their stand and at the meeting of the chairman's subcommittee on November 2 accepted the decision as valid with the Russian abstention.

On November 4 the full committee met and approved the two resolutions negotiated in the subcommittee. The Italian and German representatives availed themselves of the opportunity to abuse the Soviet Union for its refusal to vote in favor of the substantive resolution. The main resolution authorized the chairman (a) to approach immediately the two parties in Spain to secure their coöperation on the proportionate withdrawal of foreign volunteers and their agreement to the appointment of two commissions to estimate the total number of foreign volunteers and to supervise the withdrawal, and (b) to inform the parties that the states represented on the committee were willing to grant them belligerent rights on the conditions set down in the British plan. The resolution also provided for the reinstitution of land frontiers control and a strengthening of the sea observation scheme just preceding the commencement of withdrawal. The second resolution provided that the chairman "make clear to the parties the attitude and intentions of the various governments in regard to the several parts of the [first] resolution," and that the subcommittee should continue to work out the details of granting belligerent rights and the withdrawal of volunteers.

The persistence of Soviet nonobstruction and noncoöperation was motivated probably by several factors. First, she no longer wanted to be associated with the continued failures of the Non-Intervention Committee. Second, she wanted to keep her record in this affair as untarnished as possible to show the world she was not an appeaser. She was encouraged particularly by the British Labour party and a minority in the Conservative party whose opposition to the policies of the British government in respect to Spain were becoming increasingly marked.[37] Russia also may have hoped to use the position as a bargaining point in the future. But her attempts to employ this artifice failed in the same way as had her previous maneuvers of obstruction. She was always a minority of one and England and France never bothered to gain her support through compromise or concession, but were quite willing and even desirous of isolating her. Although not approving the plan, the Soviet Union did not want to leave the Non-Intervention Committee or stop the proceedings, as she had on former occasions threatened to do, because it would only open the way to a four-power pact. As a result, the Soviet Union refused to accept responsibility for the new plan, but coöperated with the committee in every other way to make the new scheme as effective as possible, offering frequent suggestions to the secretariat and to the committee.

After the resolution passed over her abstention, the Soviet Union realized her position was doing nothing to alter the scheme or the determination of Great Britain and France to carry it out. Her attitude had merely been employed by Italy and Germany as a pretext to delay agreement and would most likely be used in the future to completely negate any chance of withdrawal of volunteers from Spain. Thus her stratagem, as on previous occasions, had completely failed. Furthermore, unilateral refusal by the Soviet Union to recognize Franco's belligerency would not in international law significantly affect his status because he would have the recognition of the vast majority of the European countries. Finally, nothing was to be gained by continuance of the policy of nonsupport. The British plan certainly had many good elements from the Soviet point of view and, if it were actually carried out, the Loyalist government and collective security might still be saved. And even if the plan did not go through, as seemed very unlikely, it was better to be detached from blame and allow the fault to fall where it actually belonged—on Germany and Italy. Perhaps in the process England and France might still become cognizant of the true nature of fascism and Nazism and that only force or threat of force was going to stop Hitler and Mussolini. The Soviet leaders may also have recognized that the British in particular had no desire to save Loyalist Spain, wanted only to prevent the permanent occupation of Spain by Germany and Italy, and refused to use force for this purpose. Even if the Communists did not trust Franco, Hitler, or Mussolini to respect agreements or curb their ambitions through diplomacy, they acknowledged the British policy of negotiations was better than doing nothing. Consequently, the Soviet government reviewed its position and decided to back down and make the best of it.

At the meeting of the chairman's subcommittee on November 16, the Soviet government completely capitulated. Maisky stated:

> Today, I am in a position to inform the Sub-Committee that the Soviet Government, in order to facilitate still further the practical work of the Non-Intervention Committee for the withdrawal of foreign combatants from Spain, accepts the Resolution of the 4th November, in toto, without any reservations whatsoever, leaving along with the other Governments its interpretation of the term "substantial withdrawal" until the time when this question will come up for consideration in the Committee.[38]

The Soviet about-face was accepted in the committee with few comments. Obviously England and France had all along been confident that Russia would come around.

FURTHER ATTEMPTS TO NEGOTIATE THE BRITISH PLAN

While the committee awaited replies from the two parties in Spain to the proposals, technical subcommittees labored with the details of the three main branches of the plan; the withdrawal of volunteers, the granting of belligerent rights, and the restoration and strengthening of the observation scheme. These negotiations revealed that the committee was still a long way from final agreement. The resolution of November 4 had been merely agreements in principle, no more.[39] The disparity in interpreting the principles of the British plan became abundantly clear from the replies of the Nationalists and Loyalists. The two parties in Spain accepted the plan in name but asked for further clarification on certain questions.[40] The reply from Franco suggested that the withdrawal of 3,000 from both sides be considered a substantial withdrawal—a figure certainly not acceptable to the Loyalists or the Soviet Union. The Insurgents also demanded recognition of belligerency as a right, not as a concession. The Loyalist government objected to the failure to include the Moors as foreigners. Distinctly, securing agreement of the two parties was going to be a major hurdle.

During the month of January, 1938, England and France both in the meetings of the chairman's subcommittee and outside tried to secure agreement on details among the committee members. It is of little value at this point to trace the course of these negotiations.[41] It is only necessary to mention that in respect to these negotiations, the attitude of Germany and Italy reflected in general the military successes of Franco in Spain. The Republican capture of Teruel, a Nationalist stronghold, on January 8, 1938, decided Italy and Germany to delay temporarily any agreement in the Non-Intervention Committee. German and Italian military authorities in Spain at the time judged that Franco was going to need more help in order to win.[42] In February, 1938, when the Nationalists launched their offensive along the Ebro, breaching the Loyalist front and finally splitting the Republic into two zones, Italy and Germany were more optimistic and therefore more affable in the negotiations in the London committee. But later when the Loyalists blunted the Nationalist offensive, Italy and Germany again reversed their position in respect to an agreement on immediate withdrawal of foreign volunteers.

The Soviet tactic was rear guard defense, an attempt to prevent further concessions to the Nationalists and their allies.[43] Wherever possible, the Soviet representative tried to put teeth into the agreement so it would not become a sham, as had previous schemes. Although the Soviet attitude was certainly defensible if viewed as an effort toward effecting an honest scheme, the obstinacy of the Russians on several occasions simply obstructed agreement and gained them the enmity of the democratic powers.

The positions of France and England were in between those of Italy and Germany and the Soviet Union.[44] The British were more willing to make concessions to Germany and Italy, while the French tended toward the Soviet view. Both, however, were motivated by the same two desires. First, and this was especially true of England, they wanted to prevent a break with Hitler and Mussolini and to eliminate Spain as a source of division. Second, and this was supported particularly by France, they wanted a workable agreement that would ultimately turn Spain back into an independent state and the satellite of no power.[45] In fact the French government, in order to counteract the increasing German and Italian supplies to the Nationalists, unofficially opened the border to allow transshipment of goods to Loyalist Spain.[46] Even the British government, whose policy was basically one of appeasing Italy and Germany, would not tolerate the renewal of widespread piracy by Italy and the Nationalists against merchant shipping. The Nyon arrangement, initially successful in ending unwarranted sea attacks on merchant shipping, by the beginning of 1938 was ignored and submarine attacks were again prevalent. The British government after consultation with France and Italy sent out orders to its naval commanders to sink any unidentified submarine on sight.[47]

The negotiations during January in the chairman's subcommittee produced no results and consequently the committee enjoined the chairman, Lord Plymouth, to negotiate individually with the opposing members in an effort to find a compromise. The fate of the plan for the withdrawal of foreign volunteers was not, however, to be decided ultimately in the Non-Intervention Committee nor in the direct negotiations of Lord Plymouth. Two outside factors entered the scene and shaped the final form of the negotiations. These two factors were intertwined and formed a part of the whole picture of that fateful year of 1938—the year of Munich and the momentary capitulation of England and France. One element was the rapid overshadowing of the Spanish conflict by the new aggressive acts of Hitler in Austria and Czechoslovakia.

With these events Spain was all but forgotten and any agreement on the Spanish issue needed to be, now more than ever, a part of a settlement of the general European crisis. Prior to this, Spain comprised the exclusive area in which the conflict of interests in Europe had broken out in naked form.

Closely connected with the outbreak of these new crises was the second factor that affected the outcome of events in Spain—the attempt by Great Britain followed by France to woo Italy from the Anti-Comintern Pact. Chamberlain had been trying to bring about a *rapprochement* with the dictators. Although he may have preferred an agreement with Hitler, Chamberlain's failure caused him to divert his efforts to Italy. It is beyond the scope of this work to analyze the Anglo-Italian negotiations in detail, but the high lights must necessarily be reviewed as they touch directly on the Spanish problem.

It is interesting to note that, although in each instance the outcome was vital to Russian security, the USSR was prohibited by the Western powers from participating intimately in the crises and thus relegated to the role of an isolated spectator. In the consultations concerning the Spanish Civil War, the four powers of Western Europe time and again had attempted to bypass the Soviet Union, generally without success. In these new problems that descended on the European scene, they were at last free of Soviet influence and could settle them without Communist interference.

CHAPTER XII

APPEASEMENT: 1938

ANGLO-ITALIAN NEGOTIATIONS

THE WAY TO A *rapprochement* between Italy and England had first been opened by the signing of the Gentlemen's Agreement in January, 1937, upholding the *status quo* in the Mediterranean.[1] Further progress was made during the talks between the two countries in the summer of 1937 but was interrupted by Mussolini's visit to Berlin. At this time Mussolini tied his future to the rising force of Nazism, and British endeavors to reopen talks with Italy in October for a bilateral settlement of the Spanish problem had been to no avail. Failure to reach any agreement on the withdrawal issue in the Non-Intervention Committee during December and January induced the British to attempt once again to reopen direct conversations with Italy. By now the glow of Mussolini's trip to Berlin had dimmed and Italy found herself in a very awkward position because of the German threat to Austria, the former protégé of Italy. The actual prospect of having Hitler as a northern neighbor was not reassuring. Consequently, Mussolini was willing to renew conversations with Britain as a counterweight to Hitler's increasing strength.[2] Furthermore, Mussolini was finding the Spanish adventure an increasingly heavy burden. Although his prestige denied him retreat from Spain, his cause in Spain could be immeasurably helped by British recognition of his special interests there.

Conversations were initiated during the first part of February, 1938, preparatory to the opening of formal negotiations. One of the main obstacles was that Prime Minister Chamberlain and his Foreign Minister Anthony Eden were at odds concerning these talks. Chamberlain was anxious that they be carried through to a successful conclusion at almost any cost; Anthony Eden felt, because Italy had broken the Gentlemen's Agreement of the previous year by sending more troops to Spain only a few days after signing it, Italy could not be trusted. Consequently, any official negotiations with Italy should be predicated on some concrete solutions concerning the problems facing the two countries.[3] In a speech before the House of Commons Eden explained his position:

... In January last year, after difficult negotiations, we signed the Anglo-Italian Agreement, but within a very few days, indeed almost simultaneously, the first

---

[1] For notes to chap. xii, see pp. 166–170.

considerable consignment of Italians left for Spain. It may be held that this was not a breach of the letter of our understanding, but no one, I think, surely will contend that it did not run counter to its spirit. ...

... it is my contention that before His Majesty's Government open official conversations in Rome with the Italian Government, conversations which have, and rightly have, as an objective not only an improvement of Anglo-Italian relations, but appeasement in the Mediterranean as a whole—before that can be done we must make further progress with the Spanish problem; we must agree not only on the need for withdrawal and on the conditions of withdrawal—we have had assurances enough of that in the past—but we must go further and show the world not only promise but achievement. The withdrawal must have begun in earnest before those conversations in Rome can be held on a really solid basis of goodwill, which is essential to success.[4]

Chamberlain on the other hand was willing to overlook previous violations and to open formal negotiations with Italian token approval of the British formula for the proportional removal of volunteers. His difference with Eden led to Eden's resignation from the government on February 20, 1938.[5] In this way the last obstacle to Chamberlain's policy of appeasement and to formal conversations with Italy had been eliminated. After a brief interlude to enable the British ambassador to return home for consultation, talks were resumed in Rome during the first part of March. The choice of Rome for the discussions was itself a concession to Mussolini.

The main issue consisted of Italian withdrawal from Spain. England considered this problem of utmost importance. A compromise was facilitated by Hitler's occupation of Austria on March 12 making the *Anschluss* a fact, and the accord was signed on April 16. It reaffirmed the Gentlemen's Agreement of January, 1937, on the *status quo* in the Mediterranean and contained agreements on the Middle East, the exchange of military information, and propaganda. In regard to Spain, Italy had already, before the opening of formal talks, acquiesced in the London committee to the British formulas on withdrawal. According to Count Ciano, Italy reaffirmed "that once victory has been won by Franco's troops Italy does not intend to maintain military forces in Spain."[6] Nothing was said specifically about Italy withdrawing her troops prior to Franco's victory and certainly her support of the British compromises in the committee did not insure the success of the withdrawal plans. It was decided, however, that the coming into force of the accord was to depend on two factors: British recognition of the Italian empire in Abyssinia and withdrawal of Italian troops from Spain.

In an exchange of letters Anthony Eden and Winston Churchill discussed their opinion of the pact:

Mr. Churchill to Mr. Eden—April 18, 1938:

The Italian Pact is, of course, a complete triumph for Mussolini, who gains our cordial acceptance for his fortification of the Mediterranean against us, for his conquest of Abyssinia, and for his violence in Spain.

Mr. Eden to Mr. Churchill—April 28, 1938:

... With regard to the Italian Pact, I agree with what you write. Mussolini gives us nothing more than the repetition of promises previously made and broken by him, except for the withdrawal of troops from Libya, troops which were probably originally sent there for the nuisance value. It is now become clear that, as I expected, Mussolini continued his intervention in Spain after the conversations in Rome had opened. He must be an optimist, indeed, who believes that Mussolini will cease increasing that intervention now, should it be required to secure Franco's victory.[7]

Anthony Eden's prediction of continued Italian intervention in Spain was fulfilled.[8]

Anthony Eden's and Winston Churchill's pessimistic views of the pact, however, were not generally shared. It was widely acclaimed as a split in the German-Italian front and a particularly heartening sign to many owing to the German seizure of Austria.

After the conclusion of the Anglo-Italian accord, the next step in British policy was to bring about better relations between France and Italy. Britain had tried in vain to include France in the original pact, but owing to Italy's resistance it remained bilateral.[9] In April, 1938, Paul Boncour was advantageously replaced as foreign minister by Georges Bonnet, who was more inclined to support Chamberlain's policy of appeasement. Conversations were opened subsequently in Rome by the French, but were broken off when Hitler paid a return visit to Mussolini in May.[10]

Soviet Reactions to the Anglo-Italian Negotiations and Accord

The Soviet attitude, as expressed in the press, toward rumors and reports of the impending renewal of negotiations between Italy and England was that the Chamberlain government was drastically erring. The Soviet Union, as the British government, appreciated the value of an agreement with Mussolini, but felt the Chamberlain approach was wrong:

An agreement with Italy could bring about a favorable change in the European scene only in one case, if England obtains from Italy a refusal to take part in the bloc of aggressors. In this case, it is possible that Italy would find partners for these negotiations not only in London but also in Paris and other capitals. But these are not England's intentions.[11]

Most alarming to the Soviet Union was the old threat that these talks might lead to a four-power pact. The same editorial continued:

> The English government clearly calculates that the negotiations with Italy will open a path for wider negotiations, for the realization of the famous project of a "four [-power] pact." According to the latest information Göring and Ribbentrop are going to Rome and the Anglo-Italian negotiations will be turned into tripartite negotiations by the participation of Germany.

The resignation of Eden and the immediate opening of formal negotiations with Mussolini appears to have been considered especially ominous by the Soviet Union, and the Communist press released a flood of abuse against the British government and particularly against Chamberlain. The vitriolic attacks against Chamberlain and the "Clivedon set"[12] soon became a permanent feature of Communist propaganda. There appeared, for example, in the April issue of the *Communist International* a long article on the shift in British foreign policy with the change in foreign ministers from Anthony Eden to Lord Halifax:

> ... the circumstances surrounding this resignation of Eden were such as to bring out with the utmost sharpness the turn that they [the British fascist circles] had been preparing for so long. The whole world became aware that the Prime Minister of Britain was cringing to "a foreign despot," to the fascist aggressors.
>
> ... The Anglo-Italian and Anglo-German negotiations which began with the fall of Eden represent an increased danger for Spain and therefore for the defense of democracy and peace. Chamberlain's policy is to give belligerent rights to Franco and to remove all hindrances to Mussolini pouring into Spain fascist armies and munitions; and for this purpose to accord him a loan of millions of pounds.
>
> Hatred of Communism, hatred of the People's Front, hatred of democracy are a mainspring of Chamberlain's policy. The National Government is making a deal with fascist Italy also because it *wants* to buttress fascism.
>
> But whatever hopes certain politicians may have placed in the breaking of the Rome-Berlin axis by the strengthening of the Rome end, it is clear that in reality friendship with Mussolini is also friendship with Hitler. The new Foreign Secretary, Lord Halifax, was chosen precisely because of his extremely subservient attitude to fascist Germany, precisely because he was the candidate of the Clivedon clique of the pro-fascist millionaires.[13]

The Soviet press followed the Anglo-Italian negotiations with a jaundiced eye and, when the Anglo-Italian pact was signed in April, immediately attacked it. *Pravda* commented:

> ... One fact above all others is that Italy gained from the agreement. England did not. ...
>
> At the same time this new agreement is a clear indication of England's policy of capitulation. We have in mind the question of Abyssinia and Spain. As for Abyssinia "the solution" is unusually simple and clear: England once again as a concession to

Italy takes upon herself the dishonorable role "of legalizing" the Italian seizure of Abyssinia. As for Spain, British diplomacy in this case quite openly "gives its blessing" to Mussolini in its extensive war against the Spanish people.

England retreated from her demands of immediate withdrawal of the so-called "volunteer" Italian troops from Spain. She agreed to the demands of Mussolini that Italian troops would be removed from Spain only after the victory of the rebels.[14]

Nonetheless, in diplomatic circles the Soviet Union still maintained a friendly countenance toward the British government and was not wholly unappreciative of the Anglo-Italian agreement as a method of dividing Italy and Germany. Litvinov had the following to say about the accord:

My Government, which takes particularly to heart everything which relates to international peace, quite naturally welcomes any agreement reached between various countries removing the misunderstandings and disputes existing between them. From this point of view, one cannot but welcome the British-Italian Agreement.

But in dealing with bilateral pacts, we have to take into consideration not only their effect upon the relationship between the two parties concerned but also upon the relations between the parties and the rest of the world. We have also to take into consideration the effect which such agreements may have on those problems which are still before the League of Nations and which still remain to be dealt with. We, therefore, reserve our final judgment upon the importance of this Agreement from this point of view. We may still express the hope that these problems will certainly not suffer from that Agreement.[15]

NEGOTIATIONS IN THE NON-INTERVENTION COMMITTEE

In the light of the Anglo-Italian conversations, during the spring of 1938 the Non-Intervention Committee became merely a subordinate arena of negotiations. The success of the latter depended solely on the ability of England to obtain a concrete commitment from Italy to remove her troops from Spain in the very near future. The British government had no doubts that the Soviet Union and the Spanish government could be prevailed upon to relinquish the services of the International Brigades if the rebels could be made to send home their Italian and German divisions. In fact, the Republicans were so anxious about withdrawal that five months later they were willing to remove unilaterally all foreign volunteers from their side.[16] Another factor assured Soviet coöperation; Stalin was losing in the Loyalist struggle. As mentioned previously, since the summer and fall of 1937, the amount of material aid the Russians sent to Spain had appreciably decreased (although when the Loyalists were hard pressed by the Nationalist offensive along the Ebro, the Soviet Union rushed planes and war material). There were also indications that with the developing crisis in central Europe the Soviets wanted to pull out of Spain entirely.[17] Finally, the growing tension between the Soviet Union and Japan activated the Soviet leaders to use their resources for building up their military force in the Far East against Japanese penetration. Actually a few months later, in July, 1938, hostilities broke out between the two countries along the Manchuko (Manchurian) border.

Nevertheless, since the Anglo-Italian accord signed in April did not include a hard and fast commitment on the part of Italy to leave Spain immediately, the Non-Intervention Committee possessed little chance of successfully completing its plan for the withdrawal of troops. Mussolini inferred from his negotiations with England that the latter was not too interested in the fate of the Loyalists as long as he did not intend to keep his troops permanently in Spain.[18] Also, both England and France had recently established unofficial relations with Franco, an action indicating that they expected a Franco victory and would do nothing to prevent it. With this green light Mussolini felt free to sabotage any agreements in the London committee and reject any offers of mediation, even those made directly by the British government. He dismissed all such attempts as show pieces for popular consumption only. For example, he answered the British proposal in May to conciliate the Civil War by saying it was "out of the question to propose an armistice to Franco unless the terms are unconditional surrender by the Reds, in which case Italy could exert a moderating influence."[19]

Although Italy and Germany did not take seriously the hagglings of the Non-Intervention Committee, in an effort to win public opinion and in order to fulfil Italy's pledge made during the conversations preceding the Anglo-Italian accord, they participated in working out a plan. They were confident many weeks would lapse between negotiating an agreement and actually implementing its terms in Spain. In the meantime they hoped for Franco's quick victory. Such a possibility did not seem remote, especially after the Nationalists had cut the Loyalist territory in two by their drive to the sea in the middle of April.[20] It never occurred to Italy and Germany that the Loyalists would hold out for another year. They had predicted victory for the rebels so often and felt they could not possibly be wrong again. The "Reds" simply could not hold out very long against the superior forces of Italy, Germany, and the Nationalists.

By April, 1938, almost six months after agreement in principle, the main issues on the plan for the withdrawal of foreign volunteers and for strengthening the control scheme were still unresolved. The British time and again had attempted unsuccessfully to advance compromise proposals. The French and the Russian governments stood together on several issues:[21] they supported the original November 4 resolution that frontier control should be reëstablished only just before the evacuation of volunteers actually began, rather than as soon as the two commissions proceeded to Spain, as proposed by Italy and Germany and agreed to by the British. Furthermore, both the USSR and France felt it necessary to provide for strict control of the sea frontier as well as the land frontiers. The French favored observers in all Spanish ports and the Soviet Union favored a restoration of naval patrols. The Soviet Union, however, was willing to go along with the French idea of port observers if the system was made adequate. They also stood together in insisting that withdrawal must be by specific categories, a percentage of each category to be evacuated each day, to thus prohibit Franco's retention of the most valuable combat troops and technical help to the end. The French were less insistent than Russia on this point.

The French government at this time did not confine its coöperation with the USSR merely to siding with the Soviet representative in the committee on certain issues. The Blum and even the Daladier cabinets continued to allow Soviet equipment to be transshipped freely across France to Loyalist Spain. The United States Ambassador in France reported to the secretary of state:

Daladier said that he had opened the French frontier to Spain as completely as possible. He had even done more. After the recent successful offensive of General Franco the Russians had indicated their willingness to send 300 planes to the Spanish Government if France would make arrangements for their transshipment across France to Spain. He had transported the 300 planes across France successfully in the largest trucks available although he had had to cut down many miles of trees along the sides of roads in order that the large bombers might pass.[22]

But France did not go all the way in her support of the Soviet position. In respect to the other issues in dispute before the Non-Intervention Committee, the Soviet Union stood alone as the opposing power. The USSR still refused to accept the removal of 10,000 "volunteers" from the side with the least foreign troops as the basic figure representing "substantial progress," though it had been accepted by all the other powers. She also refused to contribute monetarily to the evacuation of foreign volunteers. She would not put herself in the position of financing the evacuation of German and Italian volunteers from Spain. The Soviet Union also found herself isolated in refusing to finance the sea observation scheme which still operated. She reiterated her view that the control of frontiers, the naval patrol, and the observation schemes were all a part of one system as agreed to by the committee in March, 1937, and to do no more than employ neutral observers on ships going to Spain was worthless.[23] When the funds of the Non-Intervention Board were almost exhausted because the Soviet Union, followed by other states, refused to contribute, the British government brought the matter before the chairman's subcommittee on April 25, 1938. The other countries consented to make additional contributions to sustain the observation scheme. The Soviet Union alone refused.

By May, Chamberlain's pressure on Daladier had taken effect and alignment in the Non-Intervention Committee changed. The British government at the Anglo-French conference at the end of April urged the French to accept the new British compromises already acquiesced to by Italy as part of the Anglo-Italian accord. France bowed to the British wishes—she had become almost a satellite of the British Foreign Office and was unable or unwilling to sustain or initiate her own policy.[24] She agreed even to reëstablish control on her frontier just as soon as the international commissions began counting "volunteers" in Spain.[25] Later she went even further than this. Without regard for when the plan would actually come into effect and even before there was final agreement in the committee, the French government closed the border sometime during the first weeks of June, 1938, although England did not urge Portugal to do the same. At about the same time the Bank of France refused to turn over to the Bank of Spain £7,500,000 of Spanish gold. Thus British pressure and the French retreat seemed interminable.[26] Germany, following Italy's lead, also agreed to the compromises. The Soviet Union alone resisted. The only Soviet concession was to accept the British proposal of 10,000 volunteers from the lesser side as constituting "substantial progress" in the removal of foreign troops from Spain.

In the end the Soviet Union remained the only hinderance to the final agreement on withdrawal. Italy and Germany, as before, turned the Soviet balking into propaganda for themselves. At the meeting of the chairman's subcommittee on May 26 the Soviet representative, S. B. Kagan (Cahan), was forced to fight the battle of the opposition alone.[27] Although he defended his position well and presented a good analysis of the German and Italian tactics, his words fell on deaf ears. The other powers could see only that the Soviet Union was obstructing and prolonging the danger of the Spanish crisis.[28] Why was the Soviet Union willing to take this lone stand after all her previous unsuccessful attempts at using the same stratagem? As the Soviet Union had ceased to send any large amounts of aid to Spain, she herself had nothing to gain by delay. If she did it to keep her record clear, she did it at the cost of further antagonizing England and France—exactly what Hitler and Mussolini wanted. She must have known her position would not significantly alter the final solution once Great Britain and France had resolved on compromise. Furthermore, she must have suspected Italy and Germany would never allow the plan to prejudice Franco's victory and would sabotage it some way or other before it could actually go into effect. The Soviet representative intimated as much somewhat later in the meeting of the subcommittee on June 28:

> One will hardly take the responsibility of denying the fact that scarcely any important decisions of the Committee survived and were not changed or annulled at the insistence of the interventionist Powers. The almost two-year existence of the Non-Intervention Committee supplies abundant evidence of this contention....
>
> In view of these experiences in the work of the Committee and the unfortunate "traditions" established in regard to decisions taken by the Committee, there is no guarantee that the Plan at present adopted will not be changed or annulled. The whole demeanour of the Interventionist Powers compels one to doubt whether the actual evacuation of "volunteers" will take place.[29]

From the beginning, therefore, the Soviet leaders must have recognized that they would not indefinitely resist agreement since it would serve no purpose.

Then why did they hold out for over a month after the French had "capitulated," and further alienate the British government in particular? There are several possible explanations for the tactics of the Russians at this time. First, under Stalin's dictatorship, decision-making was excessively centralized. Undoubtedly this matter had to be discussed and resolved in the highest echelons of the party, if not by Stalin himself. At a period when other foreign and domestic matters were pressing, this decision may have been delayed. In the meantime the Soviet representative had to continue on the basis of his old instructions—to resist any compromise. Second, there is evidence that, as a general policy, Soviet diplomats bargain hard to the very last minute regardless of how much ill feeling it causes. Soviet bargaining after the Second World War appears to bear out this contention. Finally, the Soviet course may be another indication that even before Munich the Soviet leaders had become thoroughly dissatisfied with the weakness of the democracies and no longer wanted their friendship. Such an attitude was perhaps implied by Litvinov when he stated:

... the committee not only failed completely to ensure non-intervention, it is list-ing more and more to Franco's side. Our role in the committee now resolves itself to attempts to straighten out this list to the best of our ability, and at least to prevent the intervention of the committee itself in Spanish affairs on Franco's side.[30]

Thus, if their obstructive maneuvers in the Non-Intervention Com-mittee were not popular in Britain and France, it made no difference. The British had already clearly shown they had no interest in a *rapprochement* with Russia by their repeated attempts to ostracize and bypass her in all negotiations on important European issues. The Cham-berlain government, the Soviets may have argued, was wedded to appeasement regardless of cost. For example, the frequent and some-times deliberate attacks on British shipping in Loyalist ports during the spring of 1938 no longer brought decisive action by the Conservative government to protect British rights and lives, but merely the warning from Chamberlain that "ships entering ports which are liable at any time to be the object of military operations and attack must do so at their own risk."[31] Thus it is possible that the Soviet Union intended neither to arouse the democracies nor win their friendship, but wanted rather to awaken Hitler to the strength and advantage of an alliance with the Soviet Union. Such a conclusion must be approached cau-tiously, however, because a historian looking back over events encounters the danger of reading into the facts future motives of which the partici-pants were not yet aware. This may be a case in point. The hypothesis that the Soviet Union may have already rejected a democratic alliance is based on circumstantial evidence and rational reaction to the British policy of appeasement, and may well not be the correct interpretation. For example, a *Pravda* editorial on May 7, 1938, declared, "It is clear that the united forces of England and France together with other states—those opposed to war—can easily check Fascist aggression. How-ever, to check the Fascist aggressors is possible only on the basis of organized collective security."[32] This circumstantial evidence implies that the Soviet leaders still considered the greatest bulwark of their own security to be the military power of the democracies, and they had not yet given up hope of using it in their own behalf. The Communists furthermore still were supporting the Spanish Loyalists morally[33] and materially.[34] Nor is there any real evidence that the Soviet leaders were preparing for alliance with or appeasement of Hitler. All the outward reactions of the Soviet Union to Hitler at this time indicates her belief that an alliance with Germany was of no value.

Nevertheless, against such overwhelming pressure in the Non-Intervention Committee the Soviet Union was bound eventually to give in, as she had done previously. Further resistance would have allowed the powers to exclude her, leaving her an outcast and opening the way to a possible four-power pact against her. The immediate impetus for her capitulation was the closing of the Franco-Spanish frontier as a result of British pressure, a move which gave Italy and Germany exactly what they wanted, that is, the blockade of the main flow of Russian supplies to Spain. The Soviet government now could but hope for the slim chance that the plan would actually be carried through completely. The Soviet Union first began her retreat in the chairman's subcommittee meeting on June 2, and a final agreement on all issues was completed by June 27. In backing down, the Soviet Union was able to gain one slight advantage—the posting of observers in every Spanish port at all times. Although the Soviet government officially accepted the British compromise plan in the committee, the Soviet press did not cease its criticism of the whole scheme. An editorial in *Moscow News* on June 8 quoted *Izvestiia:*

> ... the entire history of the London committee is basically a history of Fascist provocation and transparent maneuvers on the part of the supporters of aggression. ... The recent British proposals constitute a definite attempt to impose upon the London committee the functions of a direct helper of Franco and the interventionists, a direct organizer of intervention in the Spanish war against the Republic.[35]

After the German, Italian, French, and English governments agreed without the USSR to supply the funds for withdrawal and other details were settled, the compromise version of the withdrawal plan was presented to the full committee on July 5 where it received unanimous approval.

OLD ARGUMENTS REPEATED

While the London committee was attempting to work out a plan acceptable to all its members, the Spanish government again took its case before the League Council. The previous October the overwhelming majority of the Assembly had approved the resolution that should a withdrawal of foreign combatants not be accomplished "in the near future," the members would consider abandoning the policy of nonintervention. Seven months had passed since then and the London committee still had not removed a single foreign "volunteer." Had not that point "in the near future" been passed? This was the argument of the Spanish government. The Spanish government therefore proposed to the Council on May 13, 1938, a resolution that "invited the Member

States of the League who voted in favor of the draft resolution on the Spanish situation, presented to the Assembly by the Sixth Committee on October 2, 1937, to envisage, as from the present moment, the end of the policy of non-intervention."[36]

As far as the British were concerned, unquestionably such a resolution had to be defeated, since outside the League they were making every effort to effect a compromise concerning the withdrawal. The British proposed their own resolution and reiterated their previous, well-worn argument in defense of nonintervention; it had at least prevented a general European war even though it had not stopped intervention—"a leaky dam may yet serve its purpose." Likewise the Soviet Union, following her previous pattern, stood side by side with the Spanish delegate in condemning the failures of the nonintervention schemes. The main difference in this renewed debate was the attitude of some of the small non-European powers on the Council. The representative from New Zealand led the group who believed that the League should take a more active hand in light of the failure of the Non-Intervention Committee and the seriousness of the situation. The New Zealand delegate declared:

It is due to the League, as well as to our fellow Member-States, that we should have the fullest possible information. A League examination may result in our being able to make some proposals concerning the situation and a criticism of present unsatisfactory intervention. I repeat the opinion of New Zealand, that no effort should be spared to make it possible for the people of Spain to decide their own differences, and by methods other than those now being employed.[37]

Probably this "grass roots" movement prompted Britain and France to end the debate and push a vote on the Spanish resolution just a few hours after it was presented. In the final vote Spain and the USSR voted in favor, five states voted against, and nine abstained. The representatives from China and New Zealand expressed their disapproval that the vote had been forced before they could contact their governments for instructions, thus causing them to abstain. It is also probable that the number of abstentions expressed a growing dissatisfaction with the policy of nonintervention in certain countries. The Soviet Union was encouraged that "the discussion of the Spanish problem ... demonstrated the strength—and not only the moral strength—of the front which counteracts the factors of war."[38]

CHAPTER XIII

THE FORGOTTEN CRISIS

THE DISINTEGRATION OF THE WITHDRAWAL PLAN

AFTER THE UNANIMOUS APPROVAL of the program for withdrawal of foreign volunteers by the London committee, the next step was securing the acceptance of the two parties in Spain. The Soviet Union from the beginning had called the negotiations a farce and a delusion, and this they were rapidly proved to be. Even though the negotiations on withdrawal had lasted eight months in the committee, Franco still had not ensured complete victory. Because success depended upon German and Italian troops, the Nationalists refused to consider implementing the withdrawal plan.

Even though the Loyalists replied favorably on July 26 to the proposed withdrawal plan,[1] Franco delayed answering and only after frequent and urgent representations by the British agent to Nationalist Spain did he on August 15 send his views. His reply was drafted by three foreign offices—Nationalist Spain, Germany, and Italy.[2] It consented in principle but made specific acceptance of the plan conditional on several major changes. First, belligerent rights must be granted before any withdrawal could start. Second, withdrawals must be equal on both sides. It also objected to the fact that 50 per cent of the volunteers on the Loyalist side would not be affected as they came from countries not party to the Non-Intervention Agreement. Finally, it declared the presence of observers on Spanish soil "would usurp in a humiliating manner the sovereign rights of Spain." Since the Nationalist demands hit at the very fundamentals of the committee's plan, any likelihood of eventual agreement was terminated. Thus by one stroke the Nationalists and their allies wiped out almost a year of negotiations.

The Republican government in a note on August 27 met one of Franco's complaints by declaring that it was willing to remove all foreign volunteers without regard to "whether or not they were nationals of states members of the Committee of Non-Intervention."[3]

Faced with the opposition of Franco, the Non-Intervention Committee could do little. Neither Russia nor England and France were willing to grant Franco belligerent rights as a prerequisite to inauguration of the withdrawal plan. In view of the drama unfolding in central Europe, the British Foreign Office had little time to spend on trying

---

[1] For notes to chap. xiii, see pp. 170–176.

[123]

to revive a moribund plan. The British proposed, as the only solution, to send Francis Hemming, the secretary of the committee, to Nationalist Spain to try to persuade Franco to change his views. At the beginning of September Lord Plymouth in this connection consulted with the various representatives on the committee. The Soviet answer to this plan was as follows:

> ... the response of General Franco constituted no less than a rejection of the plan of the committee although agreeing "in principle" to the evacuation of "volunteers."
>
> ... any attempt to continue to make this plan work would mean the granting of new and important concessions to the rebels. The Soviet government will raise categorical objections against all these concessions. Consequently the Soviet government cannot give its assent to the proposition of sending the Secretary of the Committee, Mr. Hemming, to Spain in order to examine the withdrawal plan with the Spanish government and with General Franco by establishing "personal contact" with them.[4]

In spite of Soviet objections, Hemming set out for Nationalist Spain on October 5. But Russia's prediction concerning the mission was correct; it proved a complete failure.[5] The withdrawal plan now was certainly dead and no one made any attempt to revive it. And not only the withdrawal plan but also the entire Non-Intervention Committee was defunct. There were no more meetings of the full committee, the last having been held on July 4, nor of the chairman's subcommittee.[6] On November 29, the Belgian government withdrew from the committee and Sweden from the subcommittee. Also, Admiral M. H. van Dulm, head of the Non-Intervention Board, resigned and a successor was never appointed. But the final disbandment of the observation staff did not come until March, 1939. By November of 1938 the Non-Intervention Committee had to all intents and purposes ended its unfortunate career. Nothing marked its passing; it was simply forgotten in the rush of events just prior to the Second World War.

A FINAL APPEAL

With the nonintervention scheme a complete failure, the Loyalists found themselves in an increasingly serious plight. Except for the Communists,[7] few doubted the outcome of the war as long as Germany and Italy supported the rebels, and the Loyalists received only a trickle of supplies from Russia and elsewhere. The Loyalists' appeals to the League had also failed to bring about more favorable conditions. Consequently, as a last desperate attempt to stir world public opinion, they decided on a new artifice. They proposed unilaterally to withdraw all foreign volunteers fighting on their side to convince England and France of their sincerity.[8] The evidence circumstantially indicates the Soviet Union concurred in or perhaps initiated this move. The Soviet Union was already in the process of removing her personnel and equipment from Spain. Removal of the International Brigades was essential for disassociating as much as possible the USSR and Communism from a lost cause. Although the non-Communists and Communists in the International Brigades were considered by Stalin expendable—in fact better expended as his subsequent liquidation of most survivors testify—he did not want them in the hands of the Nationalists who might use their testimony against him. From the point of view of diplomacy Russia also may have supported the move in order to impress England and France that she was not interested in a permanent sphere in Spain which, therefore, gave her intervention an entirely different character from that of the Fascists and Nazis.

The Loyalists knew that if they carried out the removal by themselves Germany and Italy would claim it was all a hoax and contend that thousands of foreign volunteers were still fighting on the Loyalist side. As a result, they decided to request the League of Nations to supervise the withdrawal. On September 21, 1938, Negrín himself presented the request to the League Assembly at its regular session:

> The Spanish Government has decided to ask the League of Nations to set up immediately an international commission to carry out such verifications and inquiries as it may deem necessary in order to be able to satisfy the League of Nations, and through it its member States and world public opinion, that the decision for withdrawal adopted by the Spanish Government has been applied absolutely and completely.[9]

There was a move by some of the powers to transfer the task of supervision to the London committee, but both Spain and the Soviet Union strongly resisted this attempt. In fact, the Spanish representative let it be known that his government would not accept the supervision of the London committee. When the British delegate finally came out in support of the Spanish proposal, the main obstacle was overcome.[10] On September 30 the Council passed a resolution setting up an international commission "to note the measure of withdrawal taken by . . . [the Spanish] Government," but declared that the Council would assume no responsibility for "either the method of withdrawal or of the evacuation of the persons withdrawn."[11]

The international commission of the League was able to report to the Council at its next meeting on January 16, 1939, that the total number of foreign combatants counted in the two Republican zones had come to 12,673, of which 6,490 had already left Spain and the remainder were awaiting evacuation.[12]

The action of the Spanish government aroused Italy to make some gesture of withdrawal. The war was going badly for the Loyalists, and victory at last seemed assured for Franco. This, plus the growing tension elsewhere in Europe, made Mussolini willing and even eager to lessen his commitments in Spain. Thus with a great deal of fanfare, 10,000 Italian troops were withdrawn at the end of October.[13] This spontaneous gesture to effect the withdrawal of Italian troops in turn gave Franco further opportunity to demand belligerent rights.[14] Italy, however, had not really abandoned her intervention in Spain. There still remained in Spain (1) the Littoria Division of 12,000 men; (2) aviators, tank corps, artillery, and special troops; and (3) cadres (officers and noncommissioned officers) for four mixed divisions.[15]

THE ABANDONMENT OF SPAIN

The fall of 1938 marked the height of the appeasement attitude of England and France. The open intervention of Germany and Italy in Spain had come to be acknowledged and accepted officially, even by the British government.[16] In September the Munich accord had been achieved and the concessions to Hitler were declared to have secured "peace for our time."[17] The disillusionment of later months was still unknown. Caught in the myopia of the time, Great Britain sought to use Spain to round out her policy of appeasement.[18] The Communists analyzed the situation as follows:

The method of the British imperialists to fatten German fascism at the expense of other peoples still offers many possibilities.... And why should British imperialism stop at forcing France to make territorial concessions in order to "save peace." France must already foot a great part of the bill. Her system of alliances in Europe has been destroyed, the confidence of the nations in her mission has been shaken, the Daladier Government has reduced France to the role of a vassal of British imperialism. *The French people are one of the chief losers by the Munich conspiracy.*

The next victim singled out by the four men of Munich is the Spanish Republic. The "saviors of peace" have already begun to discuss the best way of throttling the Spanish people. Daladier is obviously eager to put the noose around the neck of France as quickly as possible and to see to it that after the betrayal of the Czechoslovak ally Hitler and Mussolini may build up their military positions against France on the Pyrenean frontier as well.

However, there is one hitch in the matter: the Spanish people and its heroic army have been successfully resisting the fascist aggressors for the past two years and have no intention of surrendering to any dictate of Chamberlain. They know that Chamberlain is their enemy, they harbor no illusions about Daladier and it is not news to them that the so-called democratic governments of France and Britain betray the cause of the peoples and that the Spanish people can count only on the assistance of the broad masses.[19]

More and more Chamberlain had come to be considered by the Communists as the real defiler of Europe.

Chamberlain fulfilled the Communist prophecy. As discussed previously, he was willing from the beginning to accept a Nationalist victory in Spain and was only concerned about the long-run removal of Italian troops from the strategically important Iberian Peninsula and Balearic Isles. At the same time he wanted to break up the Rome-Berlin axis and bring about a *rapprochement* at least with Italy. After the important concessions to Hitler at Munich, the need was all the more pressing to secure the Anglo-Italian alliance. Consequently, Chamberlain felt it necessary to accept the partial withdrawal of Italian troops as evidence that Mussolini would withdraw his remaining forces after the final defeat of the Loyalists[20] and ratify the Anglo-Italian agreement.[21] At the time of the signing of the agreement in April, 1938, Lord Perth, the English ambassador in Rome, had written to Count Ciano, "In this connection I hardly need to remind Your Excellency that His Majesty's Government regard a settlement of the Spanish question as a prerequisite of the entry into force of the Agreement between our two Governments." When the agreement came before the House of Commons eight months later on November 2 for ratification, Anthony Eden then in opposition asked "the House for a moment to consider how far that very reasonable condition has been satisfied."[22] Eden and the Communists were in complete agreement in calling it "an Anglo-Italian deal at the expense of Spain."[23] This was not denied by the Chamberlain government which, in forcing through ratification of the agreement, in no way attempted to conceal that it meant sacrificing Loyalist Spain. Lord Halifax on November 3 spoke quite frankly to the House of Lords: "Signor Mussolini has always made it plain from the time of the first conversations of His Majesty's Government and the Italian Government that for reasons known to us, whether we approve of them or not, he is not prepared to see Franco defeated."[24]

The Soviet reaction was to try to appeal again to the democracies' self-interest. Molotov in an important speech on November 6, 1938, discussing the *History of the Communist Party of the Soviet Union (Bolshevik)* declared:

There it is pointed out how the Fascist countries, Germany and Italy, in 1936 began an armed intervention against the Spanish Republic. Under the pretense of fighting the "reds" in Spain the German and Italian Fascists sent their fighting units to Spain, stationing themselves at the border of France as well as intercepting the sea routes of England and France to their important colonies in Africa and Asia.[25]

But from the tone of the editorials in the Soviet press, obviously the Soviets held out little hope. The British policy of appeasement was accepted as a solid fact upon which Chamberlain's policy was based.[26] The Soviet leaders were particularly disturbed by the reports of a plan for the four powers, England, France, Germany, and Italy, to settle the Spanish question without consulting other countries.[27] "Out of Munich there has developed an alternative 'peace making' plan by international reaction for the solution of the Spanish question in the manner of Czechoslovakia."[28]

From the attitude expressed in the Soviet press, it is clear that by this time the Soviet Union considered the foreign policies of Nazi Germany, Fascist Italy, and the British Conservative government to be equally the enemies of peace. Furthermore, the idea of a popular front with the democratic *bourgeoisie* was rapidly disappearing from Communist publications; more and more there was a retreat back to the class struggle between the workers and *bourgeoisie,* and events were interpreted in terms of this struggle.[29] At the same time there was no evidence as expressed in the press that the Soviet Union had yet publicly abandoned all hope of "democratic resistance to fascism." For example, the Communists still hoped that France would not, in face of the defeat at Munich, allow Spain to be sacrificed to the Fascists. They argued:

The French government is trying to excuse the Munich capitulation by declaring repeatedly that through freeing itself from all cares in central Europe, it can consider concentrating all its forces in defense of the naval and colonial positions of the country. This means first of all the defense of the Mediterranean sea lanes and the independence of Spain. Of course after the Czech events this assurance must not be taken too quickly at face value. But, be that as it may, it is not considered possible in Paris yet to arrange a second "Munich"—for Spain.[30]

The Communist press also still talked of the struggle of the Spanish masses for victory and their confidence in its achievement.[31] Within Spain the Communists demanded further resistance even after the collapse of Catalonia in January, 1939. They also led unsuccessfully the fight to prevent the coup on March 5 of Colonel Casado who overthrew Negrín to negotiate a peace with the Nationalists. The Communists were clearly under orders to continue the war at all cost.[32] Finally as late as

September of 1938 the Soviet press pointed out: "The predominant united forces of England and France on the sea, the presence of their strong air fleet and land forces, which are based on a highly developed industry and reserves of raw materials, is a force capable of beating off victoriously the Fascist aggressors."[33] Thus the Communists were still unwilling at least publicly to admit the defeat of collective security, although disillusionment in fact was probably complete by this time.[34] Until the Soviet Union could lay the basis for an alternative policy, she did not dare renounce the old one. She kept the Spanish Civil War going as long as possible to prevent Hitler from turning his entire focus on central Europe, before the USSR could come to an agreement with him. Furthermore, Stalin may have wanted to keep the war going for use as a bargaining point in negotiations with Hitler. In this he was unsuccessful because the war ended before any real bargaining had begun between the two countries.[35]

THE CONCLUSION

When the Council of the League at its meeting in January, 1939, discussed the progress report on the evacuation of volunteers from Loyalist Spain, French Foreign Minister Bonnet declared, "If that work is to be completed, the total evacuation of non-Spanish combatants from the Government zone must be followed by the total evacuation of foreign combatants from the Burgos zone." Bonnet concluded by promising the full support of his government in carrying out the task. The promise was no more than an empty phrase. The French government would not act without England. It is significant that when British Foreign Minister Lord Halifax's turn came to speak, he made no mention of the need to evacuate foreign combatants from the Nationalist zone, which again confirmed that the British government officially and without reservation accepted Italian intervention in Spain until Franco's victory over the Loyalists had been secured.[36] Thus during these last days of the Civil War, in spite of stirrings in French quarters, clearly Great Britain would make no last-minute move to prevent the final victory of the alliance of Franco, Mussolini, and Hitler over the Loyalists.[37] England and France had in fact much earlier abandoned any idea of supporting legitimacy or democracy in Spain, but merely hoped to keep Fascist and Nazi influence at a minimum. The Non-Intervention Committee had been developed into an involved machinery and its "complication and slowness served to cool the heat of the passion which reigned behind the red and white fronts in Spain. The bureaucratic machine was to act as a brake until a decision had been reached on the battlefield."[38]

When in January, 1939, France lost her last chance to stop the conquest of Catalonia and Spain by refusing to open her borders to arms shipments to the Loyalists and was seriously considering the question of recognizing the Franco regime, the Soviet press finally gave up all hope for collective action to save Spain."The developing events in Spain reveal very plainly in all their depravity the falsity of the capitalist policies of capitulation before the aggressor. The governing circles in England and France have done and are doing everything possible in order to aid Italian-German intervention in strangling Spain."[39]

The superiority of the Nationalist forces gradually narrowed Republican control to an area in central Spain. On February 27, 1939, the French and British governments recognized the Franco regime as the *de jure* government of Spain,[40] and on March 29 the final battle was over. The Soviet Union, from its precarious position of spectator and possibly the next victim in the policy of appeasement, concluded, "The betrayal of Spain means not simply the handing over of important strategic positions to the aggressors, but threatens to undermine the moral stability of democracy itself."[41]

The end of the Civil War in Spain and the complete victory of Franco came at the same time that Soviet foreign policy made its complete about-face. From preferring a policy of collective security and alliance with England and France, the Soviet leaders decided on appeasement and agreement with Hitler. It is no accident that this reversal came with the end of the Spanish Civil War. The signal for the change appears to have been the speech on March 10 by Stalin to the Eighteenth Congress of the Communist Party of the Soviet Union, although some signs of *rapprochement* appeared earlier.[42] In his report Stalin reviewed the events in Europe and Asia during the previous years and concluded that the growing crisis was caused by the failure of France and particularly England to support collective security. Stalin then declared:

Formally the policy of nonintervention might be characterized in this way, 'let each country defend itself from aggression as it wishes and as it is able.' For our part we shall trade with both aggressors and their victims.[43]

It is significant that Stalin made no mention of any intent to further follow the policy of collective security. Stalin defined the task of the party in foreign affairs:

1. To continue the policy of peace and of strengthening business relations with all countries.

2. To be cautious and not to allow our country to be drawn into conflicts by war-mongers who are accustomed to have others pull the chestnuts out of the fire for them.

3. To strengthen the might of our Red Army and Red Navy to the utmost.

4. To strengthen the international bonds of friendship with the working people of all countries who are interested in peace and friendship among nations."

The Soviet Union's experience in the Non-Intervention Committee and in the diplomatic proceedings arising from the Spanish Civil War was undoubtedly a major factor in convincing her of the bankruptcy of her collective security policy. All her attempts at joint efforts to stop Italian and German aggression in Spain had completely failed and for her trouble she had merely aroused the enmity of England and France. It is fair to say that the events surrounding the Spanish Civil War, which generally dominated the international scene in Europe from August, 1936, to July, 1938, and the Munich accord were the two most important factors that influenced the change in Soviet foreign policy in the spring of 1939 and opened the way to the Russo-German pact of August, 1939.

Great Britain, as this study has shown, until 1939 did not want and did not feel the need of an alliance with Communism against Hitler and Mussolini. France, inclined toward closer relations with the USSR but strategically bound to Great Britain, was forced to follow along. The Chamberlain government was confident that by appeasement and diplomacy it could handle the dictators and keep Spain from their hands. Actually the Spanish episode from the point of view of the Iberian Peninsula was not a British defeat. The two and a half years of struggle engaging the forces of Mussolini and Hitler at the cost of the Loyalists and the Soviet Union helped England and France to gain time. Nor did the collapse of the Loyalist government turn out as badly for England and France as many, including the Communists, had predicted. Actually the forecast of Winston Churchill came much closer to the truth:

It does not, however, follow that if General Franco wins he will be grateful to his Nazi and fascist allies. On the contrary, the probability is that the first thought of all patriotic Spaniards, once delivered from the awful plight, will be to escort their rescuers to the nearest seaport. . . .[45]

The end of the Civil War did, in fact, conclude the occupation of Spain by German and Italian troops. The allied powers, however, had to continuously cajole and appease Franco to keep him out of the Axis camp, and with the collapse of France in 1940 Franco would have abandoned his neutrality for the Nazi new order except Hitler rejected his offer.[46]

The long-range effect of the British Spanish policy, however, was unfortunate. Chamberlain's assumption that England and France could appease, outwit, and eventually outfight the Axis without Soviet support proved to be almost fatal for both democracy and communism. After almost three years of seeking collective action in Spain, the Soviet Union felt she could not wait for Great Britain to recognize the danger of this assumption. In a situation in which three hostile ideologies and forces—democracy, communism, and fascism—were vying for survival or supremacy, the Soviet Union, the least powerful of the three, feared isolation above all. Consequently, when she was unable to ally with the movement she considered less dangerous to herself and her survival, she turned to the other.

NOTES

NOTES TO CHAPTER I

The Great Powers and the Outbreak of War in Spain: July, 1936

(Pages 1–13)

[1] For a more detailed analysis *see* David T. Cattell, *Communism and the Spanish Civil War* (Berkeley and Los Angeles: University of California Press, 1955), pp. 23 ff.

[2] The Soviet interpretation of German and Italian intervention on the side of the rebel generals can be summed up as follows: "The German-Italian intervention in Spain is a prelude to world war. German and Italian fascism are playing Franco for large stakes. We are speaking of the seizure of important strategic positions on the Mediterranean basin and mineral resources. On the other hand, the Fascist aggressors, not without basis, fear that the victory of the Spanish people would undermine the strength of international fascism in world politics as well as within the Fascist countries." G. Dashevskii, "Bor'ba s fashistskoi 'piatoi kolonnoi' v Ispanii" ["The Struggle with the Fascist 'Fifth Column' in Spain"], *Mirovoe Khoziaistvo i Mirovaia Politika* (Jan., 1938), p. 61.

[3] Cattell, *op. cit.*, p. 221 n. 15. One Soviet writer, however, characterized Mussolini as being reluctant at first to commit himself to intervention in Spain and did it only at the urging of Hitler:

"The deal of Mussolini with Hitler, creating the 'Rome-Berlin Axis [October 25, 1936]' was that Italy would give up in favor of Germany its interest in a leading role in southeast Europe and direct its actions toward the Mediterranean Sea. In light of the October agreement the backstage aspects of the revolt of General Franco became clear. Intensive intervention in Spain was undertaken more quickly by Hitler than Mussolini. German Fascist intervention in Spain was calculated to accomplish two purposes: to bring into German hands on the far southwest of Europe extremely important bases for an attack on France and at the same time push Italy into an adventure on a large scale in the Mediterranean Sea in order to use this embarrassing situation to force Italy completely out of her Balkan-Danubian position.

"Characteristically in the first months of the war in Spain the predominant role in intervention was unquestionably taken by Germany. When in the beginning of November, 1936, the attack of the Fascist hordes of General Franco were beaten at the very walls of Madrid due to the heroism of the Republican forces, Germany began systematically to transport military units to Spain. By the end of the year in Spain on the side of the rebels were fighting not less than 20,000 soldiers of Hitler.

"At this time Mussolini apparently still was hesitating, having a presentiment that the Spanish adventure might be undertaken by him too far, and decided not to cut off his path of retreat.

"The turning point only came at the end of December and especially at the time of the January visit in Rome of General Göring where he together with Mussolini discussed a plan of further action of both powers in Spain. From this time Mussolini began at a furious tempo to transport to Spain one battalion after another. In February there came the first large operation of Italian forces, leading in the seizure of Malaga, but their chief blow was planned against Madrid. In the beginning of March there was concentrated in Spain not less than 70,000–80,000 Italian soldiers, of this number 40,000 (four divisions) were on the Guadalajara front. As is known, the general attack of the Italian divisions on the Guadalajara front ended cruelly for them in a rout.

"This defeat was such a smashing moral blow to Italian fascism that henceforth a quick exit of Fascist Italy from participating in Spain was out of the question.

In the course of 1937 and 1938 Fascist Italy with increasing strength continued her intervention in Spain, sending continuously newer and newer forces, planes, tanks, artillery pieces, etc...." Petr Aleksevich Lisovskii, *SSSR i kapitalisticheskoe okruzhenie* [*The USSR and Capitalist Encirclement*] (Moscow: Gos. Izdat. Politicheskoi Literatury, 1939), pp. 87–89.

⁴ Elizabeth Wiskemann, *The Rome-Berlin Axis* (New York and London: Oxford University Press, 1949), pp. 23 ff.

⁵ Göring at the Nuremberg Trials on March 14, 1946, explained the German role in Spain: "When the Civil War broke out in Spain, Franco sent a call for help to Germany and asked for support, particularly in the air. One should not forget that Franco with his troops was stationed in Africa and that he could not get the troops across, as the fleet was in the hands of the Communists, or, as they called themselves at the time, the competent Revolutionary Government in Spain. The decisive factor was, first of all, to get his troops over to Spain.

"The Führer thought the matter over. I urged him to give support under all circumstances, firstly, in order to prevent the further spread of Communism in that theatre and, secondly, to test my young *Luftwaffe* at this opportunity in this or that technical respect.

"With the permission of the Führer, I sent a large part of my transport fleet and a number of experimental fighter units, bombers and anti-aircraft guns; and in that way I had an opportunity to ascertain, under combat conditions, whether the material was equal to the task. In order that the personnel, too, might gather a certain amount of experience, I saw to it that there was a continuous flow, that is, that new people were constantly being sent and others recalled." *Trial of the Major Criminals Before the International Military Tribunal* (Nuremberg: International Military Tribunal, 1947–1949), IX, 280–281.

On the other hand, the German army did not favor intervention in Spain. "However small the shipments to Spain, they represented a dangerous drain on Germany's military resources during the most critical period of her own rearmament." Gordon A. Craig, *The Politics of the Prussian Army, 1640–1945* (Oxford: The Clarendon Press, 1955), p. 487.

⁶ P. A. M. van der Esche, *Prelude to War* (The Hague: Martinus Nijhoff, 1951), p. 13.

⁷ *See* memorandum by the foreign minister, August 7, 1936, and the ambassador in Italy to the foreign ministry, August 6, 1936, Documents 32 and 30 in *Documents on German Foreign Policy, 1918–1945*, D, III; conversations with the Hungarian minister, September 7, 1936; *Ciano's Diplomatic Papers* (London: Odhams Press Limited, 1948), pp. 36–37.

⁸ New York *Times* (July 21, 1936), p. 3.

⁹ Report of the ministry of air dated January 23, 1937, and report of the ministry of state, microfilms of Italian documents in the National Archives, Washington, container no. 412, slide nos. 062992 and 062975.

¹⁰ Cattell, *op. cit.*, p. 82; *and* Walter Görlitz, *History of the German General Staff*, (London: Hollis and Carter, 1953), p. 307.

¹¹ J. W. Garner, "Questions of International Law in the Spanish Civil War," *American Journal of International Law*, 31 (1937), 66–73.

¹² For example, Russia emphatically denied that a Soviet tanker fired on Ceuta. *Pravda* on July 25, 1936, declared: "The Italian press has readily taken up the stupid yarn fabricated by the Spanish rebel, General Franco. With his hands smeared with the blood of the Spanish toilers, this adventurer stated in writing that a Soviet ship has joined the Spanish Republican fleet which is operating against the rebels. What sort of ship specifically was it that was sent from the far away USSR to take part in the firing upon the fortifications on the coast of Spanish

Morocco seized by the blackguards of General Franco? Was it a liner, a destroyer or perhaps a submarine? Nothing of the kind. It appears that the USSR could find nothing better for the naval operations off the coast of Spanish Morocco than an oil tanker!"

[13] *See* Cattell, *op. cit.*, pp. 38–43, for a fuller treatment.

[14] J. R. Campbell, "The Movement in Great Britain in Support of the Fight of the Spanish People," *Inprecorr*, vol. 16, no. 35 (Aug. 1, 1936), 931.

[15] The Franco-Russian Alliance was signed on May 2, 1935, and was approved by the Chamber of Deputies on February 27, 1936, and by the Senate on March 12, 1936.

[16] For example: "German and Italian fascism which wages war against the Spanish people and the Spanish Republic are prepared to deal a blow to the very heart of democratic Europe.... Italy and Germany want to erect against the republic of France a third Fascist frontier, a third Fascist front. The Fascist interventionists try to seize on the coast of Spain new basic positions in the forthcoming struggle against England for the mastery of the Mediterranean." *Izvestiia* (Oct. 16, 1936). See also *Izvestiia* (Oct. 17, 1936); Hans Behrend, "Open Interference by the Nazi Government on the Side of Spanish Fascism," *Inprecorr*, vol. 16, no. 35 (Aug. 1, 1936), 934; B. Minlos, *"Voenno-fashistskii miatezh v Ispanii"* [*"The Military Fascist Rebellion in Spain"*], *Mirovoe Khoziaistvo i Mirovaia Politika* (Sept., 1936), p. 40. For additional examples *see* page 153 n. 24.

[17] Cattell, *op. cit.*, pp. 69–70.

[18] Such support was not in any way illegal. Even the Non-Intervention Agreement signed later prohibited only the sending of military equipment and ammunition. The United States chargé in the Soviet Union (Henderson) reported to the secretary of state on August 4, 1936: "A responsible Soviet official told me last night that a number of Soviet officials charged with the conduct of Soviet foreign relations were opposed to sending funds to Spain since they felt that such action would be used by Germany and Italy to justify the aid given by themselves to the rebels. These objections were overruled, however, by those Soviet leaders who take the view that if the Soviet Union is to continue to maintain hegemony over the international revolutionary movement it must not hesitate in periods of crisis to assume the leadership of that movement." *Foreign Relations of the United States, 1936*, II, 461.

[19] *Pravda* (Aug. 4, 1936).

[20] *Ibid.* (Aug. 6, 1936).

[21] Later England became the leading advocate of an agreement with Italy. *See* pp. 111 ff.

[22] The British attitude had already been expressed by the signing of the Anglo-German Naval Treaty nine months earlier, permitting German naval rearmament up to 35 per cent of the British strength in all categories—an explicit violation of the terms of the Versailles Treaty.

[23] Winston Churchill, writing on September 18, 1936, described the growing division in French society as follows: "The tragedy of the Spanish Civil War continues to play every day directly under the eyes of the French people, and its varying fortunes and invariable brutality stir profoundly every section of politics, and range in hateful and perilous antagonism not only parties but classes." Winston Churchill, *Step by Step, 1936–1939* (London: T. Butterworth, 1939), p. 47.

[24] Information concerning these early negotiations between France and Spain is to be found in newspaper reports and the letter of Ferdinando de los Ríos from Paris to José Giral dated July 25, 1936, cited in William Foss and Cecil Gerahty, *The Spanish Arena* (London: John Gifford Ltd., 1938), pp. 372–376.

[25] *Ibid.*, p. 374.

[26] Luis Araquistain described Blum at this time as "the antithesis of a man of action" and "the Hamlet of French politics." Luis Araquistain, *La verdad sobre la intervención* (Madrid: 1938), p. 40.

[27] Churchill, *op. cit.*, p. 37.

[28] The French ambassador to Italy reported his government's decision to Count Ciano, Italian foreign minister, on July 29, 1936, *Ciano's Diplomatic Papers*, pp. 21–22.

[29] Anthony Eden, *Foreign Affairs* (London: Faber and Faber, 1939), pp. 182–183.

[30] The ambassador in the United Kingdom (Bingham) to the secretary of state, March 31, 1937, *Foreign Relations of the United States, 1937*, I, 270.

[31] Britain controlled about 20 per cent of the foreign capital invested in Spain. Also British trade with Spain was extensive. Great Britain was Spain's greatest supplier and largest customer.

[32] Anna Louise Strong, sympathetic to the Communist view, described the dichotomy of the democratic peoples. "England and France are divided personalities. The common people instinctively sympathize with the Spanish people's fight, but they are confused by appeals to religion and their will is paralyzed by the reactionaries, who play upon their dread of war. Even the ruling class in these countries is divided; its national interests are on one side and its class interest on the other. A German-Italian conquest of Spain endangers both France and the British Empire, but they think it does not endanger the rule of British capitalists over British workers as does a victory of the People's Front. So class interests have proved paramount...." Anna Louise Strong, *Spain in Arms* (New York: Henry Holt and Company, 1937), p. 80.

NOTES TO CHAPTER II

THE NON-INTERVENTION AGREEMENT: AUGUST, 1936

(PAGES 14–21)

[1] The United States chargé in France (Wilson) reported to the secretary of state, August 6, 1936: "He [Minister of Foreign Affairs Delbos] said that the French Government has conclusive proof of aid given to the rebels not only by the Italian Government but by the German Government as well. Five German airplanes, three of them large transport planes, had been flown to Spanish Morocco and turned over to Franco—and this could not happen without the approval of the German Government; furthermore the French Government knew that the *Deutschland* had landed bombs in Spanish Morocco for the rebels. As regards Italian aid he said that the French Government now knew that the flight of Italian Air Corps planes to Morocco, two of which landed in French Morocco, was headed by a colonel of the Italian Air Force; that the Italian Air Corps personnel who manned the planes had been enrolled for this duty at least as early as July 20 and that a pay slip was found on one of the airmen indicating that he had drawn his pay from the Italian Air Corps in advance through July 31." *Foreign Relations of the United States, 1936*, II, 467–468.

[2] New York *Times* (Aug. 19, 1936), p. 1.

[3] Claude Bowers, United States ambassador to Spain at this time, in his book *My Mission to Spain* (New York: Simon and Schuster, 1954), pp. 281–282, supports the view that the British were the real instigators of the policy of nonintervention: "It is now fairly established that this plan was hatched in London and that Blum was practically blackmailed into acceptance. Otherwise, England would withdraw her guarantee to maintain the frontier of France and support France in a possible

war with Germany; and would consider herself released from her obligations under the Locarno Pact, unless France abandoned her right under international law, to sell arms and ammunition to the democratic republic that both England and France recognized as the legitimate, legal government. This amounted to an ultimatum, and the Blum government yielded to the threat. Mr. Churchill would have us believe that the plan was Blum's and that he acted on his own initiative. When two nations thus seek to shift responsibility, there is something of which to be ashamed."

On the other side is the report of the chargé in France (Wilson) to the secretary of state, August 20, 1936: "He [Blumel, *Chief de Cabinet* of Blum] said that the British Government at first had been rather lukewarm in its support of the French initiative for a non-intervention pact. This he explained by [apparent omission] that at first British conservative opinion, including the Army and Navy, had been that the triumph of the Spanish Government would mean Communism and disorder in Spain and that a victory of the military elements was to be desired. However, more recently the British Government seems to have shown a clearer realization of the implications to their interests of a victory of the military rebellion in Spain." *Foreign Relations of the United States, 1936*, II, 503.

⁴ For a detailed discussion *see* David T. Cattell, *Communism and the Spanish Civil War* (Berkeley and Los Angeles: University of California Press, 1955), pp. 42–43.

⁵ This follows the explanation given in the Communist press: "... How could the Soviet Government not have agreed, when in the absence of the possibility of deliveries from the USSR, practically the whole burden would rest on France and when, if the Soviet Government had rejected the French proposal the anti-Soviet campaign, the strongest incitement of the fascist war and rebellion-mongers, would have reached its climax?" *Inprecorr*, vol. 16, no. 37 (Aug. 15, 1936), 985. *See also* "Spain in the Struggle against Fascism," *Communist International* (Nov., 1936), p. 1437.

⁶ *Le Temps* (Aug. 7, 1936).

⁷ "To the Aid of the Spanish People!" *Inprecorr*, vol. 16, no. 36 (Aug. 8, 1936), 959. In the same issue of *Inprecorr*, André Marty, a leading French Communist and member of the Executive Committee of the Communist International, openly attacked the British government for its early prorebel sympathies: "As far as British imperialism is concerned, it has at least 17 warships in the Spanish ports and has sent four big aeroplanes to Lisbon. From the outset it showed its full sympathy with the Franco rebellion. It sees today, a little late, that its German and Italian rivals are the chief beneficiaries from this operation." "Liberty or Death! In Spain as During the Great French Revolution," p. 957.

⁸ Paul Nizan, "To the Aid of the Spanish Republic!" *Inprecorr*, vol. 16, no. 37 (Aug. 15, 1936), 990. See also *Humanité* (Aug. 9, 1936).

⁹ *Pravda* (Aug. 17, 1936).

¹⁰ *Ibid.* (Aug. 19 and 20, 1936).

¹¹ A report from the United States Embassy in Moscow dated August 29, 1936, in the Archives of the Department of State, Washington, D.C.

¹² Documents of the Non-Intervention Committee, N.I.S. (36) Document no. 2A.

¹³ The Soviet decree had no material effect since there were no private traders in the USSR and the Soviet government from the beginning had refrained from giving armed support to the Republican government.

¹⁴ Documents of the Non-Intervention Committee, N.I.S. (36) 2nd Meeting, p. 7.

NOTES TO CHAPTER III

The Left and Nonintervention

(Pages 22–31)

[1] Pope Pius XI on September 14, 1936, addressed some 600 Spanish refugees, bishops, priests, and laymen, whom he received in audience at Castel Gandolfo: "These tragic happenings in Spain speak to Europe and the whole world and proclaim once more to what extent the very foundations of all order, of all culture, of all civilization are being menaced. This menace, it must be added, is all the more serious, more persistent, more active, by reason of a profound ignorance and a disclaiming of the truth, by reason of the truly satanic hatred against God and against humanity redeemed by Him, all that concerns religion and the Catholic Church. This point has so often been admitted and as We just observed, openly confessed, that it is superfluous for Us to insist on the matter further, and now less than ever when the events of Spain have spoken with such appalling eloquence." *To the Spanish Refugees* (New York: The American Press, 1937).

[2] Cited in Arnold J. Toynbee, *Survey of International Affairs 1937*, vol. II *The International Repercussions of the War in Spain (1936–1937)* (London: Oxford University Press, 1938), p. 142.

[3] *L'Humanité* (Aug. 13, 1936).

[4] Reported in the *Manchester Guardian* (Sept. 7, 1936).

[5] New York *Times* (Sept. 10, 1936), p. 18.

[6] The Communists also persistently and openly criticized Blum's foreign policy: "Concerning the questions of foreign policy the Communist party of France has more than once stepped forward with criticism of the activities of the cabinet of Leon Blum and his minister for foreign affairs, the Radical Delbos. The party subjected to sharp criticism that shameful farce of 'nonintervention' which freed the hands of Hitler and Mussolini in their brigand and plundering war against the Spanish peoples." R.-R., "Smena kabineta vo Frantsii" ["Shifting of the Cabinet in France"], *Mirovoe Khoziastvo i Mirovaia Politika* (Aug., 1937).

The French Communist party, furthermore, never ceased trying to complete a united front program with the French Socialists, including joint action in respect to Spain. *See* for example J. Decaux, "On the Fourth Anniversary of the United Front Pact in France," *Communist International* (Aug., 1938), pp. 763–764, "Chamberlain's Echo," *ibid.* (Nov., 1938), p. 990.

[7] Cited in Toynbee, *op. cit.*, p. 145. *See also* Leon Blum, *L'histoire jugera* (Paris: Éditions Diderot, 1945), pp. 156–160.

[8] The Communists answered such arguments in the manner reported by Gabriel Péri at the French Communist Party Conference in the summer of 1937: "Finally they say to us, that thanks to the policy of 'nonintervention' the Spanish war has not gone beyond the borders of Spain. We answer that this is incorrect; if the Spanish war has not gone beyond the borders of Spain, it is not thanks to but in spite of the policy of 'nonintervention.' That the war has not spread is not thanks to the policy of concession to fascism but thanks to the heroism and bravery of the resistance of the Spanish people. (Applause)." *Kompartiia Frantsii v bor'be za narodnii front [The French Communist Party in the Struggle for the People's Front]* (Moscow: Partizdat TsK VKP(b), 1938), p. 58.

[9] Adolph Sturmthal, *The Tragedy of European Labor 1918–1939* (New York: Columbia University Press, 1943), p. 295.

[10] For a general discussion of the Labour party's foreign policy during this period, see G. D. H. Cole, *A History of the Labour Party from 1914* (London: Rout-

ledge and Kegan Paul Ltd., 1948), pp. 318–335, and Elaine Windrich, *British Labour's Foreign Policy* (Stanford: Stanford University Press, 1952).

[11] *The Spanish Problem*, speeches at the Trade Union Congress, Plymouth, 1936, Ref. No. 7.9/1936 (London: Trade Union Congress General Council), pp. 19, 28–29.

[12] Even the Communist party of Great Britain did not at this time urge the abandonment of the Non-Intervention Agreement, but did urge some concrete evidence of solidarity with the Spanish people:

"I believe that the following are further practical measures to be taken:

"(1) The sending of official Trade Union and other delegations to Madrid, as an indication of British support to the Caballero Government.

"(2) The organisation through the Co-operative Societies of a regular service of food ships for Spain.

"(3) The sending of official Trade Union and other delegations to take part in all demonstrations of the People's Front in France, as an expression of British and French solidarity in the fight against fascism.

"(4) The strengthening of the British Medical Unit already in Spain, and the sending of skilled mechanics and technical experts to help the Spanish Government.

"(5) The immediate convening of Parliament and of the League of Nations, in order to take a definite stand against the fascist violations of international law, which are endangering peace.

"(6) Arrangements for the care, until the fascist rebellion has been crushed, of all orphaned children who can be brought to Britain from Spain.

"(7) Really nation-wide financial assistance for the Spanish people, with a levy on all organised workers, to be collected through the shop stewards and trade union branches." (Harry Pollitt, *Spain and the T.U.C.* (London: Communist Party of Great Britain, 1936), pp. 15–16.

[13] On July 20, 1936, the leader of the Labour party, Clement Attlee, at a conference in London of the labor and co-operative movements, moved and secured the adoption of a resolution pledging "all practicable support to our Spanish comrades in their struggle to defend freedom and democracy in Spain." On July 27 the National Council of Labour opened a fund for the relief of the Spanish working class in distress, particularly the women and children. Deputations of leading representatives of labor were received by Foreign Secretary Anthony Eden on August 19 and by Lord Cranborne on September 1. On August 28, a manifesto denouncing the intervention in Spain by Italy, Germany, and Portugal was issued by a representative conference of the labor movement. To the Foreign Office on September 1, and again in Plymouth on September 4, the Labour party expressed "grave concern at the delay in bringing the Non-Intervention Agreement into force."

[14] The overwhelming support for the decision can be seen in the card vote taken on a resolution amendment proposing Congress denounce the policy of nonintervention: for the amendment 51,000; against 3,029,000. *The Spanish Problem*, p. 38.

[15] *Ibid.*, pp. 7–12.

[16] *Ibid.*, p. 18.

[17] *Ibid.*, p. 13.

[18] At the Labour Party Conference in Edinburgh Clement Attlee's statement on behalf of the Executive Committee of the party, declaring its conviction that the Fascist powers had broken their neutrality pledges and demanding an investigation, was approved unanimously on October 9.

[19] New York *Times* (Oct. 29, 1936).

[20] *Inprecorr*, vol. 17, no. 3 (Jan. 16, 1937), 48.

[21] The Communists remained critical of the Labour party for its half-hearted attempts to help Spain: "Unfortunately, we have to record the fact that the biggest obstacle to international united action is the policy of the British Labour leaders.

It needs to be placed on record that so far they have not organized a single mass demonstration in Britain on behalf of the Spanish government, nor does Spain figure in any of their current political campaigns." Harry Pollitt, "International Unity Can Bring Peace to Spain and Europe," *Inprecorr*, vol. 17, no. 26 (June 19, 1937), 594. *See also* "Sir Walter Citrine—Friend of Chamberlain," *Communist International* (Aug., 1938), p. 715.

[22] During the winter and spring of 1937, the Labour party generally supported the government's efforts to establish a system of control and merely urged it to more strenuous efforts in this direction. When by July 27, 1937, all efforts at control were obviously bound to fail because of Fascist objections, the National Council of Labour came out with a strong report demanding rescission of the Non-Intervention Agreement. The report was endorsed by the Labour Party Conference in October, 1937.

[23] Foreign Minister Anthony Eden put the government's case as follows: "Let us face the alternatives to non-intervention. They must be bluntly stated. An open and limitless competition in the supply of arms and munitions and even men to Spain, stimulated by the almost frenzied support of rival ideologies. Where must that have led Europe? What role was there for this country in such a feeding of the flames in a foreign civil strife? Unless we were ourselves prepared to intervene in Spain, ourselves willing to send men to participate in that civil war—and no one in this country advocates that course. Then clearly there was only one role for us; to continue to work patiently, persistently for the limitation and at least the cessation of all outside intervention in Spain, for the sake of the unhappy people of Spain and for the sake of Europe." Anthony Eden, Speech at Liverpool on April 12, 1937, *Foreign Affairs* (London: Faber and Faber, 1939), pp. 189–190.

[24] For the Communist reaction to the attitude of the Socialist International, *see* Georgi Dimitrov, "To Protect Despicable Terrorists is to Help Fascism," *Communist International* (Oct., 1936), p. 1245.

[25] *Inprecorr*, vol. 16, no. 49 (Oct. 31, 1936), 1308. *See also* "The Second International and Spain," *Communist International* (Jan., 1937), p. 61.

[26] For example, at the Congress of the International Federation of Socialist Students held in Oxford from July 17 to July 20, Communist representatives were present to give their point of view on united action. *Inprecorr*, vol. 16, no. 36 (Aug. 8, 1936), 979. In an article in *Inprecorr*, vol. 16, no. 35 (Aug. 1, 1936), 930, A. Komjat pleaded: "Unity of action of the Communist International, the Labour and Socialist International, and the International Trade Union Federation, only this can assure the campaign for saving of the Spanish Republic. . . . Only this unity of action can coördinate the different sections of the proletariat to assist the campaign to victory."

In the middle of August the Communist parties of Great Britain, France, and Belgium issued the following manifesto:

"We demand that the Spanish Government be allowed to obtain its requirements from Britain, France and Belgium, and that what amounts to economic sanctions should not be imposed against it.

"We demand that our governments maintain normal relations with the legal Spanish government.

"We demand that the material ordered by the Spanish government to ensure the victory of order be furnished without any restrictions.

"We demand that the port of Tangiers be opened to the warships of the legal Spanish government.

"We call on all workers and all adherents of peace to demand that the Spanish people be not made the victim of a blockade which would cripple its heroic struggle." *Inprecorr*, vol. 16, no. 38 (Aug. 22, 1936), 1017.

[27] *Ibid.*, no. 48 (Oct. 24, 1936), 1288.
[28] Georgi Dimitrov, *The United Front* (New York: International Publishers, 1938), p. 212. For the text of the resolution of the Communist International of October 28, 1936, see *Narod (Ispanskii) pobedit! [The (Spanish) People are Winning!]* (Moscow: Partizdat. TsK VKP(b), 1937), p. 11.
[29] K. Gottwald, "Unity of Action is Possible Everywhere," *Communist International* (Sept., 1937), p. 599.
[30] *See* articles in *Inprecorr:* vol. 17, no. 13 (March 20, 1937), 316: André Marty, "To Hasten the Victory in Spain after Eight Months of Fighting," vol. 17, no. 15 (April 2, 1937), 363. For the reports of negotiations between the Communist International and Socialist International during June, 1937, see *ibid.*, vol. 17, nos. 25–29. *Also see* Georgi Dimitrov, "Fascism is War," *Pravda* (Aug. 1, 1937) and the following in *Communist International:* "Spain Calls for Unity" (Aug., 1937), p. 514; "The Soviet Union and the Working Class of the Capitalist Countries" (Dec., 1937), p. 889; José Díaz, "Rally Closer the Ranks" (Jan., 1938), pp. 52 ff.; "May First Manifesto" (May, 1938), p. 412; "The Conspiracy of Munich" (Oct., 1938), pp. 884–885; Kurt Funk, "The Policy of the Labor and Socialist International and the Fascist Offensive" (Dec., 1938), pp. 1100–1101; "Spain and the Capitulators" (April, 1939), pp. 314–315. Also, *Delo Ispanii ne chastnoe delo ispantsev [The Affair in Spain is Not Just a Private Affair of the Spaniards]* Moscow: Partizdat. TsK VKP(b), 1937); Georgi Dimitrov, *Two Years of Heroic Struggle of the Spanish People* (New York: Workers Library Publishers, 1938).
[31] David T. Cattell, *Communism and the Spanish Civil War* (Berkeley and Los Angeles: University of California Press, 1955), pp. 121–124.

NOTES TO CHAPTER IV

The Soviet Union Intervenes

(Pages 32–37)

[1] For further discussion *see* David T. Cattell, *Communism and the Spanish Civil War* (Berkeley and Los Angeles: University of California Press, 1955), p. 73. See also *Soviet Shipping in the Spanish Civil War*, mimeograph ser. no. 59 (New York: Research Program on the USSR, 1954), for a description of the methods by which material was shipped to Spain.
[2] For an analysis of Soviet activities and intervention in Spain sympathetic to the Soviet position, *see* Louis Fischer, *Men and Politics: an Autobiography* (New York: Duell, Sloan and Pearce, 1941), *and* Anna Louise Strong, *Spain in Arms* (New York: Henry Holt and Co., 1937). For the Spanish Loyalist view *see* Luis Araquistain, *La verdad sobre la intervención y la no intervención en España* (Madrid: 1938), pp. 30–32, and Carlos de Baraibar, *La guerra de España en el plano internacional* (Barcelona: Editorial Tierra y Libertad, 1938), pp. 187–190, 197–199.
[3] Cattell, *op. cit.*, pp. 25–29.
[4] The Soviet press was reporting evidence of stepped-up German and Italian intervention even after the Non-Intervention Agreement went into effect on August 28. See *Pravda* (Aug. 26, 29, 31, Sept. 1, 1936), *and* Nicoletti, "Mussolini Continues Arming the Spanish Rebels," *Inprecorr*, vol. 16, no. 42 (Sept. 12, 1936), 1146.
[5] Such statements as that made by the Soviet ambassador in London on March 13, 1937, can be dismissed as wishful thinking or deception: "We have only two frontiers—in the west and in the far east—to defend, and I betray no military secret when I say that *these two frontiers during the last few years have been made well-nigh impregnable by the great fortifications, by the large armies well equipped with*

all modern appliances, and by the huge air force." Jane Degras, *Soviet Documents on Foreign Policy* (London: Oxford University Press, 1953) III, 237.

[6] *See* Maxim Litvinov, *Against Aggression* (London: Lawrence Wishart Ltd., 1939).

[7] This tactic of the Soviet leaders has become very familiar in the post-Second World War period in which the Soviet Union has made good use of Koreans, Chinese, Vietnamese, and others for her purposes in Asia, supplying them with munitions in their fight against the "imperialist powers."

[8] *See also* the editorial by A. Nikiforov, "Aggressive Plans of German Fascism against Czechoslovakia," *Pravda* (Sept. 13, 1936).

[9] Extracts from a speech by Litvinov on the international situation at an election meeting in Leningrad on June 23, 1938, in Degras, *op. cit.*, p. 293.

[10] Cattell, *op. cit.*, chap. viii.

[11] Several books were published in the Soviet Union on military strategy and organization in the Spanish Civil War. It is very interesting that the editors in the preface criticized Helmut Klotz's book, *Uroki grazhdanskoi voiny v Ispanii* [*Lessons from the Civil War in Spain*] (Moscow: Voenizdat., 1938), for minimizing the role of the air force. *See also* A. Samarin, *Bor'ba za Madrid* [*Struggle for Madrid*], (Moscow: Voenizdat., n.d.). This book reported on both the military and nonmilitary aspects of the seige of Madrid. The author ended (p. 106) by ridiculing the Italian forces: "The whole war role of the Italian corps shows their completely inferior war efficiency, absence of will, and subjectiveness to panic. It is characteristic that for the period of operations the Republicans took prisoner about 900 Italians and at the same time only 11 Moroccan war prisoners were taken."

An analysis of the Loyalist military organization by the Russians appears in *Upravlenie voiskami i rabota shtabov v Ispanskoi republikanskoi armii* [*The Administration of the Troops and Work of the Staff in the Spanish Republican Army*] (Moscow: Voenizdat., 1939). Its general conclusion was: "During the length of the whole war in Spain the problem of organizing the high command and administering the armed forces was very acute. At the outset of the war the organization underwent a series of substantial changes, but until the end of the war they had not been completely resolved." P. 5.

[12] For example, the ambassador in France (Bullitt) reported to the acting secretary of state on November 25, 1936: "The French Government is convinced that the Soviet Government desires to push the conflict to the bitter end on the theory that even though in the first instance the Soviet Government would suffer a defeat through the overthrowing of the Madrid and Barcelona Governments by Italian and German troops enlisted in Franco's army, the final result would be an attempt by the Germans to establish a new status in Spanish Morocco and an attempt by the Italians to maintain possession of the Balearic Islands which would result in war between Germany and Italy on one side and France and England on the other. This the Soviet Government anticipates would lead to eventual Bolshevization of the whole of Europe." *Foreign Relations of the United States, 1936*, II, 575.

[13] Walter Krivitsky, *In Stalin's Secret Service* (New York: Harper and Bros., 1939), pp. 73 and 76. *See also* Julian Gorkin, *Canibales politicos; Hitler and Stalin en España* (Mexico City: Ediciones "Guetzal," 1941), p. 54, *and* Franz Borkenau, *European Communism* (New York: Harper and Brothers, 1953), pp. 117, 135, and 169.

[14] Extracts from a speech by Litvinov at the Central Executive Committee, November 10, 1936, in Degras, *op. cit.*, p. 216.

NOTES TO CHAPTER V

SOVIET DIPLOMATIC MANEUVERS: SEPTEMBER AND OCTOBER, 1936

(PAGES 38–52)

[1] A year later Anthony Eden in a debate in the House of Commons described the reluctance on the part of the League to deal with the Spanish crisis: "Let me assure him [honorable Member from Derby] that the League never showed any enthusiasm to handle the Spanish problem, for the very simple reason that the League knew how sharp were the divergencies of views within that organization about Spain." Anthony Eden, *Foreign Affairs* (London: Faber and Faber, 1939), p. 230.

[2] Records of the Seventeenth Assembly, September 25, 1936, recorded in League of Nations *Official Journal* (Oct., 1936), p. 48.

[3] Maxim Litvinov, *Against Aggression* (London: Lawrence and Wishart Ltd., 1939), pp. 56–57. This is an excerpt from a speech delivered at the XVII Plenary Session of the League of Nations, September 28, 1936.

[4] *Inprecorr*, vol. 16, no. 45 (Oct. 3, 1936), 1227. See also *ibid.*, no. 46 (Oct. 10, 1936), 1249.

[5] The Communist propaganda on the danger of the Nazi menace to the West reached a high pitch during this period. *See* for example *Pravda*'s editorials on Nazism and France on September 15 and 16, 1936.

[6] Documents of the Non-Intervention Committee, N.I.S. (36) 5th Meeting, pp. 8–9.

[7] *Ibid.*, p. 5.

[8] The Soviet Union frequently deplored the slow manner in which the committee considered the accusations against Italy and Germany and avoided taking any positive action. *See* for example *Pravda*'s editorial of October 31, 1936.

[9] For the Soviet interpretation of the role of Portugal in the Spanish Civil War *see* Eugen Varga, "Portugaliia i Ispanskie sobytiia" ["Portugal and the Spanish Events"], *Mirovoe Khoziaistvo i Mirovaia Politika* (March, 1937), pp. 43 ff. *See also* Evgenii Aleksandrovich Aksanov, *Portugaliia i ee rol' v fashisitskoi interventsii v Ispanii* [*Portugal and Her Role in the Fascist Intervention in Spain*] (Moscow: Gos. Sotsial'no-ekonomicheskoe izdat., 1937). This book is a detailed analysis of Portuguese history, the intervention by Portugal in the Spanish Civil War, and Hitler's attempts to take over British hegemony in Portugal.

[10] The Soviet representative had uttered several oral complaints during the September meetings, but did not make them formally until he presented the Soviet note of October 6, 1936, to the secretary of the committee.

[11] Documents of the Non-Intervention Committee, N.I.S. (36) Document no. 77.

[12] The Portuguese representative had left the meeting in a huff when the charges of the Soviet government were presented to the committee.

[13] Note to the committee from the Soviet representative dated October 7, 1936, *ibid.*, Document no. 81. *Pravda* on October 24 explained the main legal argument of the Soviet Union as follows: "As regards the Soviet government, it naturally can have no other obligations under the agreement than those actually observed by the other signatories."

[14] The resolutions passed by the Russian workers in support of Spain were no longer just innocuous appeals for relief. Beginning on October 15 they became belligerent in tone: "We demand: either force the Fascist countries to respect international law and immediately cease aiding the Fascist rebels in Spain, or give the legal government of Republican Spain, elected by the people in accordance with the law and wishes of millions of Spanish workers, the right and possibility to receive every necessity in its struggle with the Fascist rebel bandits and the hired assassins

supported by Fascist Germany, Italy, and Portugal." *Pravda* (Oct. 15, 1936). *See also* Harry Pollitt, *Arms for Spain* (London: Communist Party of Great Britain, Oct. 30, 1936).

[15] "To Madrid, Central Committee of the Communist Party of Spain, Comrade José Díaz," *Pravda* (Oct. 16, 1936).

[16] The United States chargé in the Soviet Union (Henderson) reported to the secretary of state on October 9, 1936, the official reasons as disclosed by the Soviet government:

"The following is a brief summary of what a responsible official of the Foreign Office told me yesterday regarding the considerations responsible for the dispatch of the Soviet note of October 7 to the International Committee on Non-Intervention in Spain.

"(1) For a whole month the Committee has taken non-effective steps in the direction of seeing that the agreement of non-intervention was being carried out.

"(2) The Italian representative has continuously blocked the efforts of the Soviet representative to have investigations made of alleged violations of the agreement by insisting that it was first necessary to discuss the question of inducing other powers to become parties to the agreement to determine whether or not the agreement should be amended so as to include obligations not to give moral support, money or foodstuffs to one or the other combatants.

"(3) The British Chairman has consistently sided with the Italian representative, and the French Government instead of aiding the Soviet representative has on several occasions suggested privately to the Soviet Government that the raising of questions regarding alleged violations is likely to result only in unprofitable friction.

"(4) Portugal in the meantime has made little effort to conceal the fact that it is furnishing the rebels with military supplies, while Germany and Italy have been almost as brazenly assisting the rebels in a similar manner.

"(5) The Soviet Government has therefore come to the conclusion that unless it takes a firm stand in the matter the Committee will continue to view with equanimity violations by Germany, Italy and Portugal...." *Foreign Relations of the United States, 1936*, II, 535–536.

[17] Documents of the Non-Intervention Committee, N.I.S. (36) 6th Meeting, p. 12. *See* "Spain in the Struggle Against Fascism," *Communist International* (Nov., 1936), pp. 143 ff., for a detailed analysis of the Communist attitude toward the Non-Intervention Agreement at this time.

[18] The USSR, however, was not the first power to have violated the secrecy of the meetings of the committee.

[19] Documents of the Non-Intervention Committee, N.I.S. (36) 6th Meeting, pp. 7, 9.

[20] Ferdinand Kuhn, Jr., reported to the New York *Times* on the Russian note: "But whatever Russia's reasons may have been, her warning has irritated the British Government more than any document that has come from Moscow in years. The emotions behind it were understandable, but its peremptory tone and its brusque method of delivery were felt today to be first-class blunders by Soviet diplomacy.

"Officials here could hardly restrain themselves today when they discussed the Russian note. What on earth, they asked, could Russia hope to gain by throwing neutrality overboard at a time like this? Wasn't it plain to the Russians that in any open scramble to supply arms to Spain the Germans and Italians could supply twice as much and do it twice as quickly? And how would that help Russia's friends in Madrid?" New York *Times* (Oct. 9, 1936).

[21] The German chargé d'affaires in Spain to the acting director of the political department of Germany, October 16, 1936, *Documents on German Foreign Policy, 1918–1945*, D, III, Document no. 100.

²² *See* for example K. Gottwald, "Long Live the Spanish People, Long Live the Spanish Democratic Republic," *Communist International* (Oct., 1936), p. 1314, and Gabriel Péri, "The So-Called 'Non-Intervention Policy' is a Sham," *Inprecorr*, vol. 16, no. 47 (Oct. 17, 1936), 1267–1268.

²³ The Soviet editorial comment was hopeful about the growing sympathy for the cause of the Loyalists: "The interest and sympathy of the broadest masses all over the world and of all forward and progressive mankind is on the side of the Spanish people. Neither England nor France can ignore this enormous solidarity movement with the Spanish people." *Pravda* (Oct. 19, 1936).

²⁴ In defense of the Soviets, it must be said that they answered all accusations immediately without using dilatory tactics as did Portugal, Germany, and Italy.

²⁵ *See* Documents of the Non-Intervention Committee, N.I.S. (36) 7th Meeting, October 23, 1936, *and* 8th Meeting, October 28, 1936, at which the allegations against the Fascist states were discussed.

²⁶ Memorandum from the representative of the United Kingdom, October 23, 1936, *ibid.*, Document no. 105.

²⁷ See *ibid.*, 9th and 10th Meetings, November 4, 1936, at which the Italian and German charges against the Soviet Union were under consideration.

²⁸ *Ibid.*, 10th Meeting, p. 16.

²⁹ *Ibid.*, p. 10.

³⁰ T. Karradov, "The Unbiased Attitude of Lord Plymouth," *Pravda* (Oct. 27, 1936). Another article of a similar nature in *Pravda* on October 30, 1936, was a speech by Maisky to the committee on October 28, which, contrary to the rules of the committee, was published. He declared: "...the note [from the Portuguese government] undoubtedly shows the exceptional zeal on the part of the minister of foreign affairs of Portugal. In spite of his many duties he found time and opportunity to prepare a huge and formidable piece of work which reminds one very much of a monologue delivered by a provincial tragedian in an old-fashioned melodrama, in which the evil character is, of course, the Soviet Union. However, everything considered, Portugal seldom has the honor of appearing on the international stage, and, therefore, we can understand the desire of the minister of foreign affairs of Portugal to make all possible use of such a happy opportunity."

³¹ The Soviet Union made no direct threats to the committee that she might withdraw if her ultimatum were not accepted, nor did the newspapers publish such a threat, but a statement by the chief of the Third Western Political Division of the People's Commissariat for Foreign Affairs on October 8, 1936, contained such an intimation: "Unless the committee shows itself determined to bring about an immediate cessation of the violations of the [Non-Intervention] Agreement, the Soviet government intends to withdraw from the committee and to consider itself to be no longer under obligations to refrain from aiding Spain with military equipment. The Soviet government is not as yet prepared to make any statement with respect to what steps it will take in case it denounces the agreement. Its actions in such an event will be decided by future developments and the exigencies of the moment." United States, Department of State Archives, Dispatch from Moscow, October 11, 1936.

³² Documents of the Non-Intervention Committee, N.I.S. (36) Document no. 92, Annex A.

³³ Letter dated October 14, 1936, from the chairman of the committee to the USSR representative, Documents of the Non-Intervention Committee, N.I.S. (36) Document no. 92, Annex B. *Pravda* expressed the attitude of the Soviet Union to this new rebuff in an editorial on October 18, 1936:

"The position of the chairman of the London committee shows clearly that some states have reached the Agreement on Non-Intervention in Spanish affairs mainly to justify before public opinion their refusal to supply the legal Spanish government with the weapons needed to suppress the revolt organized by the Spanish reactionaries in agreement with international fascism. These states were ready from the beginning to overlook the continued German, Italian, and Portuguese criminal activity in their rendering assistance to the Spanish rebels. These states were only anxious to retain the fiction of noninterference. It is not surprising, therefore, that after the signing of the Agreement on Non-Intervention, the supplying of the rebels with ammunition and arms, mainly of German and Italian make, and through Portugal, not only did not desist, but on the contrary, continued to increase formidably.

* * *

"The clear and definite policy of the USSR deprives, however, the capitalist countries of the chance of continuing this game. By representing concrete demands to take practical measures against further violation of the agreement, the USSR makes the London committee face the necessity of either giving up its practice of encouraging intervention by the Fascist governments, and either truly to see to it that the agreement is not violated by any of the participants in that agreement, or openly to acknowledge that the agreement concerning noninterference and the attitude of the London committee only serve the purpose as masquerading the military assistance given to the rebels by Germany, Italy and Portugal...."

Izvestiia on October 18 in a similar article, " 'The Application' of the Agreement on Non-Intervention in Spanish Affairs," stated that the position taken by the chairman of the London committee was nothing but an encouragement of the Fascist states to further violation of the Non-Intervention Agreement which they so hypocritically signed. See also *Narod (Ispanskii) pobedit!* [*The (Spanish) People are Winning!*], (Moscow: Partizdat. TsK VKP(b), 1937), pp. 162–164.

[34] The Soviet note in part stated: "Not wishing to remain in the position of persons unwittingly assisting an unjust cause, the government of the Soviet Union sees only one way out of the situation created; to return to the Spanish government the right and facilities to purchase arms outside of Spain, which rights and facilities to [purchase] are enjoyed at present by the governments of the world; and to extend to the participants of the agreement the right to sell, or not sell, arms to Spain. In any case, the Soviet government, unwilling to bear any longer the responsibilities for the clearly unjust situation created in regard to the legitimate Spanish government and Spanish people, is compelled now to declare that in accordance with its statement on the 7th October, it cannot consider itself bound by the Agreement for Non-Intervention to any greater extent than any of the remaining participants of the Agreement." Letter dated October 23, 1936, to the chairman of the committee from the USSR representative, Documents of the Non-Intervention Committee, N.I.S. (36) Document no. 109.

The Communists outside the committee also stepped up their attack on England and France for their blind policies. A *Pravda* editorial on October 24, 1936, concluded that the work of the committee thus far "speaks eloquently that the London committee in every way avoids facing squarely the question concerning the stopping of intervention. More than that it clearly strives and even plays the role of accomplice by covering up and encouraging the perfidious activities of the foreign stranglers of the Spanish people." See also *SSSR i fashistskaia agressiia i Ispanii, sbornik dokumentov* [*The USSR and Fascist Aggression in Spain, a Collection of Documents*] (Moscow: Gos. Sotsial'no-ekonomitcheskoe Izdat., 1937), p. 9.

[35] Documents of the Non-Intervention Committee, N.I.S. (36) 8th Meeting, p. 7.

[36] There is some evidence, however, that some of the Soviet leaders were sorely tempted to withdraw from the committee: "(5) A number of foreign competent observers here are of the opinion that since his return to Moscow, Litvinov has been

striving to prevent the Kremlin from taking a step which would entirely alienate the Soviet Union from France and Great Britain and has succeeded in persuading it to adopt such an equivocal position at this time that it is free to move in either direction without altogether losing face. This opinion, in so far as I can ascertain, is based entirely upon [conjecture?]; it seems however highly reasonable." The chargé in the Soviet Union (Henderson) to the secretary of state, October 24, 1936, *Foreign Relations of the United States,* 1936, II, 542.

NOTES TO CHAPTER VI

PROPOSALS ON ENFORCEMENT: NOVEMBER AND DECEMBER, 1936

(PAGES 53–56)

[1] Documents of the Non-Intervention Committee, N.I.S. (36) 8th Meeting, p. 6.

[2] "The proceedings of the Committee have convinced the Soviet Government that at present there are no guarantees against further supply to the Rebel Generals of war material. In these circumstances the Soviet Government is of the opinion that until such guarantees are created and an effective control for the strict fulfilment of the obligations regarding non-intervention established, those Governments who consider supplying the legitimate Spanish Government as conforming to international law, international order and international justice, are morally entitled not to consider themselves more bound by the Agreement than those Governments which supply the rebels in contravention of the Agreement. Such is the meaning of the concluding part of the statement of the 23rd October.

"A different situation will only become possible from the moment when effective control over the fulfillment of the obligations for non-intervention is established on the part of all Governments participating in the Agreement. The Soviet Government has with this object made this proposal for control over Portuguese ports and is prepared to discuss the proposal of the Chairman of the Committee, Lord Plymouth, which was in the same direction, a proposal to establish, apart from this control in Portugal, also control in Spanish ports and along the Spanish frontiers. The Soviet Government raises no objection against establishing control also in the ports and on points along the frontiers not occupied by the rebels provided the consent of the legitimate Spanish Government is obtained." *Ibid.,* p. 4.

[3] It is also significant that at about this same time the Soviet representative on the committee, S. Kagan, counsellor of the Soviet embassy, was replaced by the ambassador, Jean Maisky, who had a great deal of personal charm and humor and engaged in fewer stormy exchanges with the representatives of Italy and Germany than his predecessor. For a sympathetic study *see* George Bilainkin's biography of Jean Maisky, *Maisky: Ten Years Ambassador* (London: George Allen and Unwin, 1944).

[4] David T. Cattell, *Communism and the Spanish Civil War* (Berkeley and Los Angeles: University of California Press, 1955), 98 *et seq.,* 130 *et seq.*

[5] Documents of the Non-Intervention Committee, N.I.S. (36) 10th Meeting, p. 11.

[6] *Ibid.,* 11th Meeting, p. 25.

[7] This new attitude of the Soviet Union did not, however, decrease her hostility outside the committee toward the Fascist powers or the Non-Intervention Agreement in general, which she condemned as a "farce." *See* editorials in *Pravda* (Oct. 30, Nov. 12 and 19, 1936).

[8] See page 57 ff.

[9] A memorandum by the acting state secretary of Germany dated September 22, 1936, explained the reason for the Fascist attitude: "Now, however, when the

Nationalist forces were well supplied and, on the other hand, the Madrid Government lacked war matériel, the situation had changed, and Germany and Italy now were very much interested in having the embargo strictly enforced. The attitude of the Italian representative in London, who insisted upon strict enforcement of the embargo and upon control measures, was based on these considerations." *Documents on German Foreign Policy,* D, III, Document no. 85.

[10] Italy and Germany simultaneously on November 18, 1936, recognized the Nationalist government as the legitimate government of Spain and withdrew their recognition from the Republican government.

[11] No doubt England and France were also apprehensive that the early Fascist recognition of the Nationalist government would give Germany and Italy a preferred place in rebel Spain.

[12] See *Documents on German Foreign Policy, 1918–1945,* D, III.

[13] The Soviet Union had suspected this collusion of the Fascist powers from the beginning. *See,* for example, *Pravda*'s editorial on October 26, 1936, which discussed an alleged Italian-German protocol concerning joint intervention in Spain.

[14] *Pravda* (Dec. 11, 1936). In an editorial the same day *Pravda* reviewed the Soviet policy toward the Spanish crisis, emphasizing the Soviet attitude of coöperation with England and France and also the growing intervention of the Fascists in Spain which, since their recognition of the Franco regime, had entered a new phase of sending whole military organizations.

[15] Great Britain and France also do not appear from the beginning to have hoped for success: "I do not understand that either the French or British Governments are hopeful that this *démarche* in Rome, Berlin and Moscow will be successful, but the British and French Governments are anxious for their own records that such an action should be taken especially before the meeting of the [League] Council on December 10." The ambassador in the United Kingdom (Bingham) to the acting secretary of state, December 4, 1936, *Foreign Relations of the United States, 1936,* II, 586.

[16] Yvon Delbos, foreign minister of France, called the Spanish plea to the Council "a frightful development.... It would have been better if the move had been submitted first to France for consultation since England and even Russia have advised against it." New York *Times* (Nov. 28, 1936). *See also* the ambassador in France (Bullitt) to the acting secretary of state, November 28, 1936, *and* the ambassador in the United Kingdom (Bingham) to the acting secretary of state, December 4, 1936, *Foreign Relations of the United States, 1936,* II, 578, 585.

[17] The ambassador in France (Bullitt) reported to the acting secretary of state on November 28, 1936: "He [Foreign Minister Delbos] said that Litvinov had advised the Spanish Government that he felt the League Council could do nothing effective at this moment but that he would support the position of Madrid." *Foreign Relations of the United States, 1936,* II, 578.

It was also reported by the American ambassador in France on December 8, 1936: "They [the French foreign office] understand that Litvinoff is 'furious' at the action of the Spanish Government in having brought about this meeting against his advice and that he will not attend." *Ibid.,* 595.

[18] M. Potemkin, the Soviet representative, declared: "Everyone is aware of the attitude of the Union of Soviet Socialist Republics towards the Spanish question. My Government has never regarded the aid to the legal Government of the Spanish Republic against the rebels as interference in the internal affairs of the country, as a breach of the Covenant of the League of Nations. We have always regarded the prohibition of the sale of arms to a legal government which is the victim of an aggression—particularly when the arms are supplied in virtue of contracts previously concluded—as an arbitrary and unfair measure, a measure contrary to international law.

"Nevertheless, bearing in mind certain exceptional circumstances and being anxious to do its utmost to safeguard peace, the Government of the Union of Soviet Socialist Republics felt bound to accede to the international agreement concerning non-intervention; and it has faithfully fulfilled its undertakings. . . ." 95th Session of the Council, League of Nations *Official Journal* (Jan., 1937), pp. 16–17.

NOTES TO CHAPTER VII

Foreign Volunteers and a Control Scheme: February–April, 1937

(Pages 57–70)

[1] Documents of the Non-Intervention Committee, N.I.S. (36) Document no. 177.

[2] By the end of October Germany was planning to send, in addition to the technicians and pilots already in Spain, the following German military units: one bomber group, one fighter group, one long-range reconnaissance squadron, one flight of short-range reconnaissance planes, two signal companies, two operating companies, three heavy anti-aircraft batteries, and two searchlight platoons. The foreign minister to the ambassador in Italy, October 30, 1936, *Documents on German Foreign Policy, 1918–1945*, D, III, Document no. 113. At the end of November Italy resolved to send a whole division of Black Shirts. The ambassador in Italy to the foreign ministry, November 27, 1936, *ibid.*, Document no. 130.

[3] From the evidence available it can be concluded that the Soviet personnel in Spain never reached over 5,000. For further discussion *see* David T. Cattell, *Communism and the Spanish Civil War* (Berkeley and Los Angeles: University of California Press, 1955), p. 82. For the Soviet denial of this charge, *see* Jane Degras, *Soviet Documents on Foreign Policy* (London: Oxford University Press, 1953), III, 228.

[4] For the Fascist arguments *see* the director of the legal department to the embassy in Italy, December 30, 1936, *Documents on German Foreign Policy, 1918–1945*, D, III, Document no. 175.

[5] Ambassador in Italy to the foreign ministry, December 23, 1936, *ibid.*, Document no. 161.

[6] Soviet propaganda was quick to note this delay and declared it was for the purposes of building up the Italian forces in Spain, represented by the landing of 10,000 Italian legionnaires in Cádiz on December 31 and January 2. *Mirovoe Khoziaistvo i Mirovaia Politika* (Feb., 1937), p. 124.

[7] Documents of the Non-Intervention Committee, N.I.S. (36) Document no. 220.

[8] The Soviet note declared the USSR:

"1. Agrees in principle to the extension of the Agreement to cover indirect as well as direct intervention so far as may be practicable, and;

"2. Agrees, as the first step to the extension of the agreement to cover the recruitment in, the dispatch from, or transit through the territories of the contracting parties of persons proposing to take part in the Civil War in Spain." *Ibid.*, Document no. 190. The answer of the British government was delivered on December 16, 1936, *ibid.*, Document no. 183.

[9] Five thousand Germans were reported landed at Cádiz during the end of November. New York *Times* (Dec. 2, 1936).

[10] It was reported that on December 19 Foreign Minister Anthony Eden had a conference with Joachim von Ribbentrop, the German ambassador to England, warning him of the seriousness with which the English viewed the reports of increased German forces in Spain. New York *Times* (Dec. 24, 1936). A similar conference was held by Foreign Minister Y. Delbos in Paris, *ibid.*, *and* the ambassador in France to the foreign ministry, December 24, 1936, *Documents on German Foreign Policy, 1918–1945*, D, III, Document no. 164.

¹¹ Memorandum by the foreign minister, December 31, 1936, *ibid.*, Document no. 177. *See also* the ambassador in Italy (Phillips) to the secretary of state, January 12, 1937, *Foreign Relations of the United States, 1937*, II, 227.

¹² *See* telegrams, dated December 24, 1936, addressed by the secretary of state for foreign affairs to His Majesty's ambassadors in Berlin, Rome, Lisbon, and Moscow, Documents of the Non-Intervention Committee, N.I.S. (36) Document no. 267.

¹³ *Ibid.*, Document no. 267, Annex C. Full text published in *Inprecorr*, vol. 17, no. 2 (Jan. 9, 1937), 24–25.

An editorial in *Pravda* on December 31, 1936, reviewed the Soviet attitude on this issue: "The Soviet government has determined its position in relation to the new Anglo-French proposal. This position represents a new demonstration of the unchangingly peaceful character of the foreign policies of the Soviet Union. It is perfectly clear that the agreement proposed by England and France can play a positive role only in case the conditions expressed in the statement of Comrade Litvinov are realized. Otherwise this agreement would have no greater significance than the notorious Non-Intervention Agreement which has been turned by the Fascist interventionists into a simple scrap of paper. It is to be hoped that this lesson will be taken into consideration."

¹⁴ Documents of the Non-Intervention Committee, N.I.S. (36) Document no. 267, Annex D. *Inprecorr* in an editorial concluded: "This means that if the conditions submitted by Italy and Germany are not accepted, Italy and Germany will send their troops to Spain *officially*." Vol. 17, no. 3 (Jan. 16, 1937), 44.

An editorial in *Pravda* on January 8, 1937, declared: "The German and Italian replies, which least of all speak of the desire to observe actively the agreement on nonintervention and represent an open and independent challenge to it, are primarily the result of the policies of London and Paris, policies of appeasing the aggressor." See also *Izvestiia* (Jan. 8 and 9, 1937).

¹⁵ Documents of the Non-Intervention Committee, N.I.S. (36) Document no. 267, Annex F.

¹⁶ *Ibid.*, Document no. 276, Annex C.

¹⁷ Documents of the Non-Intervention Committee, N.I.S. (36) Document no. 283, Annexes A and B. *See also* editorials in *Inprecorr*, vol. 17, no. 3 (Jan. 16, 1937), 44, and *Izvestiia* (Jan. 18, 1937).

¹⁸ These efforts were encouraged and applauded by the Soviet Union. *See* for example *Inprecorr*, vol. 17, no. 5 (Jan. 30, 1937), 87: "On the other hand, France and Britain have at last taken up a firm attitude toward Germany and Italy. Everyone remembers the explanation given by Léon Blum to the French Chamber of Deputies when the decree on the conditional banning of volunteers for Spain was passed. The French answer to Britain and the answer of the USSR were based on identical consideration, i.e., on the necessity of a rapid and effective control. In the House of Commons Mr. Anthony Eden at last defined the British attitude in strong and unequivocal terms."

¹⁹ *Pravda* (Nov. 19 and Dec. 5, 1936).

²⁰ See the feature article in *Izvestiia* (Jan. 11, 1937), p. 2, discussing the change of attitude on the part of the English intellectuals and youth in particular toward German aggression in Spain.

²¹ N. Maiorsky, "Ispaniia i vseobshchii mir" ["Spain and World Peace"], *Bolshevik*, no. 1 (1937), p. 55. Another example, *Izvestiia* (Jan. 4, 1937), in a leading article declared: "Naïve people in diplomatic quarters in France and in England hope to bind by agreements, signatures, and obligations German Fascists, who introduce into their once cultured country the cult of the bloody heathen god, Wotan, and into international life the methods of gangsters and pirates." See also *Pravda*'s editorial, "Fruits of British Politics," (Nov. 23, 1936).

[22] For example, *Izvestiia* reported in part during the first ten days of January, 1937:

January 4: 20,000 select German troops for Franco's army
4,000 Italians landing in Cádiz
6,000 more Italian troops on the way to Spain

January 7: 10,000 Italian troops reported landing in the previous two weeks in Franco Spain

January 8: 10,000 German troops fighting on the Madrid front
100 tanks sent to Spain

January 10: 300 German soldiers and 50 pilots quartered in Tangiers

[23] "... [the sinking of the *Komsomol*] is not a question of Soviet shipping nor a private affair of the Soviet Union, but ... is a matter which concerns all those whom fascism wishes to subjugate, against whom it is directing its robber plans, that is to say, in the first place, it is a matter which concerns the working people in the democratic countries." "Sinking of the *Komsomol*," *Inprecorr*, vol. 16, no. 58 (Dec. 24, 1936), 1512.

[24] An article in *Pravda* (Jan. 2, 1937), "A Joint Stock Company to Rob Spain" by L. Volynsky, reported: "As time goes on, more and more details come to light concerning the conspiracy plotted secretly by the Fascist rebels and interventionists against the Spanish people. It has become known now that side by side with the spies and the men from the Gestapo, Spain has been visited and well studied by the various 'scientific' expeditions from Germany and Italy as early as 1935."

Another example: "Victory of the Spanish people would end the threat from the Fascist sword on France from the side of the Pyrenees, would restrain bold-face aggressiveness and delay the beginning of war against France and a general war in Europe.

* * *

"The economies of the interventionists have already been strengthened significantly at the expense of the English financial magnates, although the latter have attempted to make, as the French say 'a good face through a bad game.' A large part of the copper ore and sulfur from the English Rio Tinto is being requisitioned and sent to Germany (and also Italy)." G. Dashevskii, *Fashistskaia piataia kolonna v Ispanii* [*The Fascist Fifth Column in Spain*] (Moscow: Voenizdat., 1938), pp. 94–95, 103). *See also* "The plot of the Fascist Aggressors" by N. Maiorsky, *Pravda* (Feb. 23, 1937); and *Mirovoe Khoziaistvo i Mirovaia Politika* (March, 1938), pp. 181 f. The Soviet press gave special stress to German infiltration into Morocco. For example *see* "The Germans make themselves at home in Morocco," *Izvestiia* (Jan. 3, 1937); *Izvestiia* (Jan. 10 and 13, 1937); Gabriel Péri, "The German Invasion of Morocco," *Inprecorr*, vol. 17, no. 3 (Jan. 16, 1937), 43; *and* Georges Soria, "The Background of German Penetration in Morocco," *ibid.*, no. 8 (Feb. 20, 1937), 209. Surprisingly, France was less complacent about Germans in Spanish Morocco than on the mainland of Spain and was prepared to take decisive action to prevent German penetration into this area; see *Foreign Relations of the United States, 1937*, I, 217–219.

[25] *Izvestiia* (Jan. 5, 1937). *See also* "Spain, the Western Powers and Germany," *Inprecorr*, vol. 17, no. 1 (Jan. 2, 1937), 1–2, *and* Gabriel Péri, "The 'Gentleman's Agreement,'" *ibid.*, no. 2 (Jan. 9, 1937), 23.

[26] The Communists, on the other hand, had never predicted a smooth path for the two Fascist dictators. "Although there is a community of interest on the part of the Fascist powers to uphold and secure the victory of the Fascist rebels in Spain, further development of intervention will only serve to aggravate an Italian-German clash." *Izvestiia* (Jan. 6, 1937). Thus the Soviet leaders may not have been entirely unappreciative of the British attempt to keep the dictators apart.

[27] The Soviet press followed very closely the visit of Göring to Mussolini and gave prominence to the report in the London press on January 27 that Italy and Germany had agreed to send 80,000 more troops to Spain. See *Izvestiia* (Jan. 14–28, 1937).

[28] In many ways the attitude of the French governing circles toward the USSR paralleled that of the British. Even Socialist Leon Blum was apprehensive of Russia's basic aims.

[29] "At present the only argument used and abused to justify the policy of embargo is that it is necessary in order to maintain a good understanding between France and Britain. The French press has published enthusiastic comments on Mr. Eden's speech in which he said to his constituents that Great Britain, true to the agreements she has signed, would observe her obligations of mutual assistance in respect of France if that country were victim to an unprovoked aggression. . . .

"This means, if translated into everyday language, that if France did not agree to the Hitlerisation of Spain, Britain would not respect the obligations towards France from the Locarno Pact and from the letters exchanged between Paris and London after the London conference." *Inprecorr*, vol. 16, no. 52 (Nov. 21, 1936), 1377.

[30] K. Gottwald, "For the Defense of the People and the Republic," *Communist International* (Jan., 1937), p. 13. From the very beginning the Communists had stressed the world-wide implications of the Spanish conflict and its relationship to countries like Czechoslovakia. Georgi Dimitrov, who headed the Comintern, wrote in the same vein in the *Communist International* (Dec., 1936), p. 1568: "The war undertaken by fascism against the Spanish people cannot be considered as a casual isolated act. No, this war is a link in the chain of the Fascist offensive on the international arena. No illusions must be harbored as to the war undertaken by fascism against the Spanish people being the last. Fascism is preparing to strike at democracy in France, Belgium, Czechoslovakia, and the democracy of England, Switzerland, Scandinavia, and other countries."

See also Karl Radek's article, "The Danger of War Looms Ever Nearer," *Inprecorr*, vol. 16, no. 36 (Aug. 8, 1936), 963.

[31] Positive action, however, appears to have been something the French wanted to avoid. The ambassador in France (Bullitt) to the secretary of state of the United States reported on February 15, 1937: "In conversation this morning with an official at the Foreign Office we were told that the French Government is greatly concerned over the question of foreign intervention in Spain. . . .

"This official said that France was being placed in 'an impossible situation' regarding this matter. He said that the last thing that the French Government wanted to do was to regain freedom of action and openly permit shipment of war material and passage of volunteers to Spain as Italy and Germany were now doing." *Foreign Relations of the United States, 1937*, I, 241.

[32] For details *see* Cattell, *op. cit.*, p. 82.

[33] *Documents on German Foreign Policy*, D, III, Document no. 212.

[34] Documents on the Non-Intervention Committee, N.I.S. (36) 15th Meeting, p. 9.

[35] For text of the Soviet decree *see* Degras, *op. cit.*, pp. 234–235.

[36] *Pravda* (Feb. 15, 1937). See also *Pravda* (Feb. 17, 1937), editorial by T. Karradov, and *Izvestiia*'s editorial, "Farce of Nonintervention," (Feb. 12, 1937).

[37] The German and Italian navies were assigned zones off the coast of Loyalist Spain. For the Soviet argument see *Inprecorr*, vol. 17, no. 6 (Feb. 6, 1937), 115.

[38] Documents of the Non-Intervention Committee, N.I.S. (36) Document no. 362.

[39] Gabriel Péri, correspondent for *Inprecorr*, summed up the Communist reaction: "But what is to be thought of such a resolution [prohibiting the recruitment of volunteers and establishing a control scheme for Spain] arrived at after the events

of the last two weeks, after the fall of Málaga, which was celebrated in Rome as an Italian victory." "The British Foreign Office Supports Franco," *Inprecorr*, vol. 17, no. 8 (Feb. 20, 1937), 208.

And in the next week's issue, he wrote: "... there will remain a hidden breach along the Portuguese frontier where clandestine traffic in favor of Franco will be controlled only by agents of Salazar (for the British 'supervision' can only be a farce if London continues to act as it has in the past)." No. 9 (Feb. 27, 1937), 234.

[40] *See* Documents of the Non-Intervention Committee, N.I.S. (36) Document nos. 371 and 374, 13th and 14th Meetings of the Technical Advisory Committee Number 3.

[41] *Ibid.*, Document no. 787.

[42] *Documents on German Foreign Policy, 1918–1945*, D, III, editor's note, pp. 932–933.

[43] The ambassador in France (Bullitt) reported to the secretary of state, July 2, 1937:

"... He (Chautemps) believed that the Soviet Union would not attempt to assist the Valencia Government on a great scale. The Russians were too much occupied with their own internal difficulties and Soviet Russia had come to realize that their intervention in Spain might lead to serious consequences." *Foreign Relations of the United States, 1937*, I, 348.

[44] The partial effectiveness of the control scheme was evident by the speed of the German Government in sabotaging it after it had come into operation. See pages 79–82.

NOTES TO CHAPTER VIII

OTHER ISSUES: MARCH AND APRIL, 1937

(PAGES 71–78)

[1] The Communists were very much elated over the Loyalist victory at Guadalajara for they perceived it as the beginning of the decline of fascism. D. Manuilsky expressed this view: "It is reported that the heroic struggle of the Spanish people against fascism produces a sobering effect on the Fascist governments, that Guadalajara has destroyed the warlike fervor of the German and Italian interventionists....

"It is also reported that during the past months the Fascist activities in all the capitalist countries has been on the decline, that the victory of the Spanish people has brought a severe blow to the prestige of fascism and assists a more vigorous growth of anti-Fascist activity...." *O mezhdunarodnom polozhenii, sbornik* [*Concerning the International Situation, a Collection*] (Moscow: Partizdat. TsK VKP(b), 1937), pp. 21 f.

[2] The Soviet Union had some misgivings about the French and English attitudes concerning withdrawal:

"Yet M. Yvon Delbos declared the other day in the French Senate that he was going to increase his efforts toward recalling the Loyalist volunteers. It is to be feared that France will once again take the initiative in this before any agreement is concluded or any beginning of execution is made by Italy and Germany." *Inprecorr*, vol. 17, no. 10 (March 6, 1937), 256.

[3] Documents of the Non-Intervention Committee, N.I.S. (36) Document no. 398.

[4] *See* David T. Cattell, *Communism and the Spanish Civil War* (Berkeley and Los Angeles: University of California Press, 1955), pp. 80–82.

[5] Another factor may also have been the persuasion of British Foreign Minister Anthony Eden. During the third week of March he had discussions with the interested powers to try to speed up consideration of the withdrawal of volunteers and

he may have prevailed on the USSR in the spirit of compromise to give up her position on the question of Spanish assets.

[6] George Bilainkin, *Maisky: Ten Years Ambassador* (London: George Allen and Unwin, 1944), p. 175.

[7] Joseph Davies, *Mission to Moscow* (London: Gollancz, 1944), p. 108.

[8] *Ibid.*, pp. 125 ff.

[9] Ribbentrop reported back to his government: "It seems as if Grandi was somewhat carried away by the provocation of the Soviet Ambassador." The ambassador in Great Britain to the foreign ministry, March 30, 1937, *Documents on German Foreign Policy, 1918–1945*, D, III, Document no. 239.

[10] As reported in the New York *Times* (March 25, 1937).

[11] Documents of the Non-Intervention Committee, N.I.S. (36) 19th Meeting, pp. 18–19.

[12] That the Soviet allegations of violation by Italy were not merely fabricated for propaganda purposes is clear from the German documents that repeatedly mention the sending of planes and replacement troops during this period. *See* the ambassador in Italy to the foreign ministry, April 9, 1937, *Documents on German Foreign Policy, 1918–1945*, D, III, Document no. 241; the ambassador in Spain to the foreign ministry, April 21, 1937, *ibid.*, Document no. 247.

[13] *See* the chargé in France (Wilson) to the secretary of state, March 25, 1937, *Foreign Relations of the United States, 1937*, I, 260.

[14] Documents of the Non-Intervention Committee, N.I.S. (36) Document no. 443.

[15] The Soviet press persistently sounded the alarm that the control measures "would not prevent Italy and Germany from sending new military reinforcements and armaments to General Franco." *Izvestiia* (April 12, 1937).

[16] The acting state secretary to the embassy in Great Britain, April 1, 1937, *Documents on German Foreign Policy, 1918–1945*, D, III, Document no. 240.

[17] The consul at Geneva (Gilbert) reported to the secretary of state, May 21, 1937: "I am informed as follows from confidential sources. The Spanish Government has prepared a document of presentation to the Council embodying extensive 'proofs' of German and Italian military intervention. During his recent visit to Paris Del Vayo conferred ... with the Quai d'Orsay which endeavored to persuade him to tone down his allegation." *Foreign Relations of the United States, 1937*, I, 301.

[18] Maxim Litvinov, *Against Aggression* (London: Lawrence and Wishart Ltd., 1939), pp. 81–85.

[19] The small powers of Europe in the League seemed to have been of the same mind: "... In my view however the foreign offices of the small powers will not be favorable to League action inasmuch as it might develop into a situation wherein they would be confronted with the inconsistency between their recent pronouncements of neutrality in European politics and their obligation to take a possibly partisan position under the Covenant, a situation which they have apparently preferred for the time being to leave in obscurity." The consul in Geneva (Gilbert) to the secretary of state, June 1, 1937, *Foreign Relations of the United States, 1937*, I, 316.

[20] 97th Session of the Council, League of Nations *Official Journal* (May–June, 1937), pp. 317–324.

[21] Documents of the Non-Intervention Committee, N.I.S. (36) 20th Meeting, p. 12. A Soviet *émigré* has reported that the *Komsomol* was not sunk but was scuttled by the crew to keep the arms which she carried from falling into rebel hands. *See Soviet Shipping in the Spanish Civil War*, mimeographed series no. 59 (New York: Research Program on the USSR, 1954).

[22] On December 6 the commissariat of foreign trade reported that 7 Russian ships

had been stopped; the Russian press bitterly assailed the piracy, but appeared to have let the matter drop there. *Pravda* (Dec. 6, 1936).

²³ *Izvestiia* (April 24, 1937).

²⁴ Documents of the Non-Intervention Committee, N.I.S. (36) 20th Meeting, p. 13.

²⁵ Arnold J. Toynbee, *Survey of International Affairs, 1937* (London: Oxford University Press, 1938), II, 69.

²⁶ Documents of the Non-Intervention Committee, N.I.S. (36) 21st Meeting, p. 6.

²⁷ *Ibid.*, p. 13.

NOTES TO CHAPTER IX

DEADLOCK: SUMMER, 1937

(PAGES 79–89)

¹ The Soviet Union made the same objection in respect to the bombing of the Italian naval vessel *Barletta* in the port of Palma: "It would be one thing if an attack was made on a ship which was on duty under the sea observation scheme. Majorca, as far as we know, is not within any zone allotted to the Italian Navy." Documents of the Non-Intervention Committee, N.I.S. (36) 22nd Meeting, p. 7.

² *Ibid.*, Document no. 559. The Soviet Union made a big propaganda play on this incident. *See* for example Georgi Dimitrov, "The lessons of Almeria," *The United Front* (New York: International Publishers, 1938), p. 41. This article by the head of the Comintern was reprinted many times and in many languages. *See also* Gabriel Péri, "After Almeria," *Inprecorr*, vol. 17, no. 25 (June 12, 1937), 568.

³ *Foreign Relations of the United States, 1937*, I, 318. In this connection the chargé in the Soviet Union reported to the secretary of state on June 9, 1937: "No information is available here which would indicate that the Soviet Government has directly endeavored to persuade the Spanish Government to bomb German or Italian war vessels in Nationalist waters. It seems quite possible, however, that Soviet officials in line with their general European policies did advise the Spanish Government to show stiffer opposition to Italian and German interferences and that this advice may have contributed to the Spanish decision to bomb the *Deutschland*. Regardless of whether Soviet officials may or may not have had some share of responsibility for the bombing, the Embassy is convinced from the attitude of Soviet officials and the press that the Soviet Government welcomed the incidents in the hope that they would put a stop to the temporizing policies of France and Great Britain and that it is deeply disappointed at the failure of these two powers to take a firmer stand in the matter. Both the Soviet press and the Spanish Ambassador have denied that the pilots of the planes which bombed the *Deutschland* were Soviet nationals." *Ibid.*, p. 328.

⁴ David T. Cattell, *Communism and the Spanish Civil War* (Berkeley and Los Angeles: University of California Press, 1955), chaps. x, xv.

⁵ In her note to the committee on June 8, the USSR declared: "However, while not objecting to the Non-Intervention Committee adopting measures for safeguarding naval observation vessels against incidents arising out of military activities, I have to state that negotiations regarding such measures should in my opinion, take place after discussion of the matter in the Non-Intervention Committee, and in any case with the full knowledge of all the countries represented in that Committee." Documents of the Non-Intervention Committee, N.I.S. (36) Document no. 559.

⁶ *See* for example *Pravda* (June 11, 1937), p. 5, *and* Gabriel Péri, "A New Four-Power Pact," *Inprecorr*, vol. 17, no. 26 (June 19, 1937), 587.

⁷ On June 7 *Pravda* attacked the appeasement policy of the British: "Britain is striving to coax the Fascist aggressors to return to the London committee at all

costs. The British proposals would transform the committee into a mere point of registration for the blows dealt to peace and collective security by the Fascists. Berlin and Rome may deign to return to the Non-Intervention Committee, but they stipulate for themselves the right to repeat the Almería crimes at any moment...."

[8] *See* Letter of Captain D. Euan Wallace, the acting chairman of the Non-Intervention Committee, to the Russian representative, cited in the London *Times* (June 11, 1937).

[9] Documents of the Non-Intervention Committee, N.I.S. (36) Document no. 563.

[10] *Ibid.*, Document no. 570. It is interesting to note that the Loyalist government in its answer of June 21 to the communication from the four powers on the alleged violation of the naval patrol declared: "My Government cannot but express surprise at the fact that this communication, the subject-matter of which comes fully within the application of the Non-Intervention Agreement, should be presented, not in the name of the Committee especially constituted in London to ensure the fulfillment of this agreement, but in the name of four of its members. While it is true that the note refers to questions connected with the naval control exercised by the four countries in whose name it was put forward, it is at the same time a fact that these countries act as mandatories of all the representatives on the London Committee. Besides this, the proposals made in the note would, on being put into practice, imply a fundamental modification of the control arrangements set up by the Non-Intervention Committee...." *Ibid.*, Document no. 597.

[11] For the Soviet interpretation of the following events, see *Mirovoe Khoziastvo i Mirovaia Politika* (Aug., 1937), pp. 147–149.

[12] Documents of the Non-Intervention Committee, N.I.S. (36) Document no. 571.

[13] *Pravda* (June 29, 1937).

[14] That the English were not ready for decisive action had long been recognized by many careful observers of the British scene. *See* for example the ambassador in the United Kingdom (Bingham) to the secretary of state, March 31, 1937, *Foreign Relations of the United States, 1937*, I, pp. 270–272.

The attitude of the French followed that of the British. For example the United States ambassador in France reported to the secretary of state a few weeks later on July 30, 1937: "At the close of our conversation this afternoon Delbos said to me that he believed the Committee of Non-Intervention in Spain would reach definite disagreement in the course of the next week or two and that the powers would resume liberty of action. He regarded this possibility with the utmost apprehensive feeling that it might well lead to European war." *Ibid.*, p. 367.

[15] Documents of the Non-Intervention Committee, N.I.S. (36) Document no. 592.

[16] *Ibid.*, 24th and 25th Meetings, p. 69.

[17] For the French attitude *see* the ambassador in the United Kingdom (Bingham) to the secretary of state, July 6, 1937, *Foreign Relations of the United States, 1937*, I, 355.

[18] Documents of the Non-Intervention Committee, N.I.S. (36) 24th and 25th Meetings, p. 53.

[19] *Ibid.*, Document no. 599.

[20] *Ibid.*, 27th Meeting.

[21] *See* for example *Pravda* (June 29, July 3, 7, 17, and 26, 1937).

The French beneath the surface were also very disturbed by the turn of events: "I lunched today with Delbos and Sir Eric Phipps, the British Ambassador. Delbos, somewhat to the embarrassment of Sir Eric, criticized severely the British proposal with regard to Spain. He said that he had no information that any such proposal was to be launched by the British Government. He had understood from his conversations with the British Ambassador and from Corbin's conversations in London that the British would develop some scheme which would be discussed with the

French Government and probably then would be launched by the smaller neutral states represented in the Committee on Non-Intervention in Spain. The British Government by the action it had taken had withdrawn from cooperation with France in the Spanish affair and had placed itself midway between France on the one hand and Germany and Italy on the other hand. [The] British Ambassador protested that it was not quite midway and that the dictatorships would be greatly encouraged by this act of obvious withdrawal of England from close partnership with France in the Spanish affair." The ambassador in France (Bullitt) to the secretary of state, July 15, 1937, *Foreign Relations of the United States, 1937*, I, 360.

[22] The Fascists made little attempt to hide their tactics: "We are told by the Italian Embassy that they see little possibility of arriving at a solution of the impasse in the London Non-Intervention Committee. They consider it practically impossible to work out by agreement individualistic [*sic*] or modified system of control. On the other hand they do not believe that there will be any breakdown in the negotiations which would result in the disappearance of the 'facade' of non-intervention; they feel that the discussion will drag on indefinitely; that the only real solution will be one found on the field of battle and are confident of Franco's ultimate victory." The ambassador in France (Bullitt) to the secretary of state, July 24, 1937, *Foreign Relations of the United States, 1937*, I, 365.

[23] Documents of the Non-Intervention Committee, N.I.S. (36) Document no. 626.

[24] For example *see* The London *Times* (July 27, 30, 31, and August 2, 1937); *Le Temps* (August 1 and 7, 1937); and *The Observer* (August 1, 1937).

[25] Chamberlain in direct talks with Maisky, the Soviet ambassador and representative on the committee, tried to pressure the USSR to modify its position but without success. George Bilainkin, *Maisky: Ten Years Ambassador* (London: George Allen and Unwin, 1944), p. 182.

[26] The following summary statement of Franco's diplomatic representative to Italy, García Condé, was made known to the United States ambassador in Italy who reported it to his government on April 23, 1937, and undoubtedly was also made available to the French and British governments: "The Spanish Minister confirmed that between 58,000 and 60,000 Italian troops and 18,000 Germans had in all gone to Spain and estimated that the total number of men serving in Franco's army was approximately 400,000, 65,000 of whom were raw recruits undergoing training. While additional foreign troops would be welcome, Franco now has sufficient manpower to draw from and very few soldiers are being brought from Africa. The great need, however, is for arms and ammunition and this need is being supplied by Italy. Garcia Conde [*sic*] admitting that both men and ammunition were still arriving in Spain from Italy, principally by way of Palma, then said 'I have nothing to complain about; Mussolini and Ciano continue to do more than their share.' " *Foreign Relations of the United States, 1937*, I, 288.

[27] As early as November of 1936, the West realized that the prestige of Germany and Italy was involved in Franco's victory. The ambassador in Germany (Dodd) reported to the acting secretary of state, November 19, 1936: "... Having recognized Franco as conqueror when this is yet to be proved, Mussolini and Hitler must see to it that he is successful or be associated with a failure. This a dictatorship can ill afford to do." *Foreign Relations of the United States, 1936*, II, 560–561.

[28] *Ibid.*, p. 369. On August 23, 1937, the chargé in the United Kingdom (Johnson) reported to the United States secretary of state: "... There have been a number of indications of a growing feeling in official circles, particularly since the fall of Bilbao, that it is time for Great Britain to start trimming her sails for the possibility of a Franco victory, or at least Franco in control of the greater part of Spain—and geographically the most important part of Spain from Great Britain's point of view...."

"... Franco is doubtlessly badly in need of money and since Italy and Germany have none to spare, the British Government should be able to make a satisfactory deal with Nationalist Spain in return for financial support from the City. Further-more, under ordinary circumstances Great Britain is Spain's best customer." *Ibid.*, pp. 374–375.

[29] *Ibid.*, p. 369–370. Litvinov when he was asked whether France would permit the establishment of a Fascist Franco state on the southern border of France, answered: " 'What can they do about it.' They will not do anything without England and they are doing nothing now while later it may be too late." The ambassador in the Soviet Union (Davies) to the secretary of state, July 10, 1937, *Foreign Relations of the United States: The Soviet Union 1933–1939*, p. 387.

[30] At the beginning of July, 1937, in a confidential conference with the United States ambassador, Litvinov revealed that he thought the situation "was very dark" and was not hopeful about stopping Fascist aggression: "With reference to Spain he [Litvinov] stated that conditions were bad and that the outlook was very dark due to 'cowardly conduct' of European democracies who were running away from the situation which they refused to face.... He stated that England was so intent upon preserving peace at any cost and seemed to be so anxious to appease Germany in this situation that there was danger of yielding to the Fascist states in the course of pending discussions although he could not think that England would recognize belligerent rights to Franco [*sic*]." *Ibid.*

NOTES TO CHAPTER X

THE NYON CONFERENCE: SEPTEMBER, 1937

(PAGES 90–96)

[1] The Soviet press openly accused Italy. *See* for example *Mirovoe Khoziaistvo i Mirovaia Politika* (Oct.–Nov., 1937), pp. 232 f.

[2] *See* Mussolini's speech at Palermo on August 20, 1937, cited in Arnold J. Toyn-bee, *Survey of International Affairs, 1937* (London: Oxford University Press, 1938), 11, 343.

[3] See the ambassador in Italy to the foreign ministry, August 5, 1937, *Documents on German Foreign Policy, 1918–1945*, D, III, Document no. 408.

[4] The telegram to the embassy in Italy from the German foreign minister on September 12, 1937, declared: "Please inform Ciano personally that it appears from a statement made to me by the British Ambassador here that the British have intercepted and deciphered radio messages of Italian submarines operating in the Mediterranean." *Ibid.*, Document no. 408.

[5] *Mirovoe Khoziaistvo i Mirovaia Politika* (Oct.–Nov., 1937), pp. 233–234.

[6] *See* for example *Pravda*'s editorials on August 4 and 7, 1937.

[7] *Inprecorr*, vol. 17, no. 34 (Aug. 14, 1937), 763.

[8] Archives of the Department of State, Washington, D.C.

[9] Winston Churchill, *Step by Step* (London: T. Butterworth Ltd., 1939), p. 76.

[10] Following is the full text of the note released to the press a couple of days later: "The Embassy of Soviet Russia draws the attention of the Italian government to the fact that the government of the Soviet Union has at its disposal indubitable proofs of the aggressive actions of Italian warships against merchant ships of the Soviet Union.

"These actions consist in the sinking by an Italian submarine of the Soviet ship *Timiryazev*, which while proceeding with a cargo of coal from Cardiff to Port Said was attacked on August 30, at 10 P.M., 75 miles to the east of Algiers.

"A similar attack was made upon the Soviet ship *Blagoev* while sailing from Mariupol to Sette with a cargo of pitch for asphalt, which was sunk on September 1, at 6:30 A.M., 15 miles off the island of Skyros.

"The Italian Government will undoubtedly take into consideration that these acts, committed against merchant ships sailing to open sea routes and belonging to the Soviet Union, which maintains normal diplomatic relations with Italy, are in flagrant contravention not only of the principles of humanity but of the most elementary and generally recognized precepts of international law.

"At the same time the acts of attack of Italian ships on ships sailing under the flag of the Soviet Union violate the pact concluded on September 2, 1933, between Soviet Russia and Italy providing in the first article an undertaking that each contracting party in respect of the other shall 'in no case resort either to war or to any other attack on land, sea, or air against the other side singly or jointly with one or several third Powers.'

"On the strength of the above the Embassy of the Soviet Union on behalf and upon the instruction of the Soviet government makes a most resolute protest to the Italian government.

"The government of the Soviet Union places upon the Italian government full responsibility for the political as also for the material consequences of the above-mentioned aggressive action of the Italian naval forces against merchant ships sailing under the Russian flag.

"The Embassy of the Soviet Union is authorized by its government to insist upon the resolute discontinuation of this aggression in the future and on full compensation for the damage caused by these acts to the Soviet government as well as to the seamen of the said Soviet ships or their families.

"The Embassy is authorized also to insist on exemplary punishment for the persons guilty of committing the above-mentioned aggressive actions."

[11] Louis Fischer in his book, *Men and Politics: An Autobiography* (New York: Duell, Sloan and Pearce, 1941), p. 445, reports: "A Soviet ambassador told me that the Soviet Government did not have any proof. But the Italians did not challenge Moscow to produce the evidence; Litvinov had gambled on that. He did not want Italy at Nyon. He never believed in the need of 'universality.'"

[12] The Soviet Union to the last feared France and England might come to an agreement with Italy. An editorial in *Pravda* on September 7, showed Moscow's anxiety: "Even now certain bourgeois democratic countries are unwilling to decide on any sort of resolute measures to curb these Fascist pirates."

[13] Louis Fischer, *op. cit.*, p. 447, gives another explanation for the Nyon Conference: "The national and imperial interests of France and England were threatened in Spain. In the summer of 1937, Franco had conquered the Basque coast of Spain and driven the Loyalists from Bilbao and Santander. Now the Republic could get arms from Russia only via the Mediterranean. If Mussolini cut that route, the Loyalist would be finished. That explains Nyon. France and England wished to see Russia continue her aid to Spain.

"But they were not prepared to give direct aid themselves. They did not mind a prolongation of the war at the expense of Germany and Italy and of Russia. But they would not send arms themselves."

[14] *See* extracts from Litvinov's speech at the opening session of the Nyon Conference, September 10, 1937, Jane Degras, *Soviet Documents on Foreign Policy* (London: Oxford University Press, 1953), III, 252–253.

[15] The Soviet note accepting the Anglo-French invitation alluded to the fact that the Spanish Republican government was a Mediterranean power and an especially interested party, and, therefore, should be invited. This note was published in *Pravda* (Sept. 8, 1937). See also *Inprecorr*, vol. 17, no. 38 (Sept. 11, 1937), 851.

[16] "Speeches of Comrade Litvinov at the Nyon Conference," *ibid.*, no. 40 (Sept. 18, 1937), 892.

[17] Chargé d'affaires in Great Britain to the foreign ministry, *Documents on German Foreign Policy, 1918–1945*, D, III, Document no. 413.

[18] The Nyon Agreement stated in this regard: "Whereas without in any way admitting the right of either party to the conflict in Spain to exercise belligerent rights or to interfere with merchant ships on the high seas even if the laws of warfare at sea are observed...." For the full text *see* Norman J Padelford, *International Law and Diplomacy in the Spanish Civil Strife* (New York: Macmillan, 1939), Appendix IX.

[19] *See* the foreign policy editorials in *Pravda* and *Izvestiia* for September 12, 1937. *See also* Gabriel Péri, "The Nyon Agreement," *Inprecorr*, vol. 17, no. 40 (Sept. 18, 1937), 889 f.

[20] "Speeches of Comrade Litvinov at the Nyon Conference," *ibid.*, p. 892.

[21] League of Nations *Official Journal*, Supplement 169, p. 79.

NOTES TO CHAPTER XI

NEW EFFORTS AT A COMPROMISE: FALL, 1937

(PAGES 97–110)

[1] 98th Session of the Council, League of Nations *Official Journal* (Dec., 1937), p. 919.

[2] *Ibid.*, pp. 944–945.

[3] Mexico also spoke openly in favor of the Spanish government.

[4] Maxim Litvinov, *Against Aggression* (London: Lawrence and Wishart Ltd., 1939), p. 89.

[5] League of Nations *Verbatim Record of the 18th Ordinary Session of the Assembly* (Oct. 2, 1937), p. 2.

[6] *Ibid.*, p. 2.

[7] *Pravda* (Oct. 2, 1937).

[8] *See* for example *Pravda's* editorials: "Results of the Plenum of the League of Nations," (Oct. 7, 1937), *and* "The End of Resistance by the League of Nations," (Dec. 27, 1937).

[9] David T. Cattell, *Communism and the Spanish Civil War* (Berkeley and Los Angeles: University of California Press, 1955), p. 79.

[10] Cited in *Ciano's Diplomatic Papers* (London: Odhams Press Ltd., 1948), p. 137.

[11] Documents of the Non-Intervention Committee, N.I.S. (36) Document no. 643.

[12] The Soviet Union regretted this bilateral action by the two powers in ending the sea control: "However, it is doubtful whether the abolition of the sea control, although it has a very limited significance, at a moment when Fascist intervention in Spain is strengthening, can be considered correct from the point of view of the interest of collective security." *Mirovoe Khoziaistvo i Mirovaia Politika* (Oct.–Nov., 1937), p. 236.

[13] Documents of the Non-Intervention Committee, N.I.S. (36) Document no. 668.

[14] *Ibid.*, Document no. 691.

[15] Prime Minister Chamberlain during this period was making a special effort to restore good relations with Italy. At the Conservative party conference in October, 1937, Lord Plymouth expressed this desideratum: "We are extremely desirous of returning to the good relationship which we used to enjoy with Italy before the Abyssinian war." The London *Times* (Oct. 8, 1937).

British attempts to improve relations with Mussolini can also be seen from Ciano's report of a conversation with the British ambassador in Rome, October 2, 1937: "The Ambassador, Sir Eric Drummond, who remained alone with me after the departure of the French Chargé d'Affaires, told me that during his absence from Rome he had seen with deep regret the progressive deterioration in Anglo-Italian relations which last summer had seemed to be moving towards a favorable solution." *Ciano's Diplomatic Papers*, p. 137.

[16] *See* page 99.

[17] See *Pravda* (Oct. 9, 1937). That such rumors were based on fact can be seen in the report of the German ambassador in Rome to his foreign ministry on October 19, 1937, stating that Mussolini had told the ambassador he was sending another division to Spain on Franco's request. *Documents on German Foreign Policy, 1918–1945*, D, III, Document no. 444.

[18] Even Leon Blum, the initiator of the Non-Intervention Agreement, admitted this freely in a speech on August 1, 1938: "In the Spanish affair for more than a year it has been London which has assumed the initiative, it is the position of London which has, in the final analysis, determined or carried along the positions of Paris." Leon Blum, *L'histoire jugera* (Paris: Éditions Diderot, 1954), pp. 175 f.

[19] See *Pravda* (Oct. 18, 1937).

[20] *See* for example *Pravda's* editorials on October 9 and 11, 1937.

[21] Stenographic notes of the 64th meeting of the chairman's subcommittee, October 16, 1937, Documents of the Non-Intervention Committee, N.I.S. (36) Document no. 680.

[22] The French government for her part threatened to reopen her Pyrenean border if immediate action were not taken by the Non-Intervention Committee at its forthcoming meeting. Foreign Minister Anthony Eden declared in support of France that Britain would not raise any objections if France would take such measures as she judged necessary. The Soviet Union applauded this move as far as it went, but criticized Eden for not giving the British government's unequivocal support to the opening of the French-Spanish border. See *Inprecorr*, vol. 17, no. 45 (Oct. 23, 1937), 1011, 1013.

[23] Stenographic notes of the 64th meeting of the chairman's subcommittee, October 16, 1937, Documents of the Non-Intervention Committee, N.I.S. (36) Document no. 680, p. 4. *See also* the speech of Anthony Eden on October 15, 1937, in his *Foreign Affairs* (London: Faber and Faber, 1939), pp. 219 ff.

[24] *See* page 83.

[25] James W. Gantenbein, *Documentary Background of World War II, 1931–1941* (New York: Columbia University Press, 1949), p. 469.

[26] The chargé in the United Kingdom (Johnson) to the secretary of state, October 13, 1937, *Foreign Relations of the United States, 1937*, I, 418.

[27] *See* the ambassador in France (Bullitt) to the secretary of state, October 23, 1937, *ibid.*, p. 434.

[28] The German foreign minister's report to the German embassy in Great Britain on October 25, 1937, instructed the German ambassador as follows: "We are not interested in having the non-intervention policy as carried on in the London Committee fail in the near future. We are not at present seeking a test of how Britain and especially France would act in case of the failure of this policy. On the contrary, a further gain of time will probably favor Franco's military fortunes and create a new situation which would also be advantageous for us in the Non-Intervention Committee." *Documents on German Foreign Policy, 1918–1945*, D, III, Document no. 456.

[29] Although at the time Mussolini and Hitler appeared to be very intimate and in complete agreement as to their aims in respect to Spain, German documents present some indication that whereas Mussolini was in favor of a quick victory,

Hitler was not averse to seeing the war last for another three years. Colonel Hossbach's notes on a meeting with the *Führer* in the Reich Chancellery on November 5, 1937, state:

"Following recent experiences in the course of events of the war in Spain the Führer does not see an early end to hostilities there. Taking into consideration the time required for past offensives by Franco; ... a further three years duration of war is within the bounds of possibility; on the other hand, from the German point of view, a 100 per cent victory by Franco is not desirable; we are more interested in a continuation of the war and preservation of the tensions in the Mediterranean. Should Franco be in sole possession of the Spanish peninsula, it would mean the end of Italian intervention and of the presence of Italy in the Balearic Isles. As our interests are directed towards continuing the war in Spain, it must be the task of our future policy to strengthen Italy in her fight to hold on to the Balearic Isles. However, a solidification of Italian positions in the Balearic Isles cannot be tolerated either by France and England and would lead to a war by France and England against Italy, in which case Spain, if entirely in White (that is, Franco's) hands, could participate on the side of Italy's enemies." International Military Tribunal, *The Trial of the Major Criminals before the International Military Tribunal* (Nuremberg: [1947], II, 271).

[80] Documents of the Non-Intervention Committee, N.I.S. (36) Document no. 682, p. 5, chairman's subcommittee meeting, October 19, 1937.

[81] *See* for example Anthony Eden's critical remarks concerning the Soviet Union in the debate in the House of Commons on November 1, 1937, in Eden, *op. cit.*, pp. 229–245.

[82] Documents of the Non-Intervention Committee, N.I.S. (36) Document no. 667.

[83] George Bilainkin in his biography of Maisky, *Maisky: Ten Years Ambassador* (London: George Allen and Unwin, 1944), pp. 183–184, reports that in private conversations with Anthony Eden, Maisky made still another concession: "Russia was prepared, in advance, to agree to accept the figures of the foreign auxiliaries (that was the current euphemism) in Spain as reported by the investigating commissions."

[84] The ambassador in the United Kingdom (Bingham) to the secretary of state, October 26, 1937, *Foreign Relations of the United States, 1937*, I, 436.

[85] On November 9, 1937, Ambassador Davies reported to the secretary of state: "... he [Litvinov] stated that the French and British Ambassadors had conferred with him here [Moscow] and had strongly urged that the Soviet Government should change its position on this subject and 'go along with them.' Both France and England had urgently pressed upon his government that it should cooperate in this situation, as to do otherwise would place the Soviet Union before the world as a nation that was blocking the possibility of peace and that such action would necessarily 'isolate the Soviet Union.' His reply to them, he said, was that it would be better to be isolated and to be right than to be wrong in good company and foolish as well. He then went on to add that the Soviet Union was definitely prepared to be 'isolated' and was quite prepared for this contingency." Joseph E. Davis, *Mission to Moscow* (London: Gollancz, 1942), p. 243.

[86] *See* page 86.

[87] "At the moment when the British National government had taken its latest and greatest step toward the complete betrayal of the Spanish Republic and the world democracy and peace, by announcing that it will exchange consular 'agents' with General Franco—thus granting him *de facto* recognition, what ever the Government spokesmen may say to the contrary—the British Labour movement launches its first nation-wide *campaign to aid the Spanish people*." Richard Goodman, "British Labour in Action for the Spanish Republic," *Inprecorr*, vol. 17, no. 50 (Nov. 20, 1937),

1219. Perhaps even more encouraging was the criticism expressed by the minority in the Conservative party led by Winston Churchill against appeasing Italy, as reported in detail in *Pravda* (Oct. 16, 1937).

[38] Documents of the Non-Intervention Committee, N.I.S. (36) Document no. 702.

[39] In working out the details of the plan the main problem was determining the meaning of "substantial withdrawal" in respect to the recognition of belligerency. However, during December the chairman's subcommittee after lengthy discussions was able to contour the terms of reference for the two commissions directed to go to Spain for the purpose of estimating the number of volunteers and supervising the withdrawal, though the composition of the commissions was still undecided.

[40] The Burgos government replied on November 20 and the Loyalist government on December 1.

[41] There were several issues in dispute during the January, 1938, negotiations. The biggest problem was to secure agreement on what was meant by a substantial number. Franco had suggested 3,000 from both sides, whereas the Soviet Union suggested a figure of about 12,000 for the side with the least and a proportionately higher figure for the side with the most foreign combatants. The Soviet Union claimed that only 12,000 foreign volunteers were on the Loyalist side. If this were true, it would have meant the withdrawal of practically all foreign troops before belligerency would be granted. There was also the question of when frontier control would be reinstituted—before the commissions went to Spain to start their counting or just before the actual withdrawal began. The former was supported by Germany and Italy and the latter by France and Russia. Another issue was whether or not the troops should be removed by categories. The Soviet Union felt they should be withdrawn by categories because on the Loyalist side most of the troops were combat troops, whereas on the rebel side an effective foreign combat force could remain with the rebels until the last, should the wounded and service troops be removed first. The question of observers in Spanish ports also posed a problem: how to devise a system that was adequate but still acceptable to the two Spanish factions. The Soviet Union felt the only adequate method of control was to resume the sea patrol, which did not depend on the Spanish parties for support. The Soviet position on this was weak since the report of the Non-Intervention Board proved almost conclusively its previous failure. See page 101. Finally came the matter of financing. The Soviet Union in October had discontinued her contributions to the control scheme whose only part still in operation was the system of observers on board ships traveling to Spain. The Soviets saw no value in continuing only one element of the control scheme, because the success of control depended on the functioning of the frontier, naval, and observer schemes as an integral whole. Germany and Italy in retaliation had also stopped payment, and gradually several other states began to fall into arrears.

[42] The ambassador in Spain to the foreign ministry, January 13, 1938, and memorandum by the head of Political Division IIIa, January 15, 1938, *Documents on German Foreign Policy, 1918–1945*, D, III, Documents nos. 501 and 502; *and* the chargé in France (Wilson) to the secretary of state, March 16, 1938, *Foreign Relations of the United States, 1938*, I, 162–163.

[43] The Communist press had become increasingly bitter in its attacks on the British government for its abandonment of collective security and its "cooperation with the aggressors" in Spain. *See* for example the foreign policy editorials in *Inprecorr*, vol. 18, no. 3 (Jan. 22, 1938), 43, and *ibid.*, no. 6 (Feb. 12, 1938), 102.

[44] However, there were indications that, at least until Georges Bonnet became minister of foreign affairs in April, relations between France and Great Britain were deteriorating because of their different views on the danger of the Fascist role in Spain. *See* for example the chargé in France (Wilson) to the secretary of state,

March 16, 1938, *Foreign Relations of the United States, 1938*, I, 162–163, *and* the ambassador in Spain (Bowers) to the secretary of state, March 20, 1938, *ibid.*, p. 164.

⁴⁵ The chargé in France (Wilson) reported to the secretary of state, October 16, 1937: "Léger [of the French Foreign Office] said that the sole desire of the French Government was that the Spanish conflict should be settled by the Spaniards themselves, and that while it would undoubtedly be preferable for France to have a government on the other side of the Pyrenees which was inspired by republican principles rather than a government in debt to Fascist Italy, nevertheless, France was willing to take her chances being able to deal with Franco if he should win the civil war. It was the continued occupation of Spanish territory by Italian Government forces which the French Government could no longer permit." *Ibid.*, 1937, I, p. 421.

⁴⁶ The chargé in France (Wilson) reported to the secretary of state, April 15, 1938: "We learn from Communist leaders who are usually reliably informed in this matter that for several weeks substantial quantities of airplanes and medium caliber guns have been coming from Russia, landed at Bordeaux and transported overland to Spain. The guns our informants think are obsolete but still very useful for fighting in Spain. They say that Paul-Boncour permitted transit through France and that Bonnet has intimated to them that while continuing nonintervention as a policy he will not interfere with this traffic." *Ibid.*, 1938, I, p. 177. *See also* the ambassador in the United Kingdom (Kennedy) to the secretary of state, May 9, 1938, *ibid.*, p. 191.

⁴⁷ The chargé in the United Kingdom (Johnson) to the secretary of state, February 5, 1938, *ibid.*, p. 158.

NOTES TO CHAPTER XII

APPEASEMENT: 1938

(PAGES 111–122)

¹ For a discussion of these negotiations *see* P. A. M. van der Esch, *Prelude to War* (The Hague: Martinus Nijhoff, 1951), pp. 139 ff.; Arnold J. Toynbee, *Survey of International Affairs, 1938* (London: Oxford University Press), I, 137 ff.; and *Ciano's Diplomatic Papers* (London: Odhams Press Ltd., 1948), pp. 157 ff.

² *Ibid.*, pp. 161–162.

³ See *ibid.*, p. 172.

⁴ Anthony Eden, *Foreign Affairs* (London: Faber and Faber, 1939), pp. 260–263, speech on resignation, February 21, 1938.

⁵ Sir Samuel Hoare who was closely associated with Chamberlain and his foreign policy explained their differences with Eden: "I would say that I was more inclined than he [Eden] to move step by step in the international field, and more ready to negotiate with the dictators until we were militarily stronger." Viscount Templewood, *Nine Troubled Years* (London: Collins, 1954), p. 256. Another strong Chamberlain supporter analyzed the break in such a manner: "Chamberlain's is the 'four dimensional' attitude which recognizes the element of 'time' in life, realises that it is in the nature of events to flow and seeks to canalize them towards a desirable result rather than to fix them in terms of a preconceived correctness. Eden's is the exact opposite." Duncan Keith-Shaw, *Prime Minister Neville Chamberlain* (London: Wells Gardner, Durton and Co., Ltd., 1939), p. 83.

For the Communist reaction *see* Richard Goodman, "Chamberlain Capitulates to the Fascists," *Inprecorr*, vol. 18, no. 8 (Feb. 26, 1938), 145–146. The author explained the resignation as follows:

"At this point, it became known that both Italy and Germany had told London that they would consent to negotiations being opened only if Eden were dismissed. The issue therefore became a direct one: 'Either Eden and no negotiations or negotiations and no Eden.'

* * *

"The seriousness of the position cannot be over-estimated. We must say, without the slightest exaggeration, that Chamberlain has given the Fascists the signal to attack wherever and whenever they wish."

[6] *Ciano's Diplomatic Papers*, p. 196.

[7] Cited in Winston S. Churchill, *The Second World War* (Boston: Houghton Mifflin Co., 1948), I, 283–284.

[8] *See* for example *Ciano's Diplomatic Papers*, p. 246.

[9] *Ibid.*, p. 180.

[10] Mussolini confirmed the unbridgeable gap in the Franco-Italian negotiations in a speech at Genoa on May 15: "I do not know whether we shall reach an agreement because, in a matter of extreme actuality, that is the war in Spain, we are on opposite sides of the barricades." Cited in Toynbee, *op. cit.*, p. 155.

[11] "From the Anglo-Italian Negotiations to 'a Four [Power] Pact,' " *Pravda* (Feb. 26, 1938).

[12] For the Soviet analysis of the "Clivedon set" *see* " 'Klaivdenskie Krugi' Britanii" ["Britain's 'Clivedon set' "], *Mirovoe Khoziaistvo i Mirovaia Politika* (March, 1938), pp. 85–91.

[13] R. Page Arnot, "Chamberlain Kowtows to Fascist Aggressors," *Communist International* (April, 1938), pp. 400, 402–403. *Pravda*'s editorial on March 25, 1938, sang a similar tune about betrayal: "The debauchery of the Fascist aggressions—this is the characteristic feature of the contemporary international scene. . . .

"It is not necessary to be especially clear-sighted to understand the meaning of the policies of Chamberlain. He puts his stake on the victory of Franco and the strangling of Republican Spain. There has appeared in the English press and no one refutes the information that between the English government and Franco there exists in force some kind of agreement in which the British government is bound to reserve for the rebels in the event of their victory a loan for the 'reconstruction' of Spain on the condition that Franco separate himself from his Italo-German patronage."

The Soviet Union was only a little more hopeful in respect to the policy being pursued by the French:

"M. Delbos, Foreign Minister of France, declared that France was determined to adhere loyally to the Franco-Soviet pact. He said that French diplomacy would resist the sabotage practiced against the League of Nations. What he said about Austria seems to indicate that in spite of the attempt to stifle French initiative with regard to Austria, France will not fail to pursue a policy that will prevent the establishment of a hegemony in the Danube Valley. In this connection the Foreign Minister made a comparatively satisfactory statement about the fidelity of France to the Franco-Czechoslovak pact and the necessity of strengthening and amplifying it.

"But he went no further than that. He still kept to the policy of non-intervention in Spain, and in substance repudiated the foreign policy of the People's Front which the Communists defended from the rostrum of the Chamber. A deplorable attitude to take at a time when France ought to show more than ever that she is not going to yield to the Fascist bloc." *Inprecorr*, vol. 18, no. 19 (March 5, 1938), 172.

[14] *Pravda* (April 18, 1938). In all the May Day resolutions of 1938 discussing the international scene there was an attack on "English conservatives and French re-

actionaries [who] make agreements with the Fascist aggressors to strangle the Spanish people." Georgi Dimitrov, "A Pledge of Victory for the International Proletariat," *Pravda* (May 1, 1938). See also *Pravda*'s editorials for March 24, 26, and 27, 1937, *and* Gabriel Péri, "From the Anglo-Italian Agreement to a Four-Power Pact," *Inprecorr*, vol. 18, no. 21 (April 23, 1938), 462–463.

[15] Cited in Viscount K. G. Halifax, *Speeches on Foreign Policy (1934–1939)* (London: Oxford University Press, 1940), p. 165.

[16] See page 124 ff.

[17] For example the German ambassador to the Soviet Union reported on June 20, 1938, as follows: "From ... press statements one gets the impression that the Soviets believe an understanding between the Falangist and parts of the Red Spanish side is possible. This is confirmed to a certain extent by Litvinov's statements to the French Counselor of the Embassy here, Payart, who recently returned to Moscow after being assigned to Valencia for over a year. Litvinov supposedly said that the Soviet Government would be prepared to withdraw from Spain under the proviso, 'L'Espagne por les Espagnols.' Litvinov intimated thereby that such an understanding between the two Spanish combatants was an acceptable compromise, since it would permit the Soviet Union to liquidate its Spanish adventure." *Documents on German Foreign Policy*, D, III, Document no. 615.

[18] Mussolini appears to have misunderstood the British demand that Italy remove her troops from Spain as a condition for the coming into force of the Anglo-Italian accord, or he was overconfident that Chamberlain would make further concessions. In the middle of June, 1938, Mussolini suggested the time had come to activate the agreement even though the withdrawal plan was still not finally approved and even though he had not on his own withdrawn even a token contingent of his troops. The British rejected the proposal, especially as British ships were being frequently bombed by Italian planes in Spanish waters. In the long run, however, Mussolini's assumptions did prove correct.

[19] *Documents on German Foreign Policy*, D, III, Document no. 788.

[20] The German state secretary to the embassy in Great Britain, April 7, 1938: "Since the development of the military situation in Spain permits the expectation of a speedy final victory by Franco and since the entry into force of the British plan regarding the combing-out of volunteers need therefore no longer be reckoned with, we can permit our stand on special questions to be dictated purely by considerations of tactical policy...." *Ibid.*, Document no. 563.

[21] The ambassador in the United Kingdom (Kennedy) reported to the secretary of state, May 9, 1938: "In connection with question (1) above [concerning the principal difficulties in carrying out the plan for the withdrawal of volunteers] the [British] Foreign Office informed me in strict confidence that the French have made actually more difficulties than anyone else." *Foreign Relations of the United States, 1938*, I, 190.

[22] Report dated May 9, 1938, *Foreign Relations of the United States, 1938*, I, 192. It was rumored that the French Cabinet, after the Spanish premier had made a special trip to Paris in order to plea for French help to save Catalonia from the Nationalists, seriously considered the possibility and risk of direct intervention against Franco. Toynbee, *op. cit.*, p. 314.

[23] The report of the Board of Non-Intervention itself gave some creditability to the Soviet contention. From its intelligence reports from insurance companies and shipping agencies, it declared that between April 20, 1937, and April 19, 1938, 111 ships which should have taken on observers failed to do so. Documents of the Non-Intervention Committee, N.I.S. (26) Document no. 787.

[24] An editorial on the French reversal in *Communist International* followed the usual Soviet line at this time of putting the blame on the British: "And the re-

actionary British circles have ... exerted constant pressure upon the French government in order to make it trail behind it. The aims of these circles are plain; they want to weaken democratic France in order to be able to dominate Europe. And so we see how the French government, under the twofold pressure of reactionary forces—the British Conservatives and the reactionary pro-Fascist circles in France— is supporting the policy of blockading Republican Spain, which for France is really a policy of suicide." Rosa Michel, "Two Years of the Spanish People's Heroic Struggle," *Communist International* (June, 1938), p. 533. *Izvestiia* on May 4, 1938, declared, "While, in this way, French diplomacy adapts its policy to England, while England adapts itself to the demands of Fascist aggression, Mussolini and Hitler strengthen their intervention in Spain and organize in Italy a demonstration of military power for the 'Rome-Berlin Axis.'"

[25] The Communists claimed that the reimposition of control on the Franco-Spanish border was designed to "end the war quickly" for the Fascists. *Inprecorr*, vol. 18, no. 23 (May 7, 1938), 501–502. *Pravda* on May 7, 1938, commented:

"Not only both sides [England and France] agree concerning the continuation of the scandalous policy of 'nonintervention,' they also decided to restore control on the Franco-Spanish border. Restoration of control is to take place immediately, even before the beginning of the evacuation of Italian-German troops from Spanish territory. Formally control is restored conditionally for a period of one month; if at the expiration of this period the experts dispatched to Spain do not reach results in determining the number of troops, which are subject to evacuation, the control can be again stopped. But at the expiration of the month period in the presence of the desire, anything can be found as an excuse for the further continuation of the control. And even a month has now an enormous significance for the further development of military activities."

[26] Gabriel Péri wrote that the unilateral closing of the Spanish-French frontier lost for the democracies all their bargaining power with Italy. "Two Years of Fascist Intervention in Spain," *World News and Views* [formerly *Inprecorr*], vol. 18, no. 35 (July 16, 1938), 825.

The Soviet press went so far as to interpret the unilateral closing of the Franco-Spanish border as an invitation to the Fascists to sabotage the withdrawal agreement:

"In 1938 especially after the beginning of the offensive of the interventionists on the Aragon Front (March, 1938), there took place in the policies of England and France a change to the side of open capitulation before the aggressors. This was clearly reflected in two events: [1] in the fateful agreement concerning the so-called solution on the evacuation of 'volunteers' (July, 1938) and in the unilateral closing by France of the Franco-Spanish border (June, 1938) which determined in advance the disinterest of the Fascist countries in the realization of the signed agreement. [2] Convinced of the nearness of the victory of General Franco, the British government sought in April, 1938, to conclude with Italy an agreement in which she calculates to guarantee her interests in Spain and in the Mediterranean Sea apparently in exchange for economic aid." G. Dashevskii, "Fashistskaia agressiia v Ispanii" ["Fascist Aggression in Spain"], *Mirovoe Khoziaistvo i Mirovaia Politika* (Nov., 1938), p. 41.

[27] Documents of the Non-Intervention Committee, N.I.S. (36) Document no. 744. *See also* the editorial "Under the Screen of 'Non-Intervention,'" *Pravda* (May 30, 1938).

[28] Lord Plymouth, the chairman of the Non-Intervention Committee, in the name of the other delegates at the end of May sent an urgent message to the Soviet government to accept the compromise in the name of unanimity. The ambassador in the United Kingdom (Kennedy) to the secretary of state, May 27, 1938, *Foreign Relations of the United States, 1938*, I, 199.

²⁹ Documents of the Non-Intervention Committee, N.I.S. (36) Document no. 758.

³⁰ Speech by Maxim Litvinov at an election meeting in Leningrad, June 23, 1938, cited in Jane Degras, *Soviet Documents on Foreign Policy* (London: Oxford University Press, 1953), III, 289.

³¹ Toynbee, *op. cit.*, p. 375. For a general discussion of the British attitude see *ibid.*, pp. 368 ff. For the Soviet reaction see *Izvestiia*'s editorial by Mikh. Osipov on July 3, 1938, and *Pravda*'s editorials on June 28 and 29, 1938.

³² For earlier comments along this same line by Litvinov, *see* pages 73, 129.

³³ *See* for example the May Day resolutions for 1938 and the special edition of *Inprecorr* on Spain, vol. 18, no. 24 (May 17, 1938).

³⁴ *See* page 117.

³⁵ See also *Izvestiia*'s editorial "The next step of 'non-intervention,'" by E. Aleksandrov (July 11, 1938).

The Soviet press at the same time continued to accuse Chamberlain of being directly in league with the Fascist states. *See* for example the editorial in *Izvestiia* (July 16, 1938), which charged that Chamberlain was as much responsible as Mussolini for the renewed attacks on the Spanish people and that he was becoming more and more openly involved with Mussolini's aggressive activities.

³⁶ The Spanish government in desperation was also discussing the possibility of bombarding Italian cities in retaliation for bombardment of Spanish cities by Italian planes, hoping in this way to incite England and France to action. "The British and French Governments ... expressed the opinion to the Spanish Government that in case the threat should be carried out the Italian Government would attack the Spanish Government at once with overwhelming forces and ... indicated that neither the French nor the British Governments would intervene to save the Spanish Government from destruction." The ambassador in France (Bullitt) to the secretary of state, June 26, 1938, *Foreign Relations of the United States, 1938*, I, 220.

³⁷ 101st Session of the Council, League of Nations *Official Journal* (May–June, 1938), pp. 330–331.

³⁸ Editorial by E. Aleksandrov in *Izvestiia* (May 17, 1938). *Pravda*'s editorial on May 17, 1938, by G. Anbor reviewed the session in the same light: "The discussion that was held in the session on the Chinese and in particular on the Spanish question show that the path of liquidating the League of Nations does not correspond to the interests of many states, genuinely interested in curbing the aggressors, in defending collective security. Quite characteristic of the present situation in the League of Nations is the fact that besides France the English government succeeded in receiving on the Spanish question the support of only two Fascist governments— Poland and Rumania. The majority of the members of the Council did not support the position of the English government."

NOTES TO CHAPTER XIII

THE FORGOTTEN CRISIS

(PAGES 123–132)

¹ The Loyalist answer was actually received on August 2, although the note was dated July 26. The Loyalists accepted the plan but asked several questions and requested some changes such as empowering the two commissions, which were to be sent to Spain, to investigate for themselves the veracity of the figures and estimates given them by the Loyalist and Nationalist authorities.

² See *Documents on German Foreign Policy, 1918–1945*, D, III, Document nos. 638, 641, 644–646, 649–650.

[3] Documents of the Non-Intervention Committee, N.I.S. (36) Document no. 778.

[4] Statement cited in *Journal de Moscou* (Sept. 13, 1938).

[5] *See* Hemming's report dated November 17, 1938, Documents of the Non-Intervention Committee, N.I.S. (36) Document no. 789. The Communist press reports on Hemming's visit were critical and fearful that it was being used to make new concessions to Franco.

[6] "In the summer of 1938 the deliberations of the committee slowed down imperceptibly towards a complete stop." Herbert von Dirksen, *Moscow, Tokyo, London* (London: Hutchinson and Co. Ltd., 1951), p. 212.

[7] The Communists still publicly refused to admit the inevitable victory of the Nationalists in Spain. *Izvestiia*, in an editorial on August 8, 1938, stressed the difficulties Italy was encountering in Spain—1,850 Italians killed or wounded in the ten days from July 14 through 23, 1938—and pronounced that the Loyalist cause was not lost. Even in January, 1939, the *Communist International* declared "the [Spanish] republic has gained time in which to shift the balance of forces to its own advantage. The republican government has succeeded in creating a strong, unified republican people's army, which is capable of repulsing the attacks of the enemy and even of carrying out brilliant offensive operations such as that on the Ebro...." The Communists, however, did not overlook the growing forces of appeasement. "It would nevertheless be a great mistake to shut one's eyes to the fact that since the shameful Munich agreement the danger that threatens the independence of the Spanish republic has very greatly increased." Antonio R. Jimenez, "Two and One-Half Years of War for the Independence of Spain," *Communist International* (Jan., 1939), pp. 71–72.

[8] This was probably not the only factor motivating the Loyalists to take this action. *See* David T. Cattell, *Communism and the Spanish Civil War* (Berkeley and Los Angeles, 1955), pp. 203–204, for further discussion.

[9] League of Nations *Official Journal* (Feb., 1939), p. 139.

[10] *See* resolution adopted by the Assembly, September 30, 1938, cited in Normal J. Padelford, *International Law and Diplomacy in the Spanish Civil Strife* (New York: Macmillan, 1939), p. 633.

[11] League of Nations *Official Journal* (Feb., 1939), p. 126.

[12] *Ibid.*, p. 61.

[13] *See* Kol'tsov, "The Farcical 'Evacuation' of Italians from Spain," *Pravda* (Nov. 12, 1938). The author reviews reports of the previous few months concerning new Italian forces being sent to Spain. *See also* "The Umbrella Policy," *Izvestiia* (Dec. 22, 1938).

[14] *See* Secretary Hemming's report, Documents of the Non-Intervention Committee, N.I.S. (36) Document no. 789.

[15] Foreign ministry to the German embassies in Europe, October 12, 1938, *Documents on German Foreign Policy, 1918–1945*, D, III, Document no. 678. In January, 1939, there still remained 20,000–25,000 troops. E. L. Woodward and Rohan Butler, eds., *Documents on British Foreign Policy 1919–1939*, 3d series, vol. III (London: His Majesty's Stationery Office, 1950), p. 523.

[16] Ehrenburg in an editorial in *Izvestiia* on September 29, 1938, reviewed the mass of evidence, most of it freely admitted by the Germans and Italians.

[17] The Russians looked upon the events in Spain and Czechoslovakia as "part of the general Fascist plan for aggression." *See* for example "The Forces of War and the Force of Peace," *Communist International* (Nov., 1937), pp. 783–784; *Izvestiia*, (July 3, 1938); *and* Albert Duval, "In Unity Lies the Strength of the Spanish People," *Communist International* (Aug., 1938), p. 767.

[18] "Mr. Chamberlain immediately let it be known that there would speedily be a 'settlement' in Spain—in the spirit of the settlement of Munich." Claude Bowers, *My Mission to Spain* (New York: Simon and Schuster, 1954), p. 393.

The chargé in France (Wilson) reported to the secretary of state, November 2, 1938: "As for Spain, Delbos fears that the French Government will agree to grant Franco belligerent rights after the Anglo-Italian agreement enters into force and on the basis of the withdrawal of only 10,000 Italian troops who have already left Spain. This will mean complete victory for Franco leaving a large number of Italians still in Spain, particularly Italian aviators in Majorca. France will be hurried into negotiations with Italy for the settlement of all questions in dispute between them while Mussolini continues to hold the trumps in the form of positions in Spain threatening French communications with North Africa." *Foreign Relations of the United States, 1938*, I, 251.

[19] "The Conspiracy of Munich," *Communist International* (Oct., 1938), pp. 881–882. See also "The Far Reaching Effects of the Ebro Offensive," *ibid.* (Sept., 1938), pp. 813–814. When diplomatic conversations were reopened between England and Italy, the Soviet press cynically reported, "It is supposed that they will undertake new measures to strangle the Spanish Republic." *Pravda* (Dec. 28, 1938). "Having offered Germany a free hand for expansion to Central Europe, the British Conservative government and Daladier's government seek to come to an agreement with Italy. Mussolini must receive compensation for his loyalty to the 'Rome-Berlin Axis' for which Italy without a struggle yielded her position in Central Europe in favor of her alliance to the Axis. This compensation was promised Mussolini by Hitler already in March, 1938, at the time of the German seizure of Austria. Where else could this compensation be expected than in the western basin of the Mediterranean, in Spain?" G. Dashevskii, "Fashistskaia agressiia v Ispanii" ["Fascist Aggression in Spain"], *Mirovoe Khoziaistvo i Mirovaia Politika* (Nov., 1938), p. 33.

[20] Viscount Halifax reported to Sir R. Lindsay (Washington) on October 27, 1938:

"(ii) The entry into force of the Agreement may be expected to restore to Signor Mussolini some of the liberty of action he now lacks in deciding his foreign policy; the longer the Agreement remains inoperative the more closely Rome becomes bound to Berlin, as recent events have shown.

"(iii) It is particularly important that Signor Mussolini should be encouraged to regain his liberty of manoeuvre and decision if the contact established at Munich between the Four Western Powers is to be maintained and the hope of establishing smoother relations in Europe developed.

* * *

"(vi) If we fail to take what is probably our last chance of bringing the Agreement into force and resuming our former relations with Italy, Signor Mussolini will be likely finally to conclude that we are not in fact at all anxious to resume normal Anglo-Italian friendship; and [the] Berlin-Rome Axis will be proportionately strengthened." Woodward and Butler, *op. cit.*, pp. 343–344.

[21] The Communists had predicted British ratification several months earlier even without a token withdrawal of Italian troops. See "Summary of Events," *Communist International* (Aug., 1938), p. 788. For the diplomatic documents leading to the final negotiations see Woodward and Butler, *op. cit.*, pp. 312–362.

[22] Debate in the House of Commons on ratification of the Anglo-Italian Agreement, November 2, 1938, Anthony Eden, *Foreign Affairs* (London: Faber and Faber, 1939), p. 306. Eden continued: "We have been told—it has been published to the world—that 10,000 Italian infantrymen have been withdrawn and every one has welcomed that. But the main contribution of Italy to the cause of Salamanca authorities has never been in infantry, but in technicians and armaments, and particularly aeroplanes. There has never, so far as I am aware, been any withdrawal of these."

[23] "Ratification of the Anglo-Italian Agreement which is a clearly expressed policy of openly encouraging intervention in Spain is fraught with very grave consequences for England and France." *Pravda* (Nov. 19, 1938).

[24] Cited in Claude Bowers, *op. cit.*, p. 396.

[25] *Izvestiia* (Nov. 10, 1938). In the same vein: "It is sufficient to glance at the geographical position of Spain and her possessions to realize the far-flung implications of the Fascist intervention. The seizure of Austria and to a still greater degree Czechoslovakia were the keys which opened a path for the continental expansion of German fascism through the Balkans to the shores of the Middle East, Mesopotamia, and India. Spain holds in its hands the keys to the joint expansion of German and Italian fascism on to the important sea communications of England and France with their colonial holdings." G. Dashevskii, "Fashistskaia agressiia v Ispanii" ["Fascist Aggression in Spain"], *Mirovoe Khoziaistvo i Mirovaia Politika* (Nov., 1938), p. 34.

[26] *See* for example the editorial by E. Aleksandrov in *Pravda* (Nov. 27, 1938): "The English government is prepared to assist Fascist Italy in the organization of a starvation blockade of Republican Spain and the French diplomats want to be worthy of Mussolini's favor, after the failure of Francois Poncet in Rome. It is highly probable that behind closed doors the British and French ministers have arranged a means by which it is more convenient to realize Franco's belligerency and to aid intervention by completing the ring of blockade around Spain."

[27] See *Pravda* (Dec. 2, 1938).

[28] *Pravda* (Dec. 3, 1938).

[29] Georgi Dimitrov, in his article "United Front against Fascism after Munich," *Pravda* (Nov. 7, 1938), declared: "However, the bourgeois governments did not put a system of collective security in operation. They did not do so because they did not want to; they did not do so because their policy was determined by the reactionary imperialist circles, who, out of fear of the growth of the working-class movement in Europe, of the movement of national liberation in Asia, out of hatred for the land of Socialism, sacrificed to fascism the interest of their own peoples."

The shift in the Soviet line was also reflected in the renewed and frequent reference to the dangers of capitalist encirclement and the superior Soviet strength. "The seizure of Abyssinia, Fascist intervention in Spain, rearmament, the brigand-predatory invasion of Japanese imperialism against the Chinese people, the armed seizure by Germany of Austria, the threats hanging over Czechoslovakia with the consent and agreement of the English and French governing circles, the insolent provocation by Polish fascism on the Lithuanian and Czech border—all this is linked to one aim, the development of a second imperialist military force and the preparation of a military attack on the USSR." A. Kossoi, *SSSR i kapitalisticheskoe okruzhenie* [*The USSR and Capitalist Encirclement*] (Moscow: Izdat. TsK VLKM Molodaia Gvardiia, [Nov.] 1938), p. 86. *See also* Petr Aleksevich Lisovskii, *SSSR i kapitalisticheskoe okruzhenie* [*The USSR and Capitalist Encirclement*] (Moscow: Gos. Izdat. Politicheskoi Literatury, [Feb.] 1939).

[30] *Izvestiia* (Dec. 3, 1938).

[31] For example, G. Dashevskii, "Fashistskaia agressiia v Ispanii" ["Fascist Aggression in Spain"], *Mirovoe Khoziaistvo i Mirovaia Politika* (Nov., 1938), pp. 45–50. *See also* p. 171 n. 7.

[32] For more details *see* David T. Cattell, *Communism and the Spanish Civil War* (Berkeley and Los Angeles: University of California Press, 1955), pp. 204–207.

[33] P. Gelbras, "Vneshniaia politika pravitel'stva Dalad'e ["The Foreign Policy of the Daladier Government"], *Mirovoe Khoziaistvo i Mirovaia Politika* (Sept., 1938), p. 68.

[34] It is unknown at exactly what point the Soviet leaders did actually decide on the reversal of the policy of collective security. It is not unreasonable to assume, as many have done, that it came very shortly after the Munich agreement. Interestingly, Angelo Rossi has cited evidence that Russian leaders were first considering an

alliance with Germany in October, 1938, in *The Russo-German Alliance* (London: Chapman and Hall, 1950), pp. 3 and 5. Gustav Hilger in his memoir-history of German-Soviet relations, 1918–1941, reported: "The first weak signs that the tensions [between the Soviet Union and Germany] were easing could be noticed in the summer of 1938. At that time the atmosphere created by the mutual recriminations had become intolerable, and both sides expressed the desire for a let-up. The German Embassy was the first to suggest that measures should be taken, as a token of mutual good will, to end the mud-slinging aimed at the two heads of state. The idea was Schulenburg's; but he discussed it with the first counselor of the embassy and myself before taking it up with Litvinov. The suggestion fell on fertile soil; it was discussed in various meetings, both in Moscow and in Berlin, and an agreement was finally reached. A further step in the same direction was taken in October, 1938, when Litvinov and Schulenburg came to an oral understanding that the press and radio of both states should henceforth restrain themselves and cease attacking the other country. The consequences of the agreement were the first visible indication that a change in the relations between the Soviet Union and Germany was in the offing.

"Stalin's willingness to enter into agreements of this sort was primarily a consequence of the Munich conference. From the course the conference had taken, and from the fact that the Soviet Union was kept out of it, Stalin drew the conclusions that the Western powers had no intention of showing Hitler serious resistance, and that they would even support him if he turned upon the Soviet Union. But Hitler, too, was pushed, by the events of Munich, in the direction of the settlement with the Soviet Union. Particularly, the remarks which Neville Chamberlain had made on his return to London confirmed Hitler in the opinion that he had to create additional safeguards if he wanted to gain further successes with his old methods.

"Once again the world took notice when, in late December, 1938, news came from Berlin that a German-Soviet trade agreement had been signed in the German capital. True, it was a routine affair, since the continuation of German-Soviet trade depended on the annual renewal of such business transactions; but the fact that on this occasion the agreement had been signed in time, and not with the great delay of the previous year, was regarded as symptomatic. The conclusion of the agreement served as the prologue to further German-Soviet talks that had been suggested by the trade representative of the U.S.S.R. . . ." Gustav Hilger and Alfred G. Meyer, *The Incompatible Allies* (New York: The Macmillan Company, 1953), pp. 288–289.

See also E. H. Carr, *German-Soviet Relations between the Two World Wars 1919–1939* (Baltimore: The Johns Hopkins Press, 1951), pp. 124–125; and United States, Department of State, *Nazi-Soviet Relations, 1939–1941* (Washington, D.C.: Government Printing Office, 1948).

[35] It is impossible to assume as some writers have done that the Communists purposely sacrificed Catalonia in order to appease Hitler. For a more thorough treatment *see* Cattell, *op. cit.*, pp. 206–207.

[36] This is confirmed by the Italian and British documents. *See* conversations between the Duce and Chamberlain, January 11 and 12, 1939, *Ciano's Diplomatic Papers* (London: Odhams Press Ltd., 1948), pp. 259–266, *and* conversations between British and Italian ministers, Rome, January 11–14, 1939. Woodward and Butler, *op. cit.*, pp. 518, 520–523.

Such a deal was also implied in Lord Halifax's speech in Hull on February 3, 1939: ". . . Speaking of the Mediterranean in particular, Signor Mussolini assured us that he was well satisfied with the Anglo-Italian Agreement, by which both parties undertook to respect the existing *status quo* in the Mediterranean. He also emphatically declared that, once the Spanish conflict was over, all Italian military support would be withdrawn, and he would have nothing to ask from Spain by way of territorial concessions." Viscount K. G. Halifax, *Speeches on Foreign Policy* (London: Oxford University Press, 1940), p. 218.

Izvestiia summarized Chamberlain's visit to Rome in January, 1939, as the completion of England's appeasement to Italy: "At Stresa, Simon betrayed Abyssinia. At Rome, Chamberlain betrayed Spain." *Izvestiia* (Feb. 3, 1939). *See also* "Against Munich—Working Class Unity," *Communist International* (Feb., 1939), p. 101.

For the Soviet Union the only bright star on the horizon was the united opposition of the British Labour Party to the government's foreign policy. The National Council of Labour in January, 1939, sent a letter and a deputation to the prime minister urging the removal of the embargo against the Spanish government. Clement Attlee, as leader of the opposition, also requested a special session of the House of Commons but was refused.

[37] The Soviet press was somewhat heartened in December, 1938, when Italy denounced her 1935 pact with France and relations between the two countries rapidly worsened. Further hope was expressed at the end of January when Catalonia and Minorca were being overrun by Italian troops, and France displayed a strong fear of a Franco victory in Spain. *See* editorials in *Pravda* (Jan. 26 and 28, 1939).

[38] Herbert von Dirksen, *Moscow, Tokyo, London* (London: Hutchinson and Co., Ltd., 1951), pp. 211–212.

[39] *Pravda* (Feb. 25, 1939). See also *Pravda* (Feb. 15, 1939).

[40] *See* "Daladier and Chamberlain Surrender Spain to the Aggressors," *Communist International* (March, 1939), pp. 284–285; *and* Leon Blum, *L'histoire jugera* (Paris: Éditions Diderot, 1945), pp. 206–207.

[41] "Daladier and Chamberlain Surrender Spain to the Aggressors," *Communist International* (March, 1939), p. 285.

[42] *See* p. 173 n. 34.

[43] *Izvestiia* (March 11, 1939).

[44] *Ibid.* On the following day D. Z. Manuilsky, the delegate of the Communist party of the Soviet Union to the Comintern, in his report to the congress paid strong tribute to the Loyalists of Spain and condemned the Western democracies: "For nearly three years the poorly armed Spanish nation, betrayed by the so-called bourgeois democratic states, carried on the unequal heroic struggle for its independence, for the cause of all forward-looking and progressive mankind. (Applause) It carried on this struggle against the military intervention of two large imperialistic states, Fascist Italy and Germany, and against the hidden intervention of universal reaction which adopted a blockade of the Spanish Republic under the hypocritical slogan of 'policy of nonintervention' in Europe and the policy of 'isolationism' in America." *Ibid.* (March 12, 1939).

Subsequent Communist interpretation and analysis of the Spanish Civil War has continued in much the same vein. For example I. F. Ivashin in a lecture on international relations, 1935–1939, the text of which was published in 1955, placed primary responsibility for the "Fascist rebel victory" on Italy and Germany, with England, France, and the United States playing an important secondary role. The isolationism of the United States has assumed ever greater proportions in the postwar period. Although Soviet participation on the Non-Intervention Committee was mentioned, Ivashin emphasized the ultimatums that the USSR sent to the committee and falsified the events by stating, "When the Non-Intervention Committee conclusively became an organ for coöperating with intervention and rebellion, the Soviet government withdrew its representatives." Unlike the earlier analyses that denied direct Soviet intervention, Ivashin admitted the USSR sent arms. "The Soviet Union rendered to Republican Spain not only moral and diplomatic aid but also material and military support." I. F. Ivashin, *Mezhdunarodnye otnosheniia i vneshniaia politika Sovetskogo Soiuza v 1935–1939 gg.* [*International Relations and Foreign Policy of the Soviet Union in the Years 1935–1939*] (Moscow: Vysshaia Partiinaia Shkola pri TsK KPSS, 1955), pp. 19–25.

[45] Winston Churchill, "Non-Intervention in Spain," January 8, 1937, in *Step by Step* (London: T. Butterworth Ltd., 1939), p. 76.

[46] *See* for example Winston S. Churchill, *The Second World War* (Boston: Houghton Mifflin Company, 1948) 6 vols.; Cordell Hull, *Memoirs* (New York: The Macmillan Company, 1948) 2 vols.; Sir Samuel Hoare, *Ambassador on Special Mission* (London: Collins, 1946); Herbert Feis, *The Spanish Story* (New York: Alfred A. Knopf, 1948); United States, Department of State, *The Spanish Government and the Axis* (Washington, D.C.: Government Printing Office, 1946); *and* Carlton J. Hayes, *Wartime Mission in Spain* (New York: The Macmillan Company, 1945).

BIBLIOGRAPHY

BIBLIOGRAPHY

THE MAIN BIBLIOGRAPHICAL problem in analyzing Soviet foreign relations during the Spanish Civil War has been the lack of primary material on the attitudes of the Soviet leaders and decision-making process. By the 1930's the few channels of information about policy-making in the Soviet Union were rapidly being closed. It was Stalin's order to guard closely and restrict access to top-level decisions and intelligence. In addition former leaders and top-level defectors were no longer allowed to leave the Soviet Union, but were being swallowed up by the Great Purge. Soviet bureaucrats at all levels became afraid to talk to foreigners. The lack of direct sources about this period, furthermore, is likely to be permanent. Only a radical change in the Soviet government might lead to the release of some material, but even then it is doubtful how much would become available after so many years, and after so many of the chief participants have been silenced.

Three alternative approaches to Soviet foreign policy remain. First are the official diplomatic papers of non-Communist powers, which include those of Germany (published in Washington and Moscow), the United States, and, especially important for this study, *The Documents of the Non-Intervention Committee*. But even these sources are incomplete. Great Britain has only partially published her documents for this period and the French beyond issuing a few yellow books have revealed nothing. The Italians are only beginning to publish an interwar series, although some information can be found in the jumble of archive material microfilmed by the United States occupation forces in Italy.

The second means of deriving Soviet attitudes during this period is the writings and memoirs of Communist and non-Communist participants in the events. This proved to be the least fruitful method. Except for Louis Fischer and Walter Krivitsky, no Russian or non-Russian associated closely with the Soviet role in the diplomatic events surrounding the Civil War is available or has written about them. Actually, most works written about the Spanish crisis, regardless of language, including those of Louis Fischer and Walter Krivitsky, deal almost exclusively with events in Spain and present little insight into or knowledge about the diplomatic struggle among the great powers of Europe at this time.

Finally there are the official statements by the Soviet government, the Communist party, and the press. Contrary to postwar Soviet communiques, most of these statements are revealing and forthright in character. Because the source of inspiration for Soviet ideas on foreign relations is centralized, little purpose was served by going through all the numerous articles published at the time. More than three-quarters of the material concerned events within Spain, a subject covered by the first volume of this study. Furthermore, the only important variation of pattern in this flood of propaganda and statements was the slight differentiation of emphasis in works for domestic and foreign consumption. Very often in the play of international politics the Soviet Union could be more straightforward in those publications least directly associated with herself, such as the *International Press Correspondence (Inprecorr)* and *The Communist International,* and the various publications of the Communist parties of Western Europe. In addition to the non-Russian Communist publications, *Pravda, Izvestiia, Mirovoe Khoziaistvo i Mirovaia Politika,* and occasionally *Bolshevik* provided a complete survey of official Soviet attitudes. Besides the Soviet pamphlets, periodicals, and newspapers, some books have been published in Russian on the Civil War. Most of these works were collections of documents and speeches available elsewhere or were largely concerned with events within Spain. Of the few books in Russian that attempted to analyze Soviet relations in this period, most were written subsequently and reflect the attitude of the time when they were published: I. Slobodianok, *Amerikanskie imperialisty—posobniki fashistskoi interventsii v Ispanii (1936–1939gg.)* [*American Imperialists Aid Fascist Intervention in Spain (1936–1939)*], Kiev, 1954; V. P. Potemkin, *Politika umirotvorenia agressorov i bor'ba Sovetskogo Soiuza za mir* [*The Policy of Appeasement and the Struggle of the Soviet Union for Peace*], Moscow, 1943; and B. E. Shtein, *Burzhuaznye fal'sifikatory istorii 1919–1939gg.* [*Bourgeois Falsifiers of History 1919–1939*], Moscow, 1951. The few contemporary analyses, however, were beneficial: Evgenii Aleksandrovich Askanov, *Portugaliia i ee rol' v fashistskoi interventsii v Ispanii* [*Portugal and Her Role in the Fascist Intervention in Spain*], Moscow, 1937; G. Dashevskii, *Fashistskaia piataia kolonna v Ispanii* [*The Fascist Fifth Column in Spain*], Moscow, 1938, and P. Gel'bras, *Vneshniaia i vnutrenniaia politika Frantsii* [*Foreign and Domestic Policies of France*], Leningrad, 1939.

In conclusion, these materials on Soviet foreign policy during the 1930's, in spite of important shortcomings, reveal a distinct pattern of desires of, frustrations to, and minor accomplishments by the Soviet policy-makers, as this study of the prolonged crisis surrounding the Spanish Civil War has attempted to recount.

Below are listed some of the more useful books directly and indirectly related to this subject. Additional works on the internal affairs of Spain can be found in the first volume of this study, *Communism and the Spanish Civil War,* Berkeley and Los Angeles: University of California Press, 1955.

OFFICIAL DOCUMENTS

Documents of the International Committee for the Application of the Agreement Regarding Non-Intervention in Spain. [Unpublished.] [Cited as Documents of the Non-Intervention Committee, N.I.S. (36).]

Russia. *Dokumenty Ministerstva Inostrannykh del Germanii* [*Documents of the Ministry of Foreign Affairs of Germany*]. Vol. III, *Germanskaia politika i Ispaniia (1936–1943gg.)* [*German Politics and Spain (1936–1943)*]. Moscow: 1949.

———. Ministry of Foreign Affairs. *Documents and Materials Relating to the Eve of the Second World War.* Vol. I, *November, 1937–1938;* vol. II, *Dirksen Papers, 1938–1939.* Moscow: Foreign Languages Publishing House, 1948.

Spain. Ministerio de estado. *La agressión italiana, documentos occupados a las unidades italiano en la acción de Guadalajara.* [Valencia]: 1937.

———. Spanish Embassy. *Documents on the Italian Intervention in Spain.* London: The Press Department, 1937.

The Trial of the Major War Criminals before the International Military Tribunal. Nuremberg: International Military Tribunal, 1947–1949. 37 vols.

United States. Department of State. *Documents on German Foreign Policy, 1918–1945,* ser. D, vol. III, *Germany and the Spanish Civil War 1936–1939.* Washington, D.C.: Government Printing Office, 1950. [Cited as *Documents on German Foreign Policy, 1918–1945,* D, III.]

———. ———. *Foreign Relations of the United States, 1936,* vol. II. *Foreign Relations of the United States, 1937,* vol. I. *Foreign Relations of the United States, 1938,* vol. I. *Foreign Relations of the United States: The Soviet Union 1933–1939.* Washington, D.C.: Government Printing Office, 1954–1955. [Cited as *Foreign Relations of the United States.*]

———. ———. *The Spanish Government and the Axis.* Washington, D.C. Government Printing Office, 1946.

———. ———. *The United States and Italy,* 1936–1946. Washington, D.C.: Government Printing Office, 1946.

———. National Archives. Documents of the Italian Foreign Office. Washington, D.C.: n.d. [Microfilmed.]

BOOKS

Airapetian, M. E. *Vneshnei politiki SSSR 1917–1940gg.* [*The Foreign Policies of the USSR 1917–1940*]. Moscow: Voenizdat., 1941.

Akademii Nauk SSSR. *Pravye leiboristy na sluzhbe angliiskogo i amerikanskogo imperializma* [*The Right Labourites in the Service of English and American Imperialism*]. Moscow: Gosplanizdat, 1950.

Aksanov, Evgenii Aleksandrovich. *Portugaliia i ee rol' v fashistskoi interventsii v Ispanii* [*Portugal and Her Role in the Fascist Intervention in Spain*]. Moscow: Gosudarstvennoe Sotsial'no-ekonomicheskoe Izdatel'stvo, 1937.

Allen, Jr., David Edwards. *The Soviet Union and the Spanish Civil War 1936–1939.* Unpublished Ph.D. dissertation. Stanford University, 1952.

Alvarez del Vayo, Julio. *Freedom's Battle.* London: William Heinemann, 1940.

———. *The Last Optimist.* London: Putnam and Co., Ltd., 1950.

Angles, Raoul. *La Parti radical et la question d'Espagne.* Paris: Éditions Étoile, [1939].

Araquistain, Luis. *La verdad sobre la intervención y la no intervención en España.* Madrid: 1938.

Atholl, Duchess of. *Searchlight on Spain.* Middlesex: Penguin Books, Ltd., 1938.

Bahamonde, Antonio. *Memoirs of a Spanish Nationalist.* London: United Editorial Ltd., 1939.

Baraibar, Carlos de. *La guerra de España en el plano internacional.* Barcelona: Editorial Tierra y Libertad, 1938.

Barcia Trelles, Augusto. *Un golpe de estado internacional.* Buenos Aires: PHAC, 1944.

Barcia Trelles, Camilo. *Puntos cardinales de la política internacional española.* Barcelona: Ediciones F.E., 1939.

Bardoux, Jacques. *Le chaos espagnol éviterons-nous la contagion?* Paris: Ernest Flammarion, éditeur, 1937.

———. *Staline contre l'Europe.* Paris: 1937.

Barea, Arturo. *The Clash.* London: Faber and Faber, Ltd., 1946.

Belforte, Francesco. *La guerra civile in Spagna: gli interventi stranieri nella Spagna rossa.* 4 vols. Milan: Instituto per Gli Studi di Politica Internazionale, 1938–1939.

Beloff, Max. *The Foreign Policy of Soviet Russia,* Vol. II—1936–1941. London: Oxford University Press, 1949.

Bilainkin, George. *Maisky: Ten Years Ambassador.* London: George Allen and Unwin, 1944.

Bloch, J. R. *Espagne, Espagne!* Paris: Éditions Sociales Internationales, 1936.

Blum, Leon. *L'histoire jugera.* Paris: Éditions Diderot, 1945.

Boaventura, Armando. *Madrid-Moscovo; da ditadura à república e à guerra civil de Espanha.* Lisbon: Parceria A. M. Pereira, 1937.

Bonnet, Georges. *Fin d'une Europe: de Munich à la guerre.* Switzerland: Bibliotheque de Cheval Ailé, 1948.

Borkenau, Franz. *European Communism.* New York: Harper and Brothers, 1953.

———. *The Spanish Cockpit.* London: Faber and Faber, Ltd., 1937.

Bowers, Claude G. *My Mission to Spain: Watching the Rehearsal for World War II.* New York: Simon and Schuster, 1954.

Brasillach, Robert, and Maurice Bardèche. *Histoire de la guerre d'Espagne.* Paris: Librairie Plon, 1939.

Britain in Spain by the Unknown Diplomat. London: H. Hamilton, 1939.

Campbell, J. R. *Soviet Policy and Its Critics.* London: Victor Gollancz Ltd., 1939.

Campoamor, Clara. *La révolution espagnole vue par une républicaine.* Paris: Librarie Plon, 1937.

Canovas Cervantes, S. *De Franco a Negrín pasando por el Partido Communista—historia de la revolución española.* Toulouse: "Páginas Libres," n.d.

Cantalupo, Roberto. *Fu la Spagna.* Milan: A Mondadori Editori, 1948.

Carr, E. H. *German-Soviet Relations between the Two Wars 1919–1939*. Baltimore: The Johns Hopkins Press, 1951.

———. *International Relations between the Two World Wars (1919–1939)*. London: Macmillan and Co. Ltd., 1947.

Chamberlain, Neville. *In Search of Peace*. New York: G. P. Putnam's and Sons, 1939.

Churchill, Winston S. *Step by Step, 1936–1939*. London: T. Butterworth Ltd., 1939.

———. *The Second World War*. 6 vols. Boston: Houghton Mifflin Company, 1948.

Ciano Diaries, 1939–1943. Edited by Hugh Gibson. New York: Doubleday and Company, Inc., 1946.

Ciano's Diplomatic Papers. Edited by Malcolm Muggeridge; translated by Stuart Hood. London: Odhams Press Ltd., 1948.

Coates, W. P., and Zelda K. *A History of Anglo-Soviet Relations*. London: Lawrence and Wishart and the Pilot Press, 1945.

———. *World Affairs and the U.S.S.R.* London: Lawrence and Wishart, 1939.

Code, Joseph B. *The Spanish War and Lying Propaganda*. New York: The Paulist Press, 1938.

Commission of the C. C. of the C.P.S.U.(B.), ed. *History of the Communist Party of the Soviet Union*. Moscow: Foreign Languages Publishing House, 1945.

Committee of Inquiry into Breaches of International Law Relating to Intervention in Spain. *Evidence of Recent Breaches by Germany and Italy of the Non-Intervention Agreement*. London: P. S. King and Son, Ltd., 1937.

Communist International. *VII Congress of the Communist International*. Abridged stenographic report of proceedings. Moscow: Foreign Languages Publishing House, 1939.

Craig, Gordon A. *The Politics of the Prussian Army, 1640–1945*. Oxford: The Clarendon Press, 1955.

———, and Felix Gilbert, eds. *The Diplomats, 1919–1939*. Princeton: Princeton University Press, 1953.

Dashevskii, G. *Fashistskaia piataia kolonna v Ispanii [The Fascist Fifth Column in Spain]*. Moscow: Voenizdat., 1938.

Davies, Joseph E. *Mission to Moscow*. London: Gollancz, 1942.

Dean, Vera Micheles. *European Diplomacy in the Spanish Crisis*. Geneva: Geneva Research Center, 1936.

Degras, Jane, ed. and comp. *Soviet Documents on Foreign Policy*. Vol. III, *1933–1941*. Issued under the auspices of the Royal Institute of International Affairs. London: Oxford University Press, 1953.

Delo Ispanii ne chastnoe delo ispantsev [The Affair in Spain is Not Just a Private Affair of the Spaniards]. Moscow: Partizdat TsK VKP(b), 1937.

De Wilde, John Charles. *The Struggle over Spain*. New York: Foreign Policy Assoc., Inc., 1938.

Díaz, José. *Nuestra bandera del Frente Popular*. Madrid-Barcelona: Ediciones Europa-América, 1936.

———, and Dolores Ibarruri. *España y la guerra imperlista*. Mexico, D.F.: Editorial Popular, 1939.

Dimitrov, Georgi. *The United Front*. New York: International Publishers, 1938.

Dirksen, Herbert von. *Moscow, Tokyo, London*. London: Hutchinson and Co. Ltd., 1951.

Domingo, Marcelino. *España ante el mundo*. Mexico: Editorial "Mexico nuevo," 1937.

Duroselle, Jean-Baptiste, ed. *Les relations germano-soviétique de 1933 á 1939*. Paris: Librairie Armand Colin, 1954.

Duval, Général. *Les espagnols et la guerre d'Espagne*. Paris: Librairie Plon, 1939.

———. *Les leçons de la guerre d'Espagne*. Paris: Librairie Plon, 1938.

Dzelepy, Èleuthère Nicolas. *Espejo de alevosias: Inglaterra en España y fragmentos del diario de el diplomático desconocido*. Mexico: Editorial Séneca, 1940.

———. *The Spanish Plot*. Translated by Edward Fitzgerald and Frank Budgen. London: P. S. King and Son, Ltd., 1937.

Echeverria, Frederico de. *Spain in Flames*. New York: The Paulist Press, 1936.

Eden, Anthony. *Foreign ʼAffairs*. London: Faber and Faber, 1939.

Exposición del plan secreto para establecer un "soviet" en España. Bilbao: 1939.

Falsifiers of History (Historical Survey). Moscow: Foreign Languages Publishing House, 1951.

Feiling, Keith. *The Life of Neville Chamberlain*. London: Macmillan, 1947.

Fischer, Louis. *La guerre en Espagne*. Paris: Éditions Imp. Coopérative Etoile, 1937.

———. *Men and Politics: an Autobiography*. New York: Duell, Sloan and Pearce, 1941.

Foltz, C. *Masquerade in Spain*. Boston: Houghton Mifflin Co., 1948.

Foss, William, and Cecil Gerahty. *The Spanish Arena*. London: John Gifford Ltd. [1938].

Gantenbein, James W., ed. and comp. *Documentary Background of World War II, 1931–1941*. New York: Columbia University Press, 1949.

Garcia, Khose. *Ispanskii narod v bor'be za svododu i demokratiiu protiv fashizma [The Spanish People in the Struggle for Freedom and Democracy against Fascism]*. Moscow: 1956.

García Pradas, J. *Rusia y España*. Paris: Ediciones Tierra y Libertad, 1948.

———. *La traición de Stalin, comó terminó la guerra de España*. New York: Ediciones de cultura proletaria, 1939.

Gel'bras, P. *Vneshniaia i vnutrenniaia politika Frantsii [Foreign and Domestic Policies of France]*. Leningrad: Gos. Isdat. Politicheskoi Literatury, 1939.

General'nyi shtab R.K.K.A. *Upravlenie voiskami i rabota shtabov v ispanskoi republikanskoi armii [The Administration of the Troops and the Work of the Staff in the Spanish Republican Army]*. Moscow: Voenizdat., 1939.

Gerahty, Cecil. *The Road to Madrid*. London: Hutchinson and Co., 1937.

Geroiskaia Ispaniia [Heroic Spain]. Moscow: Partizdat TsK VKP(b), 1936.

Gorkin, Julian. *Canibales politicos; Hitler y Stalin en España*. Mexico City: Ediciones "Guetzal," 1941.

Gorozhankina, N. P. *Rabochii klass Ispanii v gody revoliutsii [The Working Class of Spain in a Year of Revolution]*. Moscow: 1936.

Halifax, Viscount K. G. *Speeches on Foreign Policy (1934–1939)*. London: Oxford University Press, 1940.

Hayes, Carlton J. *Wartime Mission in Spain*. New York: The Macmillan Company, 1945.

Henderson, Nevile. *Failure of a Mission, Berlin 1937–1939*. New York: G. P. Putnam's Sons, 1940.

Héricourt, Pierre. *Pourquoi mentir? L'aide franco-soviétique à l'Espagne rouge.* Paris: Éditions Baudinière, 1937.

———. *Les Soviets et la France, fournisseurs de la révolution espagnole.* Paris: Éditions Baudinière, 1938.

Hernandez, Jesus. *Yo fui un Ministro de Stalin.* Mexico, D.F.: Editorial America, 1953.

Hilger, Gustav, and Alfred G. Meyer. *The Incompatible Allies.* New York: The Macmillan Company, 1953.

Hispanicus. *Foreign Intervention in Spain.* London: United Editorial, Ltd., 1938.

Hoare, Sir Samuel. *Ambassador on Special Mission.* London: Collins, 1946.

Hull, Cordell. *Memoirs.* 2 vols. New York: The Macmillan Company, 1948.

Huntz, Jack. *Spotlight on Spain.* London: The London Divisional Council I.L.P. [1936].

Intervention in Spain. London: The Round Table, March 1937.

Ispaniia v bor'be protiv fashizma—sbornik statei i materialov [*The Struggle of Spain against Fascism—Collection of Articles and Materials*]. Moscow: Partizdat TsK VKP(b), 1936.

Ispanskaia kompartiia boretsia za pobedu: sbornik materialov [*The Spanish Communist Party Struggles for Victory: A collection of Materials*]. Moscow: Gos. Sotsial'no-ekonomicheskoe Izdat., 1938.

Jacquelin, André. *Espagne et liberté; le second Munich.* Paris: Kérénac et cie, 1945.

Jellinek, Frank. *The Civil War in Spain.* London: Victor Gollancz Ltd., 1938.

Klotz, Helmut. *Uroki grazhdanskoi voiny v Ispanii* [*Lessons from the Civil War in Spain*]. Moscow: Voenizdat., 1938.

Knoblaugh, H. Edward. *Correspondent in Spain.* New York: Sheed and Ward, 1937.

Kompartiia Frantsii v bor'be za narodnii front [*The Communist Part of France in the Struggle for the People's Front*]. Moscow: Partizdat TsK VKP(b), 1938.

Kossoi, A. *SSSR i kapitalisticheskoe okruzhenie* [*The USSR and Capitalist Encirclement*]. Moscow: Izdat. TsK VLKM Molodaia Gvardiia, 1938.

Krivitsky, Walter. *In Stalin's Secret Service.* New York: Harper and Bros., 1939.

Kuibyshev, N. V. *Zashchita otechestva* [*Defense of the Motherland*]. Moscow: Partizdat., 1937.

Lamour, Philippe. *Sauvons, la France en Espagne.* Paris: Éditions Baudinière, 1937.

Langdon Davies, J. *Behind the Barricades.* London: Martin Secker and Warburg Ltd., 1936.

Langer, William L., and S. Everett Gleason. *The Challenge to Isolation, 1937–1940.* New York: Harper and Brothers, 1952.

Legionari di Roma in terra iberica (1936 xiv—1939 xvii). Milano: "Sagdos," officine grafiche e legatoria, 1940.

Lisovskii, Petr Aleksevich. *SSSR i kapitalisticheskoe okruzhenie* [*The USSR and Capitalist Encirclement*]. Moscow: Gos. Izdat. Politicheskoi Literatury, 1939.

List of ships interfered with, attacked or sunk during the war in Spain, July 1936– June 1938. London: Press Department of the Spanish Embassy, 1938.

Litvinov, Maxim. *Against Aggression.* London: Lawrence and Wishart Ltd., 1939. Russian edition: *Vneshniaia politika USSR, rechi i zaiavleniia 1927–1937* [*International Politics of the USSR, Speeches and Declarations 1927–1937*]. Moscow: Gos. Sotsial'no-Ekonomicheskoe Izdat., 1937.

Lorwin, Lewis L. *The International Labor Movement.* New York: Harper and Brothers, 1953.

Louzon, R. *La contra revolución en España.* Buenos Aires: 1938.

Loveday, Arthur F. *World War in Spain.* London: John Murray, 1939.

Low, Mary, and Brea. *Red Spanish Notebook.* London: M. Secker and Warburg, Ltd., 1937.

Lunn, Arnold. *Spanish Rehearsal.* New York: Sheed and Ward, 1937.

Marquès-Rivière, Jean. *Comment la Franc-Maçonnerie fait une révolucion.* Paris: Éditions Baudinière, 1937.

Marty, André. *Heroic Spain.* New York: Workers Library Publishers, 1937.

Maurras, Charles. *Vers l'Espagne de Franco.* Paris: Éditions du livre moderne, 1943.

Merin, Peter. *Spain Between Death and Birth.* London: John Lane, 1938.

Merry de Val, Marquis. *Spain's Fight for Civilization: Throwing Light upon the Origin of Spain's Plight.* New York: The Paulist Press [1936].

Mitchell, Mairin. *Storm over Spain.* London: M. Secker and Warburg, Ltd., 1937.

Mora, Constancia de la. *In Place of Splendor: The Autobiography of a Spanish Woman.* New York: Harcourt, Brace and Co., 1939.

Morgado, Aurelio Nuñez. *Los sucesos de España vistos por un diplomatico.* Buenos Aires: Talleres Gráficos Argentinos, 1941.

Moulin, Pierre. *Experiences récentes de non-reconnaissance en droit international.* Lyon: Doctoral thesis. University of Lyon, 1938.

Mussolini, Benito. *My Autobiography.* London: Hutchinson, 1939.

Namier, Lewis B. *Europe in Decay (1936–1940).* London: Macmillan and Co., Ltd., 1950.

Narod (Ispanskii) Pobedit! [*The (Spanish) People are Winning!*] Moscow: Partizdat. TsK VKP(b), 1937.

The Nazi Conspiracy in Spain. Translated by Emile Burns. London: Victor Gollancz Ltd., 1937.

Nekrich, A. M. *Politika angliiskogo imperializma v Evrope, oktiabr' 1938–sentiabr' 1939* [*The Policy of English Imperialism in Europe, October 1938–September 1939*]. Moscow: Izdat. Akademii Nauk SSSR, 1955.

Nikolaev, N. N. *Vneshniaia politika pravygh leiboristov Anglii v period podgotovki i nachala vtorio mirovoi voiny 1935–1940gg.* [*The Foreign Policy of the Right Labourites in England in the Period of Preparation and the Beginning of World War II, 1935–1940*]. Moscow: Gos. Izdat. Politicheskoi Literatury, 1953.

"Non-intervention" dans les affaires d'Espagne, Documents publiés par le gouvernement de la République espagnole.

O'Duffy, Eoin. *Crusade in Spain.* London: R. Hale Ltd., 1938.

O mezhdunarodnom polozhenii, sbornik [*About the International Situation, a Collection*]. Moscow: Partizdat. TsK VKP(b), 1937.

One Year of War 1936–1937. New York: The Paulist Press, n.d.

Padelford, Norman J. *International Law and Diplomacy in the Spanish Civil Strife.* New York: The Macmillan Company, 1939.

Pattee, Richard. *This is Spain.* Milwaukee: The Bruce Publishing Company, 1951.

Peissy, Robert. *Trois ans de Front populaire en Espagne.* Paris: Fernand Sorlot, 1939.

Pitcairn, Frank. *Reporter in Spain.* Moscow: Cooperative Publishing Society of Foreign Workers in the U.S.S.R., 1937.

Politicheskii slovar' [*Political Dictionary*]. Moscow: Gos. Izdat. Politicheskoi Literatury, 1940.

Poncins, Léon de. *Histoire secrète de la révolution espagnole.* Paris: Gabriel Beauchesne et ses fils, 1938.

Pope, Arthur Upham. *Maxim Litvinoff.* New York: L. B. Fischer, 1943.

Possony, Stefan T. *A Century of Conflict: Communist Techniques of World Revolution.* Chicago: Henry Regnery Company, 1953.

Potemkin, V. P., ed. *Istoriia diplomatii.* Tom III, *Diplomatiia v period podgotovki vtoroi mirovoi voini* [*Diplomatic History*. Vol. III in *Diplomacy in the Period of Preparation for the Second World War*]. Moscow: Gos. Izdat. Politicheskoi Literatury, 1945.

————. *Politika umirotvorenia agressorov i bor'ba Sovetskogo Soiuza za mir* [*The Policy of Appeasement and the Struggle of the Soviet Union for Peace*]. Moscow: 1943.

Prieto, Carlos. *Spanish Front.* London: Thomas Nelson and Sons Ltd., 1936.

Quero Molares, J. *Política de no-intervención, 17(VII)36–17(VII)37.* Barcelona: 1937.

Rabasseire, Henri. *Espagne creuset politique.* Paris: Éditions Fustier, 1938.

Ramos Oliveira, Antonio. *Controversy on Spain between H. A. Gwynne and A. Ramos Oliveira.* London: United Editorial Ltd., 1937.

Raynaud, Jean. *En Espagne "rouge."* Paris: Éditions du Cerf, 1937.

Remblas, José. *España vence a la Internacional Communista.* Barcelona: Ed. R. Sopena, S.A., 1939.

Reynaud, Paul. *La France a sauvé l'Europe.* Paris: Flammarion, 1947.

Rolfe, Edwin. *The Lincoln Battalion: The Story of the Americans Who Fought in Spain in the International Brigades.* New York: Random House, 1939.

Ross, M. *A History of Soviet Foreign Policy.* New York: Workers Library Publishers, 1940.

Rotbuch (Das) über Spanien; Bilder, Dokumente, Zeugenaissagen, gesammelt und herausgegeben von des Anti-Komintern. Berlin-Leipzig: 1937.

Rouvier, Martin. *Franco et la France.* Paris: Éditions de l'Aube, 1939.

Samarin, A. *Bor'ba za Madrid* [*Struggle for Madrid*]. Moscow: Voenizdat., n.d.

Sarolea, Charles. *Daylight on Spain: The Answer to the Duchess of Atholl.* London: Hutchinson and Co., Ltd., 1938.

Schuman, Frederick L. *Soviet Politics at Home and Abroad.* New York: Alfred A. Knopf, 1946.

Scheinman, M. M. *Vatikan v vtoroi mirovoi voine* [*Vatican in the Second World War*]. Moscow: Izdat. Akademii Nauk SSSR, 1951.

Sencourt, Robert. *Spain's Ordeal: a Documented Survey of Recent Events.* London: Longmans, Green and Co., 1938.

Sheinman, M. M. *Vatikan vo vtoroi mirovoi voine* [*The Vatican in the Second World War*]. Moscow: Izdat. Akademii Nauk SSSR, 1951.

Shtein, B. E. *Burzhuaznye fal'sifikatory istorii 1919–1939gg.* [*Bourgeois Falsifiers of History 1919–1939*]. Moscow: Izdat. Akademii Nauk SSSR, 1951.

Simon, O. K. *Hitler en Espagne.* Paris: Denoël, 1938.

Slobodianok, I. *Amerikanskie imperialisty—posobniki fashistskoi interventsii v Ispanii (1936–1939gg.)* [*American Imperialists Aid Fascist Intervention in Spain (1936–1939)*]. Kiev: Izd-vo Kievskogo Un-ta, 1954.

S.S.S.R. i fashistskaia agressiia v Ispanii, sbornik dokumentov [The USSR and Fascist Aggression in Spain, a Collection of Documents]. Moscow: Gos. Sotsial'no-ekonomitcheskoe Izdat., 1937.

Strong, Anna Louise. Spain in Arms. New York: Henry Holt and Co., 1937.

Sturmthal, Adolf. The Tragedy of European Labor 1918–1939. New York: Columbia University Press, 1943.

Tansill, Charles Callan. Back Door to War. Chicago: Henry Regnery Company, 1952.

Thomson, Charles Alexander. Spain: Civil War. New York: Foreign Policy Assoc., Inc., 1937.

————. Spain: Issues behind the Conflict. New York: Foreign Policy Assoc., Inc., 1937.

————. The War in Spain. New York: Foreign Policy Assoc., Inc., 1938.

Toryho, Jacinto. La independencia de España, tres etapas de nuestra historia. Barcelona: Editorial Tierra y Libertad, 1938.

Toynbee, Arnold J., assisted by V. M. Boulter. Survey of International Affairs, 1937. Vol. II, The International Repercussions of the War in Spain (1936–1937). Survey of International Affairs, 1938. Vol. I. London: Oxford University Press, issued under the auspices of the Royal Institute of International Affairs, 1938.

Trainin, I. P. Baski v bor'be za svoiu natsional'nuiu nezavicimost' [The Basques in the Struggle for Their National Independence]. Moscow: Partizdat, 1937.

United States Congress. The Communist Conspiracy: Strategy and Tactics of World Communism. Part I, Communism Outside the United States, Section D, Communist Activities around the World. House Report no. 2243. Washington, D.C.: Government Printing Office, 1956.

Upravlenie voiskami i rabota shtabov v Ispanskoi respublikanskoi armii [The Administration of the Troops and the Work of the Staff in the Spanish Republican Army]. Moscow: Voenizdat., 1939.

Vanni (Ettore). IO, Comunista in Russia. Bologna: Cappelli Editore, n.d.

Varfolomeeva, R. Reaktsionnaia vneshniaia politika Frantsuskikh pravikh sotsialistov, 1936–1939gg. [The Reactionary Foreign Policy of the French Right-Wing Socialists, 1936–1939]. Moscow: Gos. Izd.-vo. Polit. Lit.-ri., 1949.

Varga, Eugen. Ispanii i revolyutsiia [Spain and Revolution]. Moscow: Partizdat. TsK VKP(b), 1937.

Vedovato, Guiseppe. Il non-Intérvento in Spagna. Florence: Studio Fiorentino di Politica Estera, 1938.

Weinberg, Gerhard L. Germany and the Soviet Union, 1939–1941. Leiden: E. J. Brill, 1954.

White, F. War in Spain: A Short Account. London: Longmans, Green and Company, 1937.

Wiskemann, Elizabeth. The Rome-Berlin Axis: A History of the Relations between Mussolini and Hitler. New York and London: Oxford University Press, 1949.

Wolfers, Arnold. Britain and France between Two Wars: Conflicting Strategies of Peace Since Versailles. New York: Harcourt Brace and Company, 1940.

Woodward, E. L., and Rohan Butler, eds. Documents on British Foreign Policy 1919–1939. 3d series, vol. III. London: His Majesty's Stationery Office, 1950.

Yakhontoff, Victor A. USSR Foreign Policy. New York: Coward-McCann, Inc., 1945.

Ypsilon. Pattern For World Revolution. Chicago–New York: Ziff-Davis Publishing Company, 1947.

PAMPHLETS

L'action du groupe communiste au Parlement, Rapport du Groupe Communiste Parlementaire pour le IX Congrès National de Parti Communiste Français, Arles 25–29 Décembre 1937. N.p.: n.d.

Aguirre, José Antonio de. *Discours prononcé par s. Ex. Le Président du Gouvernement Basque aux postes de radio de Catalogne le 21 décembre 1938.* Paris: Librairie Bloud et Gay, n.d.

——. *Speech, December 22, 1936.* Bilbao: La Editorial Vizcaina, n.d.

Alvarez del Vayo, Julio. *Deux discours prononcés par M. Alvarez del Vayo à la 101me Session de la Société des Nations.* Paris: 1938.

——. *L'Espagne accuse!* Paris: Édité par le Comité Franco-Espagnol, n.d.

Atholl, la Duchesse d'. *L'Espagne et l'Europe.* Paris: Edité par le Comité International de Coordination et d'Information pour l'Aide à l'Espagne Républicaine, n.d.

Azaña, Manuel. *Discours prononcé par s. Ex. M. Azaña, Président de la République espagnole à Valence, 21 janvier 1937.* Switzerland: n.d.

Barrister, A. *I Accuse France.* Reprinted from the *Catholic Herald*, n.d.

Bougoin, E., and P. Lenoir. *La finance internationale et la guerre d'Espagne.* Paris: Centre d'Etudes de "Paix et Démocratie," 1938.

Dimitrov, George. *Fascism is War.* New York: Workers Library Publishers, 1937.

——. *Spain and the People's Front.* New York: Workers Library Publishers, 1937.

——. *Spain's Year of War.* New York: Workers Library Publishers, 1937.

——. *Two Years of Heroic Struggle of the Spanish People.* New York: Workers Library Publishers, Aug. 1938.

The Financial Relations between the Spanish Government and Great Britain. Three articles from the *Financial News*, March 25, April 6, and Nov. 2, 1937. London: The Friends of Spain, 1937.

Gannes, Harry. *How the Soviet Union Helps Spain.* New York: Workers Library Publishers, Nov. 1936.

Gunther, John. *Inside Europe.* New York: Reprint for American Friends of Spanish Democracy, n.d.

IFTU, LSI International Solidarity Fund. *Aid for Spain: Two Years Aid for Spain.* Paris: n.d.

Ivashin, I. F. *Mezhdunarodnye otnosheniia i vneshniaia politika Sovetskogo Soiuza v 1935–1939 gg.* [*International Relations and Foreign Policy of the Soviet Union in the Years 1935–1939*]. Moscow: Vysshaia Partiinaia Shkola pri TsK KPSS, 1955.

Lemin, Iosif Mikhailovich. *Obrazovanie dvugh ochagov voiny i bor'ba SSSR za kollectivnuiu bezopasnost' (1931–1938)* [*The Development of Two Breeding Places of War and the Struggle of the USSR for Collective Security (1931–1938)*]. Moscow: Izdat. "Pravda," 1951.

Marty, André. *Avec l'Espagne pour nos libertés et la paix!* Paris: Éditions du Comité Populaire de Propagande, Sept. 5, 1936.

Negrín, Juan. *L'Adieu de Président Negrín aux combattants internationaux, discours prononcé par le Dr. Juan Negrín, Président du Conseil espagnol, le 9 octobre 1938, à Barcelone, à l'occasion du départ d'Espagne des volontaires étrangers.* Paris: Délégation de Propagande, n.d.

————. *Discours de Dr. Juan Negrín, Président du Conseil des Ministres d'Espagne* (*Madrid, 18 juin 1938*). Paris: Édité par le Comité International d'Aide au People Espagnol, n.d.

————. *The Italo-German Aggression against Spain*. Three Speeches of Sr. Juan Negrín, Geneva, September, 1937. Paris: "Coopérative Etoile," n.d.

Negrín y Prieto culpables de alta traición, informe sobre las Comisiones de Compras, la Subsecretaria de Armamento y el despilfarro escandaloso de las finanzas de la República. Buenos Aires: Ediciones del Servicio de Propaganda España, June, 1939.

Péri, Gabriel, Alvarez del Vayo et Vaillant Couturur. *Vive l'Espagne! Vive la paix! Discours prononcés à la session du Comité central du Parti comuniste français des 22 et 23 juillet 1937*. Paris: Éditions de Comité populaire de propagande, n.d.

Peuple de France aux côtes de l'Espagne republicaine, Extraits des rapports et interventions IX Congrès du Parti comunist francais, le. Paris: Éditions du Comité populaire de propagande, n.d.

Pollitt, Harry. *Arms for Spain*. London: Communist Party of Great Britain, October 30, 1936.

————. *Pollitt Visits Spain*. London: International Brigade Wounded and Dependents' Aid Fund, Feb., 1938.

————. *Spain and the T.U.C.* London: Communist Party of Great Britain, Sept. 17, 1936.

Pope Pius XI. *To the Spanish Refugees*. Address delivered on Sept. 14, 1936, to the 600 Spanish refugees, bishops, priests, and laymen whom he received in audience at Castel Grandolfo. New York: The America Press, 1937.

Pour la paix avec l'Espagne républicaine, interprellation de Gabriel Péri prononcée le 4 décembre 1936, discours de Maurice Thorez prononcé le 5 décembre 1936, explication de vote de Jacques Duclos prononcée le 5 décembre 1936. Paris: Éditions du Comité populaire de Propagande, n.d.

Robert, Pierre. *Avec les camarades Espagnols! Leur lutte, c'est notre lutte!* London: Societé d'Éditions Internationales, Oct., 1936.

Rubinshtein, N. L. *Tridtsat' let sovetskoi vneshnei politiki* [*Thirty Years of Soviet Foreign Policy*]. Moscow: Vsesoiuznoe Obshchestvo po rasnpostraneniiu politicheskigh i nauchnygh znamii, 1948.

Soviet Shipping in the Spanish Civil War. New York: Research Program on the USSR, 1954.

The Spanish Problems. Speeches at the Trade Union Congress, Plymouth, 1936. London: Trade Union Congress General Council, 1936.

Thorez, Maurice. *Main dans la main pour la rounde de la paix*. Paris: La Brochure Populaire, March, 1938.

————. *La securité francaise et l'Espagna*. Paris: La Brochure Populaire, Jan., 1939.

INDEX

INDEX

Abyssinia, British recognition of Italian sovereignty over, 112

Air attacks, agreement on, signed and results, 94

Albania, votes against League resolution, 99

Almería, bombed by German naval forces, 79–80

Alvarez del Vayo, Julio: presents Spanish case to League Council, 75; presses resolution condemning Italy and Germany in League, 98; Spanish ambassador to USSR, 2

Anarchist movement, membership, 1

Anglo-German Naval Treaty, 1935, 137 n. 22

Anglo-Italian Agreement of January 4, 1937, 111, 112; announced, 62

Anglo-Italian Agreement of 1938: contents, 112; ratified by House of Commons, 127; Soviet reaction to, 113–115

Anglo-Italian negotiations, 110–115

Anti-Comintern Pact, 57, 110; effect of Anglo-Italian accord on, 62

Appeasement: British policy of, viii, 120; peak of, 126–127. *See also* Great Britain *and* Chamberlain

Armaments race, Soviet-German, 33–37

Attacks on merchant shipping. *See* Piracy

Austria: German threat to, 111; seizure of, effect on Spain, 109–110, 112, 113

Azaña government, 1–2

Bagnari, B. A., of Clerks and Administrative Workers of Great Britain, 25

Balearic Islands, 144 n. 12; Italian interest in, 3

Barletta, Italian naval auxiliary vessel: 79; Soviet attitude toward bombing of, 157 n. 1

Belgium: appointment of, to Chairman's subcommittee, 21; Socialist party of, denounced by Comintern, 30; withdraws from London committee, 124

Belligerency: attitude of Nationalists toward, 123; attitude of USSR toward, 85, 87; in British plan, 86; demanded by Franco, 126; France fears recognition of, 171 n. 18; in German and Italian plan, 84; and Nyon Conference, 95–96; recognition of, 77; Soviet refusal to approve British plan of, 105–107; technical subcommittees consider, 108–110

Blockade, attempted by Nationalists, 77

Blum, Leon: admits France's policy set in London, 163 n. 18; allows transshipment of Soviet aid to Spain, 117; attacks Soviet policy, 23–24; attitude toward aid to Spain, 11; attitude toward Communists, 64; attitude toward Italy and Germany, 14; defends nonintervention policy, 23–25 *passim;* foreign policy of, criticized by Communists, 140 n. 6; government of, 7–12 *passim;* seeks nonintervention agreement, 14

Boncour, Paul, replaced as French foreign minister, 113

Bonnet, Georges: becomes French foreign minister, 113; hopes for complete evacuation of volunteers, 129

Bova-Scoppa, Italian representative in Geneva, 99, 102

Bowers, Claude, U. S. ambassador to Spain, 138 n. 3

Bramhill, British ship, 48

British plan for control: accepted by Germany and Italy, 104; French attitude toward, 158 n. 21; origin of, 85–86; reconsidered, 104–110. *See also* Control schemes

Bulgaria, foreign minister of, meets at Nyon, 94–96

Burgos government. *See* Spain (Nationalist)